This Book Comes With Lots of
FREE Online Resources

Nolo's award-winning website has a page dedicated just to this book. Here you can:

KEEP UP TO DATE. When there are important changes to the information in this book, we'll post updates.

GET DISCOUNTS ON NOLO PRODUCTS. Get discounts on hundreds of books, forms, and software.

READ BLOGS. Get the latest info from Nolo authors' blogs.

LISTEN TO PODCASTS. Listen to authors discuss timely issues on topics that interest you.

WATCH VIDEOS. Get a quick introduction to a legal topic with our short videos.

And that's not all.
Nolo.com contains thousands of articles on everyday legal and business issues, plus a plain-English law dictionary, all written by Nolo experts and available for free. You'll also find more useful **books, software, online apps, downloadable forms,** plus a **lawyer directory.**

Get updates and more at
www.nolo.com/back-of-book/USCIT.html

⚖ NOLO The Trusted Name
(but don't take our word for it)

"In Nolo you can trust."

THE NEW YORK TIMES

"Nolo is always there in a jam as the nation's premier publisher of do-it-yourself legal books."

NEWSWEEK

"Nolo publications…guide people simply through the how, when, where and why of the law."

THE WASHINGTON POST

"[Nolo's]…material is developed by experienced attorneys who have a knack for making complicated material accessible."

LIBRARY JOURNAL

"When it comes to self-help legal stuff, nobody does a better job than Nolo…"

USA TODAY

"The most prominent U.S. publisher of self-help legal aids."

TIME MAGAZINE

"Nolo is a pioneer in both consumer and business self-help books and software."

LOS ANGELES TIMES

8th Edition

Becoming a U.S. Citizen

A Guide to the Law, Exam & Interview

Ilona M. Bray, J.D.

Eighth Edition	SEPTEMBER 2016
Cover Design	SUSAN PUTNEY
Production	SUSAN PUTNEY
Proofreading	ROBERT WELLS
Index	UNGER INDEXING
Printing	BANG PRINTING

ISSN: 2163-3673 (print)
ISSN: 2372-3459 (online)
ISBN: 978-1-4133-2304-7 (pbk)
ISBN: 987-1-4133-2305-4 (epub ebook)

This book covers only United States law, unless it specifically states otherwise.

Please note

We believe accurate, plain-English legal information should help you solve many of your own legal problems. But this text is not a substitute for personalized advice from a knowledgeable lawyer. If you want the help of a trained professional—and we'll always point out situations in which we think that's a good idea—consult an attorney licensed to practice in your state.

Acknowledgments

This book was inspired by the efforts of my former clients, many of whom overcame huge obstacles in order to become U.S. citizens. A couple of memories stand out in particular. There was Eduardo, who in the last months before his death from cancer, madly studied the U.S. history and government exam questions so that he could become a citizen before he died—and succeeded.

Then there was Jose, who, after failing the English writing requirement during his first interview, passed it during the second one with the sentence "the sky is blue," and happily proclaimed this phrase to the world during the whole trip home.

I couldn't have written this without the help of others, who generously shared their knowledge and experience. Particular thanks go to Robert Mautino, who lent his considerable legal knowledge and experience with current practices and procedures, to the task of updating the sixth edition. I'm also grateful to Christine Stouffer, who provided sample documents and insights on the latest procedures. Barbara Horn answered many obscure questions. Susan Bowyer helped greatly with the material on disability waivers. Lynette Parker and Carmen Reyes-Yossiff also contributed invaluable information. Though this book helps you avoid certain types of attorneys, it's ones like Robert, Christine, Barbara, Susan, Lynette, and Carmen who show what it truly means to be in a service profession. Justin Kimball, a citizenship instructor, also made valuable contributions.

Thanks also go to present and former staff at Nolo: Mary Randolph and Janet Portman, who can organize anything into sensible shape; Amy DelPo and Rich Stim, unfailingly careful and encouraging editors even as my comma placement became increasingly erratic; and the magicians who turn stacks of paper into books, including Jaleh Doane, Susan Putney, and Rebecca Bond.

About the Author

Ilona Bray, J.D. came to the practice of immigration law through her long interest in international human rights issues. Before joining Nolo as legal editor in charge of immigration, she ran a solo law practice and worked for nonprofit immigration agencies including the International Institute of the East Bay (Oakland) and the Northwest Immigrant Rights Project (Seattle). Ms. Bray was also an intern in the legal office at Amnesty International's International Secretariat in London. She received her Bachelor's degree in philosophy from Bryn Mawr College, and her law degree and a Master's degree in East Asian (Chinese) Studies from the University of Washington. Ms. Bray is a member of the American Immigration Lawyers Association (AILA). She has authored other books for Nolo, including *Fiancé & Marriage Visas: A Couple's Guide to U.S. Immigration* and *U.S. Immigration Made Easy.*

Table of Contents

Your Companion on the Path to U.S. Citizenship

This book will guide you through the process of applying for U.S. citizenship through what's called "naturalization," and explain U.S. Citizenship and Immigration Service (USCIS) procedures and rules. We'll help you determine whether you're eligible, fill out the right forms, prepare for the latest version of exams, present yourself at your citizenship interview, and enjoy your new rights as a U.S. citizen.

But let's not get ahead of ourselves. Not everyone who wants to become a U.S. citizen will qualify. To save you some time and heartache, let's make sure you're on the right track.

- **Are you already a U.S. citizen?** It's unlikely, but possible that you acquired citizenship automatically through your parents or, in rare cases, your grandparents if they were born or naturalized U.S. citizens. This could have occurred even though you were born outside the United States. In order to determine this, you'll need to do some research. Start with Nolo's online, free articles at www.nolo.com. Look for the article entitled "U.S. Citizenship by Birth or Through Parents." If, after reading this information, you have unanswered questions, consult a lawyer.

- **Do you have a green card?** If you don't have a green card, you can't apply for citizenship. It doesn't matter if you've just married a U.S. citizen, won the visa lottery, or invested $1 million in the U.S. economy. Before applying for U.S. citizenship, you must first apply to become, and spend time as, a "lawful permanent resident" (also called a "permanent resident" or a "green card holder"). (The one exception is for certain people who have served in the U.S. military, as discussed in Chapter 2, Section A.)

- **Are you old enough to apply for citizenship?** The naturalization process is only open to immigrants older than age 18. If you're under 18, however, look again at whether you might have gained U.S. citizenship through your parents.

If you've answered these questions and still believe that U.S. citizenship is a possibility for you, then this book can help. Since U.S. citizenship is the highest status you can receive under the immigration laws, the laws strictly limit who can become a U.S. citizen. However, once you have citizenship, it's very difficult for the government to take it away.

Here's how this book will guide you through the process of applying for U.S. citizenship:

- **Chapter 1** will explain the advantages and disadvantages of applying for citizenship. Keep in mind that applying for citizenship may uncover flaws in your green card approval that could lead to your being deported.

- **Chapter 2** will help you learn whether you're eligible for U.S. citizenship, covering such topics as whether you've had your green card for the appropriate length of time, whether you've spent enough of your time as a green card holder living in the United States, whether you have good moral character, whether you can pass the English language and U.S. history and government exams, and more.

CAUTION

You have the burden of proving that you are eligible for citizenship. That's why it's important that you start at the beginning of this book, rather than launching straight into filling out the application form. Filling out the paperwork and hoping for the best could lead not only to your being denied citizenship, but also, in certain circumstances, to your being removed from the United States.

Once you've analyzed your eligibility, you'll move into the procedural parts of this book. If all goes normally, your quest for citizenship will require you to:

- file a written application

- attend an interview at a local USCIS office (usually several months later), and

- after you're approved, attend a "swearing-in" ceremony (usually several weeks after your interview).

Here's how the later chapters will help you accomplish these steps:

- **Chapter 3** takes you through the written application, including how to fill out the forms and guard against losses and delays by USCIS.
- **Chapter 4** describes how to deal with the often long wait for your interview, explains how to inform USCIS if you've moved, and tells you how to question USCIS regarding delays.
- **Chapter 5** includes tips on learning English for the exam portion of your citizenship application.
- **Chapter 6** prepares you for the U.S. history and government portion of the citizenship exam, including USCIS's official list of sample questions.
- **Chapter 7** advises you on procedures to follow if you are disabled and need extra accommodations or waivers in regard to your interview.
- **Chapter 8** guides you through the interview at the USCIS office.
- **Chapter 9** provides some preliminary advice on what to do if your case is denied at the interview—you may need to seek expert legal advice.
- **Chapter 10** explains how to find a good lawyer and how to make the most out of your legal relationship.
- **Chapter 11** describes the swearing-in ceremony and gives you advice on enjoying your new rights as a citizen—including how to obtain proof of your new status, register to vote, and determine which family members you can now help to immigrate.

CAUTION

If you are or have ever been in removal or deportation proceedings—that is, Immigration Court proceedings in which the INS or Immigration and Customs Enforcement (ICE) tried to remove you from the United States—you must see a lawyer. If the proceedings aren't over or are on appeal, you may not be allowed to apply for citizenship through naturalization at this time. Even if the proceedings are over, you should ask a lawyer whether the outcome affects your current application.

Note: USCIS is a branch of the Department of Homeland Security (DHS), which was established in 2003. With the creation of DHS, the agency known as the Immigration and Naturalization Service (INS) was eliminated. USCIS took over most of the INS's service-related duties. This book will mainly use the word "USCIS" when referring to the agency in charge of immigration, except when talking about something historical that happened under the old INS.

References to the Immigration Laws in This Book

Throughout this book are references to the federal immigration laws that govern U.S. citizenship and to the USCIS regulations that describe how USCIS will apply those laws to you. (They look like this: "I.N.A. § 319(a), 8 U.S.C. § 1430(a)" or "8 C.F.R. § 316.5.") We include these references where we feel it is important to indicate our sources for information and to help you research the immigration laws on your own. See Chapter 10 for more detail on what these references mean and how you can look them up.

Get Updates and More Online

When there are important changes to the information in this book, we'll post updates online, on a page dedicated to this book:

www.nolo.com/back-of-book/USCIT.html

You'll find other useful information there, too, including author blogs.

Deciding Whether to Apply for Citizenship

M any people spend their entire lives in the United States without ever trading in their green cards for citizenship—and their friends may never know it. Their reasons vary: Some of these longtime permanent residents want to show their loyalty to their native country, some are worried that they'll fail the citizenship exam, and some just never get around to applying.

For many green card holders, however, the advantages of U.S. citizenship—for example, security from deportation (technically called "removal"), freedom of travel, and eligibility for public benefits—far outweigh the drawbacks. And as we'll see, citizenship offers some refuge from political decisions that whittle away at green card rights.

In this chapter, we'll discuss the advantages and disadvantages of applying for and obtaining U.S. citizenship.

> **CAUTION**
> **Read this chapter even if you are sure you want to apply for U.S. citizenship.** Focus in particular on Section A1, where we explain how applying for U.S. citizenship can lead to your removal or deportation, either if your original green card application should not have been approved or if you've committed acts since receiving your green card that make you removable (deportable).

A. The Disadvantages of Applying for Citizenship

We'll start with the negative aspects of applying for and receiving U.S. citizenship—but not because they outweigh the positive aspects. We simply want you to fully appreciate the risks and possible pitfalls of applying for or receiving U.S. citizenship. These include:

- If you got your green card fraudulently or have since become removable, applying for citizenship may bring you to USCIS's attention and result in your deportation (removal from the U.S.). (See Section A1.)
- Your native country may not allow dual citizenship (see Section A2).

- Carrying a U.S. passport may be a security risk in some countries (see Section A3).
- You may not be allowed to serve your home country in times of conflict (see Section A4).

1. The Risk of Removal From the U.S.

If something happened in your past that makes you removable or deportable, you should not apply for U.S. citizenship—or, at the very least, you should talk to a lawyer before doing so. The citizenship process may uncover whatever it is you're hiding and send you directly into removal proceedings.

Perhaps your green card should never have been approved in the first place because you lied on the application, or maybe you've committed a crime that Immigration and Customs Enforcement (ICE) hasn't noticed yet. Either way, applying for citizenship gives USCIS a chance to review your whole immigration history, from the time you entered the United States to the present. If something isn't quite right, you could find yourself fighting removal in Immigration Court.

In this section, we look separately at the two most common types of problems:

- a green card that shouldn't have been approved in the first place, and
- a green card that USCIS can take away because you've done something that violates its terms.

a. If Your Green Card Application Shouldn't Have Been Approved

USCIS would be the first to admit that it makes mistakes, sometimes approving people for green cards who were not eligible for them. You probably already know if you committed outright fraud—that is, lied or deliberately covered something up—on your green card application. Common types of fraud include faking a marriage, hiding a criminal conviction in one's home country, and creating false documents to show a sponsor who doesn't exist.

However, you might also have unintentionally lied—for example, gotten a green card through a relative whose own green card had already been revoked (canceled or taken away), or turned 21 before you got a green card, not realizing that the category for "children" of permanent residents applied only while you remained younger than age 21.

> **EXAMPLE 1:** Rodrigo got his green card through the farmworker amnesty program in the 1980s. In truth, he was a car mechanic, but he bought a letter from a farmer stating that he had picked strawberries during the required time period. During the citizenship interview, the USCIS officer asks Rodrigo how high he had to reach to pick the strawberries. Rodrigo answers, "Oh, no more than eight feet." The officer, knowing that strawberries don't grow on trees, takes a look at Rodrigo's old INS file. She notices that the employer who swore to Rodrigo's work was one whom USCIS believes to have made a lot of money selling fake letters. Rodrigo's citizenship application is denied, and he is placed in removal proceedings.

> **EXAMPLE 2:** Leonora applied for a green card as the unmarried child of a U.S. permanent resident. She was on the waiting list for a number of years, during which time she fell in love and married her sweetheart. Finally, her green card came through. She didn't say anything about her marriage, and the U.S. consulate forgot to ask. However, had the marriage been revealed, her green card would have been denied, because the category she applied in was meant only for unmarried children. When Leonora applies for citizenship, she lists the date of her marriage. The USCIS officer notices that the marriage occurred before Leonora's green card was approved—in other words, Leonora was ineligible for her green card. Leonora faces removal proceedings.

If you are unsure about whether you really deserve your green card, see a lawyer. The lawyer can request a copy of your USCIS file and analyze it for problems.

b. If You've Become Removable After Getting Your Green Card

U.S. laws contain a list of activities that can cause a green card holder to lose the right to live in the United States. Commit one of these activities and you become removable. If anything on the list below looks like something you've done, do not file your citizenship application until you see an immigration attorney. (We can't give you extensive details on each of these activities, so don't rely on this list alone.)

- You were inadmissible when you last entered the United States (see "Actions and Conditions That Make You Inadmissible," later in this chapter, for more about inadmissibility).
- You have violated a condition of your U.S. stay.
- You were unsuccessful in turning your conditional residence into permanent residence (primarily affecting people who married a U.S. citizen or immigrated on an investor visa).
- You have helped smuggle someone into the United States within five years of when you entered the country (with limited exceptions for close family).
- You have entered into a fake marriage to try to get a green card.
- You have committed a crime of moral turpitude within five years of becoming a U.S. resident (or ten years if you got your residency after living in the United States illegally, by paying a penalty fee under Section 245(i) of the I.N.A.). There is no official list of crimes of moral turpitude (see "What Constitutes Moral Turpitude?" below).
- You have committed a crime of moral turpitude for which the judge could have imposed a sentence of one year or more.
- You committed two or more separate crimes of moral turpitude.
- You have committed an aggravated felony.
- You have committed a drug-related crime (except a single conviction for possession of 30 grams of marijuana or less).
- You use or are addicted to illegal drugs.
- You have committed a gun-related crime (such as selling, possessing, or using a gun illegally).

- You have violated federal laws regarding spying, treason, sedition (insurrection against the U.S. government or providing support to an enemy government), or assisting others to enter or leave the United States illegally.
- You have committed a domestic violence crime or violated anti-stalking, child abuse, neglect, or abandonment laws.
- You deliberately failed to notify the INS or USCIS of your new address within ten days of moving.
- You have fraudulently acquired a visa or other official document (that is, you got it by lying or deliberately omitting information).
- You have falsely claimed to be a U.S. citizen.
- You are a threat to public safety, national security, or U.S. foreign policy.
- You have tried to overthrow the U.S. government.
- You have assisted in Nazi persecution.
- You have engaged in genocide.
- You became a public charge (received welfare payments) within five years of your approval for U.S. residency.
- You have voted in a U.S. election. (Green card holders cannot vote in the United States.)

In many cases, whatever you did wrong will have come to the attention of the INS or USCIS right after it happened. For example, USCIS checks the names of people in jail and asks the police to turn over criminal immigrants. If you've been out of the country, the border officer normally checks whether you are admissible, looking in particular at whether you stayed away too long or resettled elsewhere.

But sometimes violations go undetected by the U.S. government. For example, a person who pleads guilty to a crime but never goes to jail may escape USCIS's attention. Similarly, border patrol officers sometimes let in green card holders when they should have kept them out.

In short, if you've done something to make you removable and USCIS hasn't yet caught up with you, applying for U.S. citizenship will give the agency the perfect opportunity.

If You Divorce Your U.S. Sponsor

People who received a green card through marriage to a U.S. citizen or permanent resident but later divorce, often worry about how this will affect their citizenship application.

As long as your marriage was the real thing—that is, not a sham for purposes of acquiring your green card—and you got all the way to being approved for permanent (not merely conditional) residence, divorce will not invalidate your green card. Many people get divorced, and the immigration laws recognize that the United States may have become home to the divorced immigrant, with or without the ex-spouse.

The divorce may, however, make the USCIS officer interviewing you for citizenship wonder whether you faked it through the green card application process. USCIS officers won't automatically *assume* from your divorce that your marriage was a sham—but they may want some reassurance.

Prepare for this by gathering documents that prove your marriage was genuine (and make sure they're more recent than the documents already in the USCIS file from your green card application). Don't include these documents with your citizenship application. Instead, make copies and take these, with the originals, to your citizenship interview. The following documents may help:

- ☐ rent receipts or a home title in both your and your ex-spouse's names (showing that you lived together)
- ☐ birth certificates of children born to the two of you
- ☐ a letter from your spiritual or psychological counselor describing your meetings—particularly where your marriage was discussed. (If possible, the letter should emphasize that you worked hard to save your marriage and that the issues you discussed were the thorny ones faced by people truly trying to share their lives.)
- ☐ evidence of joint bank accounts, credit cards, and club memberships
- ☐ photographs of the two of you on vacations or sharing important occasions (preferably where the camera has automatically inserted the date), and
- ☐ subscriptions to magazines and newspapers at your shared address.

Another problem may arise if the divorce was caused by your adultery. See Chapter 2, Section D12, "You've Committed Adultery."

EXAMPLE 1: Matilda got her green card as a result of marrying a U.S. citizen. She and her husband have fiery tempers, and their arguments sometimes become physical. After one violent encounter, Matilda's husband had her arrested for domestic violence. She tried to have him arrested too, but since he was bleeding a lot more than she was, the police checked him into a hospital instead. Matilda pled guilty to a domestic violence charge in order to avoid jail time. When Matilda applies for citizenship, the USCIS officer notices the conviction on her FBI record. Since domestic violence is grounds for removal, the officer places Matilda into Immigration Court proceedings.

EXAMPLE 2: Patrick's U.S. employer got him a green card. He lived and worked in the United States for two years and then went back to his native Britain for two years. After that, he returned to the United States using his British passport (British citizens can enter the United States without a visa). He then used his U.S. green card to live and work in the United States for the next five years. Although his two-year stay in Britain meant that Patrick had given up his green card, his employer had no way of knowing this, because he still held the physical card that he could show to his boss. When Patrick applied for citizenship, the USCIS officer determined that Patrick had abandoned his U.S. residence during the two years in Britain and it was therefore inappropriate for Patrick to claim green card status after he reentered the United States. USCIS places Patrick in removal proceedings.

EXAMPLE 3: Leticia applies for U.S. citizenship. She has one minor crime on her record—fraudulent use of an ex-friend's credit card. However, USCIS considers this a crime of moral turpitude (see "What Constitutes Moral Turpitude?," below). Even though a single crime of moral turpitude isn't grounds for removal, it is grounds for denying Leticia readmission to the U.S. if she left and attempted to return. After being released from jail, Leticia took a trip to Canada. When she returned to the United States, the border patrol officer didn't ask about her criminal record. Since Leticia was inadmissible during that entry, she is removable now. After Leticia applies for citizenship, the USCIS officer at her interview realizes that an error occurred at the U.S. border, denies citizenship, and places Leticia in Immigration Court proceedings.

What Constitutes Moral Turpitude?

According to the Board of Immigration Appeals, a crime of moral turpitude is inherently base, vile, or depraved, contrary to social standards of morality, and done with a reckless, malicious, or evil intent. In short, this is a subjective, catchall term that can be used for any crime that USCIS considers offensive. For example, USCIS has judged moral turpitude to be present in crimes involving great bodily injury, sexual offenses, kidnapping, stalking, fraud, theft, embezzlement, bribery, and unlawful use of a Social Security number.

RESOURCE

To read the law on removability, see I.N.A. § 237(a), 8 U.S.C. § 1227(a). You can find this at your local law library or at www.uscis.gov. Click "Laws," then "Immigration and Nationality Act." After reading the law, you will still need the help of an immigration lawyer to answer questions about whether or not you have done something that makes you removable. Many of the terms used in the law, like "moral turpitude" and "aggravated felony," are unique to the immigration laws, and you won't be able to tell by looking at your court record whether you've committed one.

CAUTION

Every law has its exceptions. Removability rules are not always as harsh as they first appear. Some come with exceptions and waivers (opportunities to apply to USCIS for legal forgiveness). So, even if you have done something that makes you removable, you might be able to save yourself—and your chances of becoming a citizen—by qualifying for one of these exceptions or applying for a waiver. We're unable to cover the various exceptions and waivers in this book, but an immigration lawyer can alert you to the ones that apply.

Actions and Conditions That Make You Inadmissible

No, you're not seeing double. The activities that make you inadmissible overlap in many ways with the activities that make you removable. Inadmissibility affects whether you can enter the United States, regardless of whether it's for the first time or with a green card (although, if you had a green card and you reentered the U.S. after April 1, 1997, you're affected by these only if you were out of the U.S. for 180 days or more, or did something illegal during your trip).

If you've committed any of the activities below, USCIS can keep you from entering. And if you were let into the United States when you shouldn't have been—that is, when you were inadmissible, USCIS will deny you citizenship and can take away your green card.

You are (or were) inadmissible if, when entering the United States, you:

- had a communicable disease of public health significance, such as active tuberculosis or smallpox
- had a physical or mental disorder that makes you harmful to others
- were likely to become a public charge (receive welfare benefits)—something USCIS determines based on your current income, ability to work, and family resources
- were a drug abuser (if you've tried illegal drugs more than once in the past three years, that's enough for USCIS)
- had committed or been convicted of a crime of moral turpitude

CAUTION

You can access the law on inadmissibility (I.N.A. § 212(a), 8 U.S.C. § 1182) at your local law library or at www.uscis.gov. Click "Laws," then "Immigration and Nationality Act."

Actions and Conditions That Make You Inadmissible (cont'd)

- had been convicted of two or more crimes (whether misdemeanors or felonies), where the total sentence you received was five years or more
- had been convicted of certain specified crimes, such as prostitution or drug trafficking
- are the immediate family member of a drug trafficker and have knowingly benefited from their illicit money within the last five years
- had committed espionage or sabotage against the United States
- were a member of the Communist Party or other totalitarian organization
- were a Nazi or had participated in genocide
- were seeking entry as a health care or other certified worker but had failed to meet licensing requirements
- had previously violated the immigration laws or lied or committed fraud during immigration procedures
- had falsely claimed to have U.S. citizenship
- had spent time in the United States unlawfully or hadn't obtained proper documentation to enter the United States (not an issue for immigrants who hold valid green cards)
- had previously been removed or deported from the United States
- advocated, practiced, or planned to practice polygamy (being married to more than one person at the same time)
- had committed international child abduction (taking a child across international borders), or
- were on a J-1 or J-2 exchange visitor visa and were subject to the two-year foreign residence requirement.

2. Some Countries Won't Allow Dual Citizenship

If USCIS approves your citizenship application, you will attend a ceremony where you will have to swear to "absolutely and entirely renounce and abjure all allegiance and fidelity to any foreign prince, potentate, state, or sovereignty of whom or which [you] have heretofore been a subject or citizen."

Does this mean that you must give up the citizenship (and passport) of your country of origin? Not necessarily. It depends on both U.S. law and the law of your home country. Many people today successfully hold dual citizenship—that is, they are simultaneously U.S. citizens and citizens of another country.

Dual citizenship can be important for a number of reasons. You may feel a huge sense of loss in giving up the passport of the country you once called home. More practically, the laws of your home country may require that you give up other important rights along with your citizenship—such as your rights to a pension, to receive government-paid health care if you are elderly or disabled, to vote, or to own land.

U.S. law concerning dual citizenship is very vague. Nowhere does it say that you can be a dual citizen—but then, nowhere does it say that you can't. Historically, the U.S. government has used this vagueness as an opportunity to make people believe that choosing U.S. citizenship excludes all others. The oath that people take at their swearing-in ceremony (quoted above) would make anyone think that they were agreeing to give up all other citizenships right then and there.

However, the United States will not actually stop you from keeping your citizenship in your home country after becoming a U.S. citizen—if that is what you want, and provided your home country allows it.

Because the U.S. government does not formally sanction dual citizenship, there are no particular procedures to follow. No one will give you a certificate or other evidence that the U.S. government recognizes and approves your dual status. Your home country, however, may require more. First, find out whether your home country will cancel your citizenship if you are naturalized as a U.S. citizen. If cancellation isn't automatic, find out whether you have to take special steps to keep your home citizenship. Some countries allow it automatically, others allow it after an application process, and still others offer something less than full citizenship, with or without an application.

This book is published in the United States, and we don't pretend to be experts on the complex laws of every other country in the world. But, take heart—the majority of countries around the globe do allow dual citizenship, at least in some form.

Since we don't have space to provide all of the procedures for and limits on retaining your non-U.S. citizenship, you should look for further information on your own. A good starting point is the embassy of your home country in the United States. It is probably in the Washington, DC area; or find Internet links to the various embassies at www.embassy.org.

3. Carrying a U.S. Passport in Unfriendly Territory

As a large and powerful country, the United States is a focus of public opinion and debate, both positive and negative. Unfortunately, anger against the U.S. government is sometimes directed against its citizens traveling overseas. There is no way to predict whether, where, or how a guerrilla or terrorist group might make you a scapegoat for U.S. foreign policy. You'll have to assess the risks yourself, based on where you plan to travel and what you observe of world events.

Of course, if you have dual citizenship, you can always carry the passport of your home country on a trip—but you'll need to show your U.S. passport when you depart and return to the United States. You can use the other passport to travel with—that is, show it on entry to other countries. However, if you do so, the U.S. consulate there may refuse to help you if you get into a jam. Also, don't flaunt your non-U.S. passport when you return to the United States. U.S. border officials are suspicious of people who carry two passports, and they will probably question you to confirm that everything is aboveboard.

4. You May Not Be Allowed to Serve Your Native Country During War

The United States requires that its citizens demonstrate loyalty in any conflict. In fact, you'll be asked on the citizenship application if you're willing to serve in the U.S. military, either in combat or in a supporting role, if the need arises. (We'll discuss this more in Chapter 3, which covers how to fill out the citizenship application.) This also means that the United States may take action against you if you join your own country in a war that's against the United States or its allies or interests.

B. The Advantages of U.S. Citizenship

U.S. citizenship is definitely an improvement over permanent resident status. At the very least, you won't have to renew your green card every ten years—or even carry the card around. But wait, there's more! As a U.S. citizen you get:

- the right to vote and obtain certain federal jobs (see Section B1)
- security from anti-immigrant laws (see Section B2)
- security from removal (see Section B3)
- the right to live or take long trips outside the United States (see Section B4)
- special rights and protections when traveling outside the United States (see Section B5)
- an unquestioned right to return to the United States (see Section B6)
- the ability to bring other family members to the United States (faster than you could as a permanent resident) or to pass citizenship to your children (see Section B7), and
- the right to apply for public benefits (see Section B8).

1. The Right to Vote and Hold Certain Federal Jobs

Green card holders cannot vote in any U.S. election, be it local, state, or federal. (If you *did* vote, see an immigration lawyer immediately—this could result in denial of your application for citizenship.) Once you receive U.S. citizenship, however, you can make your voice heard in local and national elections. Politicians are increasingly aware of the voting-bloc power of immigrants—and are offering meaningful choices and reforms to immigrant voters as a result.

In addition to voting, U.S. citizenship will open the door to many federal job opportunities. The federal government is a huge employer, offering good salaries and job stability. You may not realize how many U.S. government branch offices are in your community—the Social Security Administration, the Environmental Protection Agency, and more. Many U.S. Foreign Service jobs also require U.S. citizenship. If you've got political aspirations, you can run for elected office—although you'll never be able to run for U.S. President or Vice President. (You must be born in the U.S.A. to qualify for either of these jobs.)

2. Security From Anti-Immigrant Laws

U.S. sentiment toward immigrants has its ups and downs, but sometimes you can't open the newspaper without seeing a proposed change toughening up the federal immigration laws. These new laws primarily affect people who are here illegally or don't have green cards—but even legal immigrants with green cards aren't immune. Individual U.S. states are, more than ever before, experimenting with legislation to discourage undocumented immigrants from living there. And the U.S. Congress—limited only by Constitutional guarantees like free speech and equal protection—can change the rights of green card holders at any time.

A dramatic example of this occurred in the late 1990s, when Congress decided to make green card holders ineligible for various federal benefits such as Supplemental Security Income (SSI). Thousands of elderly and disabled immigrants with low financial resources were suddenly cut off from their lifeline of cash support and medical or nursing home care. (The decision reportedly led to some suicides.) Congress subsequently softened this law, but tight restrictions remain. For example, immigrants who entered the United States after August 22, 1996, can qualify for SSI only if they've had a green card for five years and have worked 40 quarters (ten years) in the United States—or fall into one of a few similarly narrow categories.

More recently, Congress has responded to U.S. security concerns by requiring that all airport baggage and passenger screeners be U.S. citizens.

As a U.S. citizen, you can stop worrying about Congress's latest idea. You'll have the same basic rights as any other U.S. citizen.

3. Security From Removal

Although most green card holders can live in the United States for years without problems, an unfortunate number become removable and lose their green cards. (We provided a list of the reasons for removal in Section A1, above.) Others may become inadmissible, and therefore ineligible to return to the United States once they've left.

With U.S. citizenship, the specter of removal is eliminated. The grounds of removal do not apply to U.S. citizens. However, USCIS— although it rarely does so—can take away your citizenship if it finds you lied when seeking your green card or citizenship.

4. The Right to Live Outside the U.S. or to Take Long Trips

A green card holder who spends more than six months abroad, or shows signs of resettling elsewhere, can lose permanent residence rights. Ironically, becoming a U.S. citizen allows you to spend less time in the United States—even to make your home elsewhere if you wish. No one will take away your citizenship as a result. In addition, and unlike U.S. permanent residents, you will be allowed to continue receiving any retirement or other benefits you've earned from Social Security while you're living abroad.

Even if you want to retain your primary home inside the United States, gaining citizenship will be a huge help if you travel a great deal or have close family members or other obligations outside the United States. If family emergencies arise, you'll be able to attend to them, confident of your easy return to the United States.

5. Special Rights and Protections When Traveling Outside the U.S.

If you enjoy visiting other countries, you'll find your U.S. passport helpful. Many countries lighten their visa requirements and restrictions for citizens of the United States and other developed nations.

You'll also enjoy the protection of the U.S. State Department while you're traveling. The State Department takes very seriously its role in protecting U.S. citizens abroad. If you are injured, robbed, or run into other problems beyond your control, you'll get help from the local U.S. consulate, such as arranging your care and transportation home.

If you're arrested abroad, the State Department will help you find an attorney and see that you're treated humanely. (However, if you've actually committed a crime, don't count on the State Department to pressure the foreign state to stop your punishment. The degree of help you get depends on the seriousness of your crime and the relations between the United States and the foreign government.)

For a fuller picture of these services see the State Department's website (www.state.gov).

6. Ease in Returning to the U.S.

Remember those long lines for green card holders that you stood in when you last entered the United States? The lines are much shorter for U.S. citizens. You'll still have to pass border patrol officials, but at least they won't be asking questions designed to see whether they should take away your green card. You will no longer be subject to inadmissibility rules when you reenter the United States.

As we indicated in Section A1, above, green card holders must meet admissibility standards when they enter the United States after a long trip, and failing to meet these standards can result in being barred from entry and from citizenship.

RESOURCE

For more on inadmissibility, see Nolo's website, www.nolo.com. Look for the article in the Immigration section entitled "Inadmissibility: When the U.S. Can Keep You Out." Also see *U.S. Immigration Made Easy,* by Ilona Bray (Nolo).

7. Increased Ability to Help Family Members Immigrate

As a U.S. citizen, your existing children with green cards, any children you adopt, and any children born to you after you receive your citizenship automatically (well, almost automatically, depending on the circumstances) become U.S. citizens. For more on passing citizenship to your children, see Chapter 11.

In addition, you can submit a petition to sponsor certain other family members for U.S. green cards (but not citizenship—they'll have to wait a few years just like you did). You'll be able to submit petitions for your parents, your children, your spouse, and your brothers and sisters.

Unfortunately, not every petition results in your family member getting a green card right away. If your children are older than 21 or are married, they'll be put on a waiting list that usually lasts several years. Your brothers and sisters will also be put on a waiting list that averages at least 12 years in length. Without your citizenship, however, the same family members would either wait much longer or have no rights to immigrate at all.

For more information on how your citizenship can help your family members to immigrate, see Chapter 11.

8. Eligibility for Public Benefits

If your life takes a difficult turn and you discover you can't pay for your own food or medical care, you'll have a much easier time qualifying for government help if you're a U.S. citizen. You will be permitted to apply for SSI (if you're disabled and have a low income), federal food stamps, general assistance (cash support), nonemergency medical services, and a variety of state assistance programs—all of which are off limits or severely restricted while you're a permanent resident. Even if you never plan to rely on government help, knowing it's available in an emergency can be reassuring.

Are You Eligible for U.S. Citizenship?

No matter how eager you are to become a U.S. citizen, you should start with an honest assessment of whether you are eligible. If you're not entitled to citizenship, the application process could do you more harm than good—wasting your time and energy, or worse, sending you into removal proceedings.

If, after reading this chapter, it looks like you aren't eligible, consult with an attorney. If your attorney agrees, you will have saved yourself a lot of aggravation and difficulty. If you conclude that you are clearly eligible, congratulations! You can continue through the application process with confidence.

CAUTION
If you are in the United States illegally, you have a temporary visa or status, or you are in removal (deportation) proceedings, stop now—this book can't help you. No matter who you are or how you came to the United States, you have to start the citizenship process by getting a green card. You cannot jump from having no immigration status to U.S. citizenship. The only exceptions are for the children who may have acquired citizenship at birth from U.S. citizen parents; and for service people who served honorably and on active duty during certain military operations.

If you meet all of the following criteria, you are eligible for U.S. citizenship:

- You have had permanent residence (a green card) for the required number of years—usually five, but fewer for certain categories of applicants (see Section A).
- You have been "physically present"—that is, lived in the United States—for at least half your required years of permanent residence (usually two and a half out of five years) (see Section B).
- You have been "continuously present" in the United States—that is, have not spent long stretches of time (six months or more) overseas (see Section B).
- You have lived in the same U.S. state or USCIS district for three months before applying to the USCIS there (see Section B).

- You are at least 18 years old at the time of filing the application (see Section C).
- You have demonstrated good moral character in the years leading up to your application for citizenship—for example, by paying your taxes and child support and not committing any crimes (see Section D).
- You can speak, read, and write English (see Section E).
- You can pass a brief oral test covering U.S. history and government (see Section F).
- You are willing to affirm loyalty to the United States and serve in its military if necessary (see Section G).

In this chapter, we'll briefly explain how to prove that you meet each of these requirements.

 PAPERWORK REMINDER

Keep your eyes out for this icon. It alerts you to unique situations when you may have to submit extra documents (and explanations) with your citizenship application.

A. Confirming Your Permanent Resident Status

Before you can become a citizen, you must—with some exceptions (see Section A3, below)—have been a lawful permanent U.S. resident for at least five years. It's important to be accurate when determining your time as a lawful permanent resident—every day counts. In the following sections, we'll help you analyze the length and status of your permanent residency.

1. Are You a Lawful Permanent Resident?

Your green card—not a work permit, visa, or other temporary right to live in the United States—is what demonstrates that you are a permanent resident. Your green card should look similar to the one shown in Section 2, below.

It's not enough to possess the card; you also have to "deserve" it. If you have been ordered removed or have violated the terms of your stay, you may have lost your legal right to permanent residence even though you still carry your card. Similarly, if you didn't really deserve the green card in the first place, as described in Chapter 1, Section A, applying for U.S. citizenship won't help you. Not only could you be ineligible for citizenship, but you risk removal by applying for it.

However, if your green card expired (which it does every ten years)—you are still a permanent resident. It's a good idea to renew your card before applying for citizenship. Instructions for renewal are in Chapter 3.

2. How Long Have You Been a Permanent Resident?

To determine how many years you've been a permanent resident, calculate from the date that the INS or USCIS approved your permanent residence—it's shown on your green card, as seen in the picture below.

As you calculate the time, don't round it off to calendar years. In other words, four years, 11 months, and 20 days does not equal five years. When it comes to determining the date at which you can apply for citizenship, USCIS wants you to count full 365-day years.

> **EXAMPLE:** Loc was granted permanent residence on December 15, 2011. On January 15, 2016, he incorrectly decides that he has been a permanent resident for five years and files his citizenship application. (In actual years, he has been a permanent resident for only four years and one month.) His application will be returned, and Loc will not be eligible for citizenship until December 15, 2016 (although, as we'll see in Section 3, below, a special provision allows him and other applicants to file applications three months before they're eligible).

What if your first two years of U.S. residence are "conditional" rather than "permanent"? Conditional residence is like permanent residence, but it gives USCIS a chance to reevaluate your case at the end of two years (when the conditional residence automatically expires). Often, people who marry U.S. citizens must go through these two years of conditional residence before applying for permanent residence. Similarly, immigrants who get their green cards as entrepreneurs (by investing at least $500,000 in a U.S. business) must spend two years as conditional residents before becoming permanent residents.

If you spent two years as a conditional resident, there's good news: When it comes to applying for citizenship, those two years count as permanent residence so long as you successfully became a permanent resident at the end of them. Count your years of residence starting at the date you were approved for conditional residence. You'll find that date on your green card.

Old-Style Green Card (Front)

Date of Residency

Old-Style Green Card (Back)   **New-Style Green Card (Front)**

EXAMPLE: Tam invested $500,000 in NetMiser, a U.S. company, and was approved for conditional residence on April 7, 2012. USCIS approved Tam for permanent residence in July, 2010. Tam is eligible for citizenship on April 7, 2017—five years from the date he was approved for conditional residence.

Some conditional residents find that USCIS takes so long to decide on their I-751 petitions to remove the conditions on residence that they reach the date upon which they become eligible for naturalization in the meantime. If this happens to you, you can go ahead and apply for citizenship. This may push USCIS to approve your permanent residence. In fact, the USCIS officer who reviews your application for citizenship may request the file containing your Form I-751 petition to remove the conditions on residence, and decide on both at once.

TIP
Conditional residents who married U.S. citizens—more good news! Assuming your marriage to your U.S. citizen spouse hasn't broken up, you have to wait only three years as a permanent resident before applying for citizenship. That means you can apply one year after the end of your conditional residence.

3. How Many Years of Permanent Residence Are Required?

In this section, we'll help you determine the earliest possible date upon which you can turn in your citizenship application. For most people, that will be after five years of permanent residence, but for some— depending on their circumstances—that date may be sooner.

CAUTION
Don't count on USCIS to tell you that you've counted the days wrong. Although USCIS tries to advise people of errors in their application date soon after they submit it, some applications are bound to slip through the cracks. In other words, you could arrive at your interview only to be told you have to file again. For that reason, do your best to count your permanent-residency time accurately.

a. The 90-Day Early Application Rule

You can turn in your citizenship application 90 days before your required years of permanent residence have passed. This 90-day period compensates for the fact that USCIS may not act on your application (call you in for an interview) for at least that amount of time.

This doesn't change the fact that you're eligible for citizenship only after the full number of years have passed. But in this rare instance, USCIS allows you to become eligible after you submit your application, not before. If your local USCIS office is moving quickly and calls you in for an interview within that 90-day period, you won't be approved on that day. Current USCIS procedure is to go ahead and conduct the interview, but to wait to approve you until you've reached the full required number of years of permanent residence.

> **EXAMPLE:** Sean became a permanent resident on December 15, 2011. He carelessly counts off five years on his fingers and decides that he can apply for citizenship in 2016. He turns in his citizenship application in August 2016. His application comes back in the mail—he is told he applied too early and must reapply. If he'd waited another month, he could have applied legally on September 15, 2016 (five years minus 90 days from December 15, 2011).

b. The Five-Year Requirement

Most immigrants must wait for a full five years of permanent residency before they are eligible for citizenship. In other words, if you were approved for permanent residency on December 15, 2012, you would not be eligible for citizenship until December 15, 2017. (Due to the 90-day period discussed in Subsection a, above, you could file your application on September 15, 2017.)

c. Exceptions to the Five-Year Requirement

You don't have to accumulate five years of permanent residence before applying for citizenship if you are:

- a spouse of a U.S. citizen who stays married and living together for three years (see Subsection i, below)
- a battered spouse of a U.S. citizen, even if divorced or separated (see Subsection ii, below)
- a refugee or asylee (see Subsection iii, below)
- in the U.S. military or a military widow or widower (see Subsection iv, below), or
- a spouse of a U.S. citizen in certain overseas jobs (see Subsection v, below).

Below, we'll give you the "fine print" on these exceptions and alert you to special documentation you'll need to provide to claim the exception. However, if you can't tell whether you fit into one of these exceptions, or if you have additional questions about how these exceptions apply to your case, consult with an immigration attorney.

i. Spouses of U.S. Citizens Who Stay Married for Three Years

You can apply for citizenship after three years if, during that time, you have been a permanent resident and have been married to and living with a U.S. citizen. (See I.N.A. § 319(a), 8 U.S.C. § 1430(a).) It doesn't matter whether you got your green card through this marriage. You will, however, need to stay married to your citizen spouse all the way through your citizenship interview. This exception won't apply and you will be required to wait five years if:

- you separate or divorce legally prior to your interview
- you choose to stop living with your spouse, or
- your spouse dies.

Also, your spouse must be a citizen during all of your three years of permanent residency. If, for example, your spouse had a green card when you got married and became a naturalized citizen one year later, you'll have to wait three years from the date he or she became a citizen—that is, for a total of four years.

PAPERWORK REMINDER

Married with documentation. If you are married to a U.S. citizen and eligible to apply after three years, you'll need to prove it. Include with your application a copy of your marriage certificate, a copy of your spouse's U.S. passport, citizenship certificate, or other proof of citizenship, certificates showing that your and your spouse's previous marriages (if any) were legally ended by death, divorce, or annulment, and materials to show that the two of you are actually living as man and wife, such as your children's birth certificates, a home title, or rental receipts showing both your names, copies of joint credit card statements, and more. At least three solid pieces of evidence is the standard. Unfortunately, USCIS will not allow you to simply bring your U.S. citizen spouse to your naturalization interview as a witness.

ii. Battered Spouses or Children of U.S. Citizens, Even After Divorce or Separation

Under previous laws, battered spouses of U.S. citizens were left with a tough choice: They could stay in an abusive marriage for three years so that they could obtain U.S. citizenship, or they could leave their spouse—but had to wait longer before applying for citizenship.

Now, permanent residents in physically or emotionally abusive marriages can leave their spouse and still apply for U.S. citizenship three years after obtaining their permanent residence. Children are also eligible under this section, though the child must still reach age 18 before applying for citizenship.

If you want to use this rule, the law requires that you got your green card through your marriage to the U.S. citizen—and that in getting the green card, you used special legal provisions that allow the battered spouse to file portions of the paperwork without the abusive spouse's cooperation (either through a self-petition on Form I-360, through cancellation of removal, or through obtaining a waiver of the joint filing requirement on Form I-751). (See I.N.A. § 319(a), 8 U.S.C. § 1430(a).)

If you've already suffered through an abusive marriage to your U.S. citizen spouse for three years, you can apply after three years just like any spouse of a U.S. citizen. But, if you're not living with your U.S. citizen spouse now, this new section could help. You won't need to prove the abuse all over again.

iii. Refugees and Asylees

If you got your green card because of your refugee or asylum status, part of your time as a refugee or asylee can be counted as if you were a permanent resident (known as "rollback").

If you were granted refugee status while you were in another country, you can count the date you entered the United States as the beginning of your permanent residence. It doesn't matter how many years you lived in the United States as a refugee as long as you eventually become a permanent resident—all those years will count as if you were a permanent resident. (See 8 C.F.R. § 209.1(e).)

> **EXAMPLE:** Seyoum comes to the United States as a refugee in January 2013. He waits until the year 2016 to apply for permanent residence, and USCIS grants it in January 2017. Seyoum can apply for citizenship in January 2018, because his four years of refugee status and one year as an actual permanent resident all count as part of his five years of permanent residence.

The rules differ for immigrants who were granted asylum after they reached the United States. The maximum rollback for asylees is one year—if you waited longer than a year to apply for your green card, that extra time won't be counted toward your permanent residency period. In summary, you can apply for citizenship four years after the actual date of your approval for permanent residence. But watch out—USCIS will backdate your permanent residence approval date on your green card by one year anyway, so you'll have to wait five years from the date shown on your card. (See 8 C.F.R. § 209.2(f).)

> **EXAMPLE:** Takalin arrives in the United States on a tourist visa in 2009 and applies for and receives asylum in 2010. In 2010, he applies for permanent residence, and his application is approved in March 2014—but USCIS enters his approval date on his green card as March 2013. Takalin can apply for U.S. citizenship in March 2018, four years after he qualified for permanent residence. Only one year of his time as an asylee is counted toward his permanent residence.

CAUTION

Despite rollback benefits, refugees and asylees are subject to the same requirements as other applicants regarding how much time they must spend inside the U.S.—as opposed to traveling—before applying for citizenship. (See Section B, below.)

PAPERWORK REMINDER

If you take advantage of the rollback rules, make it clear to USCIS when you apply. Mention it in your application cover letter, and include a copy of USCIS or State Department documents proving the date you entered the U.S. (if you're a refugee) or became a permanent resident (if you're an asylee). USCIS should have these dates in its files, but the office that first handles your citizenship application may not have those files.

iv. U.S. Military Personnel and Their Spouses, Widows, and Widowers

People serving in the U.S. military and their families make a special commitment to the United States. For that reason, the immigration law provides certain exceptions for those applying for U.S. citizenship. These exceptions cover people who have performed active or reserve service in the U.S. Army, Navy, Marines, Air Force, or Coast Guard, as well as service in a National Guard unit while the unit was federally recognized as a reserve component of the U.S. Armed Forces. (See 8 C.F.R § 328.1.)

People with one year of service. If you have served honorably in the U.S. Armed Forces for one year (it doesn't have to have been continuous) and your discharge (if any) was honorable, you can apply for citizenship without waiting beyond the date you get your green card.

However, if you have been discharged, you must apply for citizenship no later than six months after your discharge, so don't delay. If six months have already passed, you will—unless you qualify for one of the other exceptions in this chapter—most likely have to prove five years of permanent residence before applying for citizenship. (See I.N.A. § 328, 8 U.S.C. § 1439.)

Spouses of U.S.-citizen military personnel. If you are married to a U.S. citizen serving in the military and stationed abroad, and you have accompanied and are residing with him or her on this overseas posting under official military orders, you have special rights under the immigration laws (I.N.A. § 319(e), 8 U.S.C. § 1430(e); and I.N.A. § 284(b), 8 U.S.C. § 1354(b)). First of all, you can count your time living with your spouse overseas as if it were time spent in the United States. Second, you can take advantage of the law allowing you to apply for citizenship after three years of permanent residence. Third, you don't have to return to the United States to apply for citizenship if you don't want to, but can instead complete all parts of the naturalization and swearing in process abroad.

 PAPERWORK REMINDER

Planning to naturalize abroad as a military spouse? You'll have to take extra steps in filing the application, including:

- When filling out Form N-400, in Part 1, "Information About Your Eligibility," check box 5, "Other," and write in "319 (e) Overseas Naturalization."
- Include a cover letter with your N-400. Your letter should be directed to the Nebraska Service Center and explain your desire to naturalize abroad. Include also your current address abroad (both local and APO/FPO), and say whether you qualify based on three years or five years of marriage to a U.S. citizen. Also state which U.S. consulate or overseas USCIS is most convenient for you to attend an interview at.
- Include a completed Form DD-1278, "Certificate of Overseas Assign-ment to Support Application to File A Petition for Naturalization," in which your military spouse's commanding officer certifies that you are authorized to have joined your military spouse abroad under "concurrent travel orders."
- Include two completed fingerprint cards (FD-258). You can have these done at a military base, an overseas USCIS field office, or a U.S. embassy or consulate.

If you're also applying after only three years based on your marriage to a U.S. citizen, you'll also need to include:

- A copy of your marriage certificate. This provides proof of your current marriage. If you or your spouse has been previously married, also include the applicable death or divorce certificates to prove that those marriages ended.
- Proof that your spouse is a U.S. citizen. This could be a copy of a valid U.S. passport, birth certificate, certificate of naturalization, certificate of citizenship, or registration of birth abroad.
- Evidence of your marital relationship, such as birth certificates for your children, copies of joint bank statements, credit card statements, joint tax returns, and so forth.

You will need to mail your completed naturalization application to:
Nebraska Service Center
N-400 319(e)
P.O. Box 87426
Lincoln, NE 68501-7426

After mailing in your N-400, you will also need to separately request overseas processing from the U.S. State Department (DOS). To do so, fill out a DHS form called "Request for Overseas Processing for spouses of active duty members of the U.S. Armed Forces, currently stationed abroad." (As of the time this book went to print, this form could not be found on the USCIS website, but a Google search would pull it up.) Send the form via email to either CIS-Seoul.Natz@dhs.gov (if you're requesting processing in Japan, Korea, or another part of East Asia, Southeast Asia, the Pacific Islands, or Australasia) or to Rome.Natz@dhs.gov if you're requesting processing in Europe, the Middle East, or Africa.

Surviving spouses of U.S. citizens killed in action. If you were married to a U.S. citizen who died while honorably serving on active duty with the U.S. Armed Forces, and if the two of you were married and living together at the time of your spouse's death, you can apply for citizenship without waiting—provided you are a permanent resident by the time you apply for citizenship. (See I.N.A. § 319(d), 8 U.S.C. § 1430(d).)

Service people during certain conflicts. If you served honorably and on active duty with the U.S. Armed Forces during one of the wars or periods of hostility listed below, and enlisted (signed up) while you were still on U.S. territory (including the Canal Zone, American Samoa, Swains Island, or a noncommercial U.S. ship), you don't even need a green card or permanent residence to apply for U.S. citizenship. You can, assuming your citizenship application is approved, go straight from having no legal status to becoming a citizen—a rare opportunity in the immigration law world. (See I.N.A. § 329, 8 U.S.C. § 1440.) The conflicts that qualify include:

- World War I (April 6, 1917 to November 11, 1918)
- World War II (September 1, 1939 to December 31, 1946)
- the Korean hostilities (June 25, 1950 to July 1, 1965)
- the Vietnam hostilities (February 28, 1961 to October 15, 1978)
- the Persian Gulf War (August 2, 1990 to April 11, 1991), and
- September 11, 2001, until a date to be determined by the U.S. President.

To take advantage of your right to apply immediately, you'll need certification from the military showing when and where you served and that your service and discharge (if any) were honorable. If you are currently serving in the military and at some later date you are dishonorably discharged, your citizenship can be taken away.

TIP

In addition to the conflicts listed above, the U.S. President can later add more by executive order. Check for new additions on the immigration section of Nolo's website (www.nolo.com).

PAPERWORK REMINDER

Put proof in your application packet. If you plan to claim one of these conflicts exceptions, include an explanation in your application cover letter and file Form N-426, which USCIS will use to request proof of your military service and discharge. You also need a separate letter saying your service and discharge were honorable.

v. Spouses of U.S. Citizens in Certain Overseas Jobs

If your spouse has a job requiring the two of you to live overseas, you may be able to apply for citizenship without five years of permanent residency. If you're willing to come back to the United States to apply, you can file your application any time after you receive your permanent residence.

There are a number of limitations on who can use this provision:

- You must be regularly stationed abroad because of your spouse's job.
- You must declare your intention to live in the United States as soon as your spouse's job ends.
- Your spouse's employer must be either:
  - the U.S. government (for example, the CIA, the military, the American Red Cross, or the Peace Corps)
  - a U.S. institution of research recognized as such by the attorney general (listed at 8 C.F.R. § 316.20(a))
  - a U.S. firm or corporation (or a subsidiary) engaged wholly or partly in the development of U.S. foreign trade and commerce
  - a public international organization in which the United States participates by treaty or statute (listed at 8 C.F.R. § 316.20(b) and (c)), or
  - a religious denomination with an organization within the United States, for which your spouse performs ministerial or priestly functions or works solely as a missionary.

Posthumous Citizenship for Soldiers Killed in Action

The law allows family members of a noncitizen who died from injury or disease caused during active duty with the U.S. Armed Forces during specified periods of military hostilities to apply for citizenship for their dead relative. (See I.N.A. § 329A, 8 U.S.C. § 1440.)

The closest relative should be the one to file the application—in other words, first choice would be a spouse, then a child, a parent, and last choice a brother or sister. If someone lower on this list than a spouse (namely a parent, child, or sibling), wants to be the one to submit the application, that person must first get permission from the spouse and anyone else higher on the list. A committee of relatives can also get together and prepare the application. This permission must be in the form of a signed affidavit.

You must apply within two years of the military person's death. Alternatively, a representative of the serviceperson's estate can file the application, as can a guardian, conservator, service organization with VA recognition, or someone designated by the U.S. Department of Defense.

To apply, fill out and send Form N-644 (Application for Posthumous Citizenship) and required documents to the USCIS California Service Center. Form N-644 and more detailed instructions and the address are available on the USCIS website at www.uscis.gov/n-644.

Immediate family members (spouses, parents, and children) of the deceased soldier may apply for green cards as the relative of a U.S. citizen. Although in ordinary situations, parents of U.S. citizens must wait until the child is 21 to apply for permanent residence, this requirement doesn't apply to the parent of a deceased service member who never reached age 21. However, the parents must file a visa petition within two years of the person's death. (This represents an amendment to the original law, which specifically refused immigration benefits to family members. See Public Law 108-36 §§ 1701–1703, enacted November 24, 2003.)

What if you start out as a conditional rather than a permanent resident? It becomes a matter of timing. If you can manage to not only apply for citizenship, but have your application approved and attend your swearing in ceremony before you've been a conditional resident for one year and nine months—in other words, before the date when you'd be expected to submit your Form I-751 petition asking to remove the conditions and become a permanent resident—you're fine. You can be naturalized without having had to submit this form. The naturalization examiner will, however, take a look to make sure you still deserve permanent residence, and may ask you, for example, for proof that your marriage is bona fide.

If the timing doesn't work out, however, and your citizenship application is still pending at the one-year-and-nine-month date at which you're expected to submit your Form I-751, then you'll need to go ahead and submit that form.

For more information, review I.N.A. § 319(b), 8 U.S.C. § 1430(b), as well as 8 C.F.R. § 319.11, and consult with an attorney.

 PAPERWORK REMINDER

If you plan to claim this overseas job exception, make sure to raise it in your application packet. Include an explanation in your cover letter and proof that you qualify for the exception.

B. Your Physical Location During Permanent Residency

In this section, we discuss three separate but overlapping citizenship requirements concerning your physical location—that is, where your feet were planted (on U.S. soil or overseas)—during the required years of permanent residence leading up to your citizenship application. The three requirements are:

- You spent most of your time during your required years of permanent residence on U.S. soil—called the "physical presence" requirement (discussed in Section B1).

- None of your absences from the United States lasted longer than six months—called the "continuous residence" requirement by USCIS (discussed in Section B2).

- You lived in the same U.S. state or USCIS district for three months before submitting your citizenship application (which we've named the "state stay" requirement, as discussed in Section B3).

We'll refer to these three requirements collectively as the "location" requirements.

1. Time Requirements for Physical Presence in the U.S.

In Section A3, we discussed how many years of permanent residence are required before applying for citizenship. But having a green card for the right number of years isn't enough to qualify you for citizenship. You must have spent as much time inside the United States as outside of it during those years.

This is the physical presence requirement, the purpose of which is for you to strengthen your ties to the United States. During those years, you'll become an active participant in U.S. society, start to understand its system of law and governance, and make a transition away from your old country.

If you are required to complete five years of permanent residence before applying for citizenship, then you must have spent two and a half of those years (30 months) in the United States. (This applies to refugees and asylees, too.) If you're required to complete three years of permanent residence, then you must have spent one and a half of those years (18 months) physically present in the United States.

EXAMPLE 1: Jorge was approved for his green card as a skilled worker. He has a five-year wait before he's eligible for U.S. citizenship. During those five years, he takes several business trips outside of the United States, adding up to two years' total time. He is eligible for citizenship, because he was physically present in the United States for more than two and a half years.

EXAMPLE 2: Graciela received her green card as a result of her marriage to a U.S. citizen (she is still married to him). She has a three-year wait from the date she got her green card before she's eligible for U.S. citizenship. She and her husband love to travel, and have spent a total of two of the last three years outside of the United States. This leaves her with only one year's physical presence since getting her green card—she has a physical presence requirement of 18 months. She'll need to spend another six months within the U.S. before she can apply for citizenship.

> **CAUTION**
> **Your sleeping hours must have been spent in the U.S., too.** If you've been working in the U.S. but commuting back and forth to your home in Canada or Mexico, you can't fulfill the continuous residence requirements.

If you fall into one of the exceptional categories of applicants who don't have to spend a specific number of years as a permanent resident, then you probably won't have to worry about the physical presence requirement. We'll talk more about these exceptional categories in Section B4, below.

The physical presence requirement is not the only way you have to prove that you made your home in the United States. Next, we'll discuss the requirement that you've lived here continuously.

Tallying Up Your Time In and Out of the United States

You'll need to know exactly when you were inside and outside the United States—preferably with exact dates.

Unless you have a fabulous memory or haven't taken many trips, you probably can't figure this out without a little research. Get out your passport, your calendar, your credit card receipts, and your frequent flier records and fill in the table below. This table is taken directly from the citizenship application, so skipping over it will only postpone the inevitable.

If your records don't reveal the information, be creative. For example, ask your employer for your time sheets and look for the vacation dates. Try to remember details of your trips that will help establish the dates. For example, think about which house or apartment you were living in when you took each trip and whether any trips were for special occasions that you can attach dates to, like your father's 60th birthday or your brother's wedding.

On the table below, enter every trip that lasted 24 hours or longer. Day trips—if you got there and back within 24 hours—don't count. If you can't determine the exact date, approximate (for example, giving the month and year). If you really can't remember the dates, write down what you can remember, such as "traveled to Mexico for the Christmas holiday every year—spent no more than two weeks each trip." (Although some USCIS officers will not accept approximations, it's better to provide some information than to hide the fact that you took trips.)

Date You Left the U.S. (Month/Day/Year)	Date You Returned to the U.S. (Month/Day/Year)	Did Trip Last Six Months or More?	Countries to Which You Traveled	Total Days Out of the U.S.
		☐ Yes ☐ No		
		☐ Yes ☐ No		
		☐ Yes ☐ No		
		☐ Yes ☐ No		
		☐ Yes ☐ No		
		☐ Yes ☐ No		
		☐ Yes ☐ No		
		☐ Yes ☐ No		

2. Continuity: Living Outside the U.S. for More Than Six Months at a Time

Taking short trips outside the United States is fine—in fact, it's one of your rights as a permanent resident. However, if during the required years of permanent residence leading up to your citizenship application, any of your trips lasted six months or more, you've got an eligibility problem. You can be said to have broken the continuity of your U.S. residence. Note that residence "in the U.S." can include living not only in one of the 50 states, but in any of the U.S. territories (Guam, Puerto Rico, or the U.S. Virgin Islands).

USCIS presumes that a six-month trip (or longer) means that you made your main home in another country and that your period of U.S. residence is no longer continuous. Even one day more than six months may raise USCIS's concern (though some USCIS offices are less strict than others).

That doesn't mean you're ineligible for citizenship. If your trip was under one year in length, you may be able to persuade USCIS that its presumption was wrong, and that you always intended to make your home in the United States. Your chances are improved if—during your trip—you maintained your primary residence in the U.S.

But a trip of more than one year breaks the continuity of your U.S. residence automatically and you are ineligible to apply for citizenship until you have completed a continuous permanent residency period.

CAUTION

USCIS could decide that you not only broke the continuity of your U.S. residence, but abandoned your U.S. residence altogether. If USCIS believes you planned to make your primary home elsewhere, it can deny your citizenship and send you to immigration court for a decision on whether you should be removed. It can take this action for any trips you took during your years of permanent residence. For example, if you've been a permanent resident for 25 years, USCIS could review a trip you took 20 years ago and determine you took that trip with the intention of abandoning your life in the United States. The USCIS officer at your citizenship interview has the power to decide that the border officials—were they let you back into the country—were too easy on you. Your case may then be handed over to a judge. If this could be an issue for you, see a lawyer.

> **CAUTION**
>
> **Tax breaks = continuity breaks!** If you claimed to be a nonresident of the United States in order to avoid paying U.S. income taxes, USCIS will determine that you have broken your continuous U.S. residence. This doesn't happen often, so we don't cover it in further depth here. If this might be an issue in your case, see a lawyer.

Though their underlying theme is the same—USCIS wants you to live in the United States—the physical presence and continuous U.S. residence requirements are different. Keep in mind that you could meet one while failing to meet the other.

EXAMPLE 1: During his five years as a permanent resident, Kelepi takes 25 vacation trips outside the United States. Each trip lasts 40 days. His total absence from the U.S. is 1,000 days (about two years and nine months). Although he can't meet the physical presence requirement—having spent more than two and one half years outside the U.S.—he has not broken the continuity rule, since no single trip was longer than six months.

EXAMPLE 2: During her five years as a permanent resident, Manawune spends eight months abroad with her ailing mother. Manawune has met the physical presence requirement—having spent over two and one half years in the United States—but she has broken the continuity of her U.S. residence. Unless she can persuade USCIS that she didn't intend to cut ties with her home in the United States, she is ineligible for citizenship until she completes a continuous five years of permanent residency.

There are exceptions to the continuity rules. Certain people who are working or stationed overseas can spend longer than six months outside the United States without hurting their eligibility for citizenship. These are discussed in Section B4, below.

In summary, your options, if you have broken the continuity of your U.S. residence, include the following:

- If your trip was more than six months but less than a year, provide evidence arguing that you didn't mean to break the continuity of your U.S. residence. (See Subsection a, below.)
- If you obviously broke your continuous U.S. residence or if you lived outside the United States for a year or more (but you didn't go so far as to abandon your U.S. residence), wait for a certain amount of time from the date you returned before applying. (See Subsection b, below.)

If you haven't yet spent six months outside the United States, but you know that you'll need to because of a job, you may have an additional option: to apply for advance permission to take a long trip. This is discussed in Subsection c, below.

a. Proving You Didn't Break Your Continuous U.S. Residence

As long as you were not outside the United States for more than one year at a time, you can argue that you didn't intend to break your continuous U.S. residence.

SKIP AHEAD

If you were gone for more than a year at a time, there's no point in arguing with USCIS or providing the documents described in this section. Go straight to Subsection b, below, to find out how long you'll have to wait before you'll be eligible for citizenship.

The key facts that will convince USCIS that you didn't intend to break your continuous U.S. residence are that you:

- kept a job with an employer in the United States (whether you were on leave, sent to work for an overseas office, or otherwise)
- continued to pay U.S. taxes
- left close family members in the United States
- kept a home or apartment in the United States to which you still had full access (that is, didn't rent out)

- continued your car registration, health insurance, and other such protections
- didn't take a new job overseas, or
- were prevented from returning to the United States by unexpected circumstances.

The more factors you match, the better. You'll need to provide supporting documents, and we've created a checklist below to help you. This is not an exhaustive list. Provide any relevant documents to prove that the United States remained your home during your absence. You might also want to get an attorney's help—USCIS has been known to deny a surprising number of applications because of continuity breaks.

 PAPERWORK REMINDER

Put the proof in your application. If you're explaining your continuity break to USCIS, describe what happened in your cover letter and include proof that you didn't break the continuity of your U.S. residence in your citizenship application packet.

b. Dealing With Continuity Breaks

Unless you were kidnapped or forcibly removed from the United States— rare exceptions—any stay of over one year outside the U.S. will break your continuity. If you've stayed over a year, or if USCIS rejects your arguments regarding trips of six months to a year, you'll need to redetermine your necessary years of U.S. residence. If you were required to have five years' permanent residence and were away for a year or more, you'll have to live in the United States for four continuous years and one day after the date you returned from your trip before applying for citizenship. (That way, there's no time during the previous five-year period when you were out of the U.S. for a year.)

If you qualify to apply for citizenship after three years, you must wait two years and one day after returning from the trip that broke your continuous U.S. stay to submit your citizenship application.

If you're applying after one of these waiting periods, don't count on using the 90-day early submission policy described in Section A3. Under these circumstances, most USCIS offices won't allow you to submit your application early.

Documents Demonstrating an Unbroken Stay

The following documents can help demonstrate an unbroken stay in the U.S.:
- ☐ copies of pay stubs showing you kept a job with a U.S. employer
- ☐ original IRS Form 1722 listing your tax information for the past three years or, if you can't obtain this, copies of your last three years' U.S. income tax returns
- ☐ copies of rent or mortgage payments showing you kept a home or apartment in the United States
- ☐ evidence that your family remained in the United States while you were away, such as copies of school, medical, and employment records, and rent or mortgage receipts
- ☐ copy of your U.S. car registration
- ☐ copies of your health insurance and other contracts and receipts
- ☐ your written explanation of the purpose of your trip and the reason it lasted so long, or
- ☐ if you were prevented from returning by unusual circumstances (for example, you broke your hip and couldn't travel), a letter from your doctor or another authority who can verify what happened.

CAUTION

Even the fixes described in this section won't help you if you not only broke the continuity of your U.S. residence, but abandoned your U.S. permanent residence altogether. If there's any strong basis upon which USCIS could claim that you meant to make your home outside the United States, consult with an immigration attorney before submitting your application. For instance, if you didn't merely divide your life between two places, but actually sold your U.S. home and car, took your children out of school, and gave your dog to a neighbor before leaving, USCIS is likely to suspect that you abandoned your U.S. residence.

c. Applying for Permission to Take a Long Trip

With a little advance planning, you can—under some circumstances—apply for USCIS permission to stay outside the United States for a year or more without breaking your continuous U.S. residence. You are allowed to do so if you have a job that takes you out of the United States for long stretches of time. You will, however, need to have lived in the United States as a permanent resident for one year before leaving (except religious workers, who can do their one year after returning). And you'll need to come back after two and a half years or else start over counting your years of permanent residence when you return to the United States. Upon return, you will need to prove that you really spent the time doing the designated job.

You are eligible to apply for permission if you are an employee of:

- the U.S. government
- a U.S. research institution (if the institution is recognized by the U.S. attorney general)
- a U.S. firm or corporation (more than 50% U.S. owned) involved in the development of U.S. trade and commerce
- a public international organization of which the United States is a member by treaty or statute, or
- a religious denomination or interdenominational mission organization having a bona fide organization within the United States, where you are authorized to perform ministerial or priestly functions or serve as a missionary, brother, nun, or sister.

(See I.N.A. § 317, 8 U.S.C. § 1428; 8 C.F.R. § 316.5(d)(2).)

You can file an application to preserve your continuous U.S. residence *after* you've left the United States, but you must turn it in *before* you've been away for a whole year. (Religious workers again receive an exception—they can file their application after returning to the United States.) Use Form N-470, Application to Preserve Residence for Naturalization Purposes, to apply. (We do not cover this application process in this book.) For the form and further instructions, see the USCIS website (www.uscis.gov).

PAPERWORK REMINDER

If you've already filed a Form N-470 application and received permission from USCIS to stay away for more than a year, include this proof in your citizenship application packet. Also include evidence that you actually returned on time, such as a copy of your plane ticket.

CAUTION

Don't confuse applications to preserve your continuous U.S. residence for citizenship purposes (Form N-470), with the Application for Travel Document (Form I-131). The latter application allows permanent residents to obtain a Reentry Permit to return to the United States after a long trip. Such permission does nothing to maintain your continuous U.S. stay for citizenship purposes—it merely protects you from being refused reentry at the U.S. border. If you're contemplating an extended trip abroad, consider filing for a Reentry Permit to protect against possible allegations of "abandonment" of permanent residence.

3. State Stay: Three Months of Residence in the State or District Where You Will Apply

You must live in the same U.S. state or USCIS district for three months before submitting your citizenship application to USCIS—we'll call this the "state stay" requirement. In other words, if you live in Maine, but move to Arkansas, you'll have to wait for three months before sending in your citizenship application. A few people who move to another state won't have to worry, because they'll remain in the same USCIS district. But this occurs only in smaller states, where USCIS serves several states with just one district office. Ask by calling USCIS at 800-375-5283.

If you have already submitted your citizenship application and then move to a different state or district, your case can no longer be considered by USCIS in the state or district you left behind. Your file must be transferred (which can delay it by many months, as we'll discuss in Chapter 4). Make sure you're comfortably situated somewhere before sending in your citizenship application.

Military personnel can submit their citizenship application in the state in which they're stationed, in the one where their spouse or minor children live, or in the one where their home address is (as shown in their military file). (See 8 C.F.R. § 316.5(b)(2).)

College students can apply in their home state or in the state where their school is located. (8 C.F.R. § 316.5(b)(2).)

4. Exceptions to the Location Requirements

If you're stationed or working overseas, meeting the various location requirements—physical presence, continuity, and state location—can be difficult. The government understands the difficulty and has made special exceptions for:

- U.S. military personnel (see Subsection a, below)
- widows and widowers of U.S. military personnel (see Subsection b, below)
- employees of the U.S. government and certain religious and other organizations (see Subsection c, below)
- spouses of U.S. citizens in certain occupations (see Subsection d, below)
- employees of certain U.S. nonprofits (see Subsection e, below), and
- service people on nonmilitary U.S. ships (see Subsection f, below).

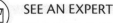 SEE AN EXPERT

We briefly discuss each of the location exceptions in this chapter. If you need more detailed information, consult with an attorney who is an expert in immigration matters.

a. U.S. Military Personnel

If you've served honorably with the U.S. military for a total of one year and you're either still serving or ended your service no more than six months ago, you can apply for citizenship without worrying about location requirements. If it's been more than six months since you left the military, you'll have to follow the rules for ordinary permanent residents—except that USCIS will count your overseas service as residence within the United States for purposes of the location requirements.

PAPERWORK REMINDER

Planning to claim this military service exception? Include a filled-out Form N-426 and a certified statement from the appropriate military authorities showing that each period of your service during the required year was honorable and that you've never had a dishonorable discharge—not even outside the one year. You'll also have to show that you made your primary home in the United States during any breaks in your military service. Use the types of evidence described in Section B2, above.

b. Widows and Widowers of U.S. Citizens in the Military

If you are an immigrant and your U.S. citizen spouse was killed during honorable service on active duty with the U.S. Armed Forces and you and your spouse were married at the time of death, you can apply for U.S. citizenship without worrying about location requirements. (See 8 U.S.C. § 1430(d), I.N.A. § 319(d).) (And as you already know from Section A3, you don't need to worry about how long you've been a permanent resident, either.) You can submit your citizenship application as soon as you have a green card.

PAPERWORK REMINDER

To claim the widow/widower exception, obtain a statement from the military authorities stating that your spouse's service was honorable and that he or she was killed during the course of this service. Include this and a copy of your marriage certificate with your citizenship application.

c. Employees of the U.S. Government or Research, Religious, and Other Organizations

You may, through an application process, avoid the continuous U.S. residence requirement if you work for:

- the U.S. government
- a U.S. research institution (if the institution is recognized by the U.S. attorney general; see the list at 8 C.F.R. § 316.20)
- a U.S. firm or corporation (more than 50% U.S.-owned) involved in the development of U.S. trade and commerce
- a public international organization of which the United States is a member by treaty or statute, or
- a religious or missionary organization for which you work as a priest, missionary, brother, nun, or sister.

(See I.N.A. § 316(b)(1), 8 U.S.C. § 1427(b)(1).)

However, you'll need to apply for advance permission to spend more than six months outside the United States without breaking the continuity of your residence. To do so, however, you'll need to fill out USCIS Form N-470. Regardless of this exception, you will still need to meet the physical presence and state stay requirements for citizenship.

d. Spouses of U.S. Citizens in Certain Overseas Occupations

If your spouse is a U.S. citizen whose job requires that the two of you regularly live overseas, you may be able to avoid the location requirements. (See I.N.A. § 319(b), 8 U.S.C. § 1430(b).) Specifically, your spouse must be:

- employed by the U.S. government
- employed by a U.S. research institution recognized as such by the attorney general
- employed by a U.S. firm or corporation (or its subsidiary) that is engaged wholly or partly in the development of U.S. foreign trade and commerce
- employed by a public international organization in which the United States participates by treaty or statute, or

- serving as a priest, minister, or missionary on behalf of a religious denomination or interdenominational mission that is organized within the United States.

If any of these employment descriptions apply, you don't have to worry about the physical presence, continuous U.S. residence, or state stay requirements. You can submit your N-400 application from overseas and designate any USCIS office (in the U.S.) you want for your interview. You'll have to declare your intention to take up residence within the United States as soon as your spouse's employment is over.

> ⬚ **SEE AN EXPERT**
> **You'll need to seek personalized advice from an experienced immigration attorney to take advantage of this overseas employment exception.**

e. Employees of Nonprofits That Promote U.S. Interests

If you work for a communications-related nonprofit that requires you to live overseas, and you've worked for that nonprofit for at least five years after becoming a permanent resident, you may be able to avoid the location requirements. (See I.N.A. § 319(c), 8 U.S.C. § 1430(c).) You must work for a nonprofit that is:

- a bona fide U.S. incorporated nonprofit
- involved in communications media
- primarily involved in disseminating information that significantly promotes U.S. interests abroad, and
- recognized as meeting the above criteria by the attorney general.

If this section applies to you, you don't have to worry about any of the location requirements—physical presence, continuous U.S. residence, or state stay. You must come to the United States to claim your citizenship, and you must declare your intention to take up residence within the United States as soon as your employment is over.

SEE AN EXPERT

You'll need to seek personalized advice from an experienced immigration attorney to take advantage of this nonprofit exception.

f. Workers on Nonmilitary U.S. Ships

If you were living outside the U.S. while working on a nonmilitary U.S. ship, your time on board won't be subtracted from the time you were physically present in the United States and won't break the continuity of your U.S. residence. However, you will still have to remain in one U.S. state or USCIS district for three months before submitting your citizenship application.

A qualifying nonmilitary ship is one that's:

- operated by the U.S. government, or
- registered under U.S. law to a U.S. citizen or corporation and has its home port in the United States.

Time spent working on a *foreign* vessel doesn't count toward your U.S. physical residence requirements. To take advantage of this section, you must also have demonstrated good conduct and honorable service on the ship. (See I.N.A. § 330, 8 U.S.C. § 1441.)

SEE AN EXPERT

You'll need to seek personalized advice from an experienced immigration attorney to take advantage of this U.S. ship exception.

g. Translators or Interpreters Employed by the U.S. Government in Iraq or Afghanistan

If you were employed as a translator for either the U.S. Chief of Mission or the U.S. Armed Forces, or for a firm under contract with one of them, and at least some of your working time was spent in Iraq or Afghanistan, then your entire absence from the United States—even if your work as a translator or interpreter also took you to other countries—will not be considered to break your period of continuous residence. However, if you did a different job altogether for part of your time outside of the

U.S., that period of time won't be covered by this exception. (See Section 1059 of the National Defense Authorization Act.)

Also, you still must meet the physical presence requirement in order to apply for citizenship. But you can take care of this if you file and receive approval of your "Application to Preserve Residence for Naturalization Purposes," using Form N-470, as described earlier in this chapter.

You'll need to provide documentation affirming that you performed qualifying services in Iraq or Afghanistan. Ideally, this will be a letter from your employer. But if such a letter is impossible to obtain, you may present other evidence of your eligibility, such as travel orders or your employment contract.

C. The Age Requirement

To use the naturalization process described in this book, you must be at least 18 years old at the time you apply.

If you're younger than 18, there's an alternate route to U.S. citizenship. If one of your parents is or becomes a citizen, you may qualify for citizenship through your parent. For details, see Chapter 11. You can also refer to the article titled "U.S. Citizenship by Birth or Through Parents" at www.nolo.com.

D. Demonstrating Good Moral Character

To qualify for citizenship, you must demonstrate good moral character during your permanent residency, with a particular focus on the last five years (or fewer, if you fall into one of the exceptional categories that can apply earlier). The longer you've shown good moral character, the stronger your case.

What is good moral character? According to USCIS, it's the moral standard of an average member of the U.S. community.

As a general rule, USCIS doesn't ask for proof that you're good; it looks for evidence you've been bad. So, if you've gone about your every-day business, paid taxes and, if need be, child support, and avoided trouble with the law (either in the United States or abroad), you should have no problem establishing your good moral character.

However, if you have some minor negative behavior to account for—for example, a series of traffic tickets or a past drinking problem—you will need to balance out your bad acts by providing specific evidence of the good things you've done (as discussed in Section D17). Keep in mind that the USCIS determination of your moral character is a subjective, unscientific analysis in which the interviewing officer weighs your good and bad actions and decides which show the real you.

If you've committed more serious transgressions—for example, murder or another serious crime—you may not be able to outweigh them with your good deeds. Immigration laws detail a variety of actions that can destroy your good character. Certain actions will permanently prevent you from becoming a U.S. citizen; others will delay your citizenship, at least until you take some other corrective action. If the law requires it, the USCIS officer may be forced to deny your citizenship, no matter how sympathetic your case.

If you have a criminal conviction, see an attorney before applying for citizenship. If USCIS discovers your criminal convictions (and it probably will, through your fingerprints), it may not only deny you citizenship, but the agency may send you to Immigration Court for removal proceedings. (Note: USCIS usually won't hold juvenile convictions—when you were younger than 18—against you. Still, it's wise to see a lawyer for a full analysis.)

CAUTION

You may have a criminal record and not know it. You may have been arrested for something minor and signed a paper saying you're guilty, then never gone to jail. Or you may have received "diversion," with no guilty plea, or perhaps your case was "expunged"—that is, erased from your record years later. Keep in mind that these crimes still count against you for immigration purposes (with rare exceptions). Worse yet, if you state on your citizenship application that your record is clean, you may run into serious problems if USCIS later accuses you of lying. If in doubt, consult with an immigration attorney, who will help you run a criminal check on your fingerprints.

The checklist below summarizes the most common ways—but not all the ways—in which moral character can be undermined. Check any boxes for which you answer "yes" or aren't sure, and then review the appropriate sections.

Recent Years of Good Moral Character May Not Be Enough

Although your main task is to prove that your moral character has been good for the required (usually five) years of permanent residence leading up to your citizenship application (I.N.A. § 316(a)(3), 8 U.S.C. § 1427(a)(3)), USCIS is allowed to consider your actions before this time period began. This is especially true if your earlier actions shed light on the type of person you are today (I.N.A. § 316(a)(3), 8 U.S.C. § 1427(a)(3)).

For example, if the USCIS officer suspects that you make a lifestyle out of drinking and brawling, then a disorderly conduct conviction from six years earlier could weigh into the final decision. On top of this, there are certain actions that no amount of time will cure—for example, USCIS will never allow a convicted murderer to become a citizen.

Therefore, if you have any criminal or moral issues that arose prior to the last five years of your permanent residency (or fewer years, if you're using an exception to apply early), consult an attorney to determine the effect on your citizenship application.

---

1. You Have a Criminal Record

If you have ever been prosecuted for criminal activity, you'll need to see an immigration attorney for a full check of your record and what it means in immigration law terms. Don't try to interpret what's a serious crime and what isn't.

To give you an idea of what your attorney will need to analyze, we provide a brief overview of the most serious crimes that will permanently bar you from citizenship (Subsection a, below) and of the various other crimes that will block or delay your qualifying for citizenship (Subsection b, below).

Good Moral Character Checklist	
☐ Have you committed any crimes?	See Section D1.
☐ If you have committed a crime, have you since completed all probation, parole, or similar obligations?	See Section D2.
☐ Have you helped or encouraged anyone to enter the United States illegally?	See Section D3.
☐ Have you lied to obtain immigration benefits?	See Section D4.
☐ Have you pretended to be a U.S. citizen or voted illegally?	See Section D5.
☐ Have you received government assistance (such as welfare) through fraud or within five years of any U.S. entry?	See Section D6.
☐ Have you paid all court-ordered child support?	See Section D7.
☐ Have you paid all your income taxes?	See Section D8.
☐ Have you had drinking problems or been arrested for drunk driving?	See Section D9.
☐ Have you been a drug addict or abused drugs?	See Section D10.
☐ Have you been part of a bigamous or polygamous marital relationship?	See Section D11.
☐ If you're male, did you register for the U.S. Selective Service on time?	See Section D13.
☐ Have you deserted the U.S. military or evaded the draft or service by claiming to be a nonresident?	See Section D14.
☐ Have you advocated Communist or totalitarian systems or attempted to overthrow the U.S. government?	See Section D15.
☐ Have you done anything else that society disapproves of, such as committing a minor crime or adultery?	See Section D16.

> **CAUTION**
> **Crimes committed overseas count, too.** See a lawyer about any criminal prosecution in your past—even if it occurred overseas. Note: USCIS will not deny citizenship to refugees and asylees who were victims of inappropriate government prosecution—but talk to a lawyer anyway, just to be safe.

a. Crimes That Permanently Bar You From Citizenship

If you've ever been convicted of one of the following, you are permanently denied U.S. citizenship:

- murder, or
- an aggravated felony (if the conviction was after November 29, 1990).

These bars are automatic—that is, the USCIS officer reviewing your citizenship application will have no choice but to deny your citizenship, no matter how long ago the crime occurred. In addition, you'll probably be placed in removal proceedings.

USCIS's definition of aggravated felonies includes more than the standard list of rape, sexual abuse of a minor, drug trafficking, firearm trafficking, racketeering, running a prostitution business, child pornography, and fraud of $10,000 or more. It also includes crimes that local and state courts sometimes classify as misdemeanors.

For example, any crime of violence, or theft or burglary that resulted in a prison term of one year or more will be considered an aggravated felony.

> **EXAMPLE:** An immigrant who stole a car stereo was sentenced to six years in prison. The federal circuit court decided that this was an aggravated felony—a crime of violence, the court said, because the immigrant had pried the car door open first. (See *U.S. v. Alvarez-Martinez*, 286 F.3d 470, 2002 WL 538939 (7th Cir. 2002); 8 U.S.C. § 16.)

Resisting arrest has also been found to be a crime of violence. Even driving while under the influence of alcohol is sometimes considered a crime of violence, particularly if it involves reckless or intentional behavior.

Helping to smuggle an alien into the United States is also considered an aggravated felony—unless it was a first offense to help your spouse, child, or parent. Note that this exception doesn't cover smuggling grandparents, brothers, sisters, aunts, uncles, cousins, fiancés, and friends.

There are many tragic stories of immigrants innocently or negligently led into criminal acts that are later classified as aggravated felonies—for example, someone who befriends a drug dealer, buys a fake green card, or has sex with an underage girlfriend. Because this area is so complex, see a lawyer if you believe your criminal record could affect your citizenship quest.

b. Crimes That Temporarily Bar You From Citizenship

Some crimes make you only temporarily ineligible for citizenship. (See I.N.A. § 101(f), 8 U.S.C. § 1101(f).) If, after the date you committed the crime, you wait out the same number of years that you must have to meet your permanent residence requirement, you may be able to receive U.S. citizenship. We say "may" because USCIS can still consider your past actions in reviewing your application—and choose to deny your application. But at least you'll have a chance to prove that the good side of your character outweighs your past bad acts.

Here is a summary list of the crimes that make you temporarily ineligible for citizenship:

- You operated a commercial vice enterprise—for example, you were a prostitute, ran a call-girl ring, or sold pornography.
- You participated in illegal vice activities—for example, you hired a prostitute.
- You have been convicted of or admitted to a crime involving moral turpitude, such as fraud.
- You spent 180 days or more in jail or prison for any crime.
- You committed any crime related to illegal drugs other than a single offense involving 30 grams or less of marijuana.
- You have been convicted of two or more crimes, the combination of which got you a total prison sentence of five years or more.
- You get most of your income from illegal gambling or have been convicted of two or more gambling crimes.

If anything on your record remotely resembles an entry on the list above, see a lawyer. The lawyer can determine whether there's a problem and confirm how many years you should wait after the conviction date before you apply.

c. Other Crimes

If you've committed a crime that is not on any of the lists in the previous sections, you are not automatically barred from citizenship. But USCIS can still use its discretion to claim that your crimes demonstrate your lack of good moral character. USCIS considers such factors as whether anyone was injured, whether or not you cooperated with the police and the courts, and whether you were drinking or carrying an illegal weapon. As with all crimes, you should see an attorney to evaluate the situation.

2. You Haven't Completed Probation, Parole, or Similar Obligations

If, after being convicted of a crime, you are placed on probation or parole, you must successfully complete it before you can be approved for citizenship. (See 8 C.F.R. § 316.10(c)(1).) Your citizenship application will not be approved while you are on probation or parole—no matter how minor the crime. USCIS will either postpone a decision on your application until your probation or parole is completed or ask you to reapply later.

3. You Helped Someone Enter the U.S. Illegally

If USCIS finds out that you helped someone enter the United States illegally (often called "alien smuggling"), your application for citizenship will be denied—and if you smuggled the alien within five years of your last entry into the United States, you can be removed from the United States. (See 8 C.F.R. § 316.10.)

Alien smuggling doesn't just refer to what professional lawbreakers, sometimes called "coyotes," do in escorting someone across the U.S. border for a fee. It can also refer to someone who gives friendly assistance or encouragement to another—for example, by pretending a cousin is part of the family on a car trip back from Mexico, or by lending a green card to one's twin sister. Even if the friend or relative fails in the attempt to enter the United States, the people who tried to help will have a problem obtaining citizenship.

If you weren't convicted, how might USCIS find out that you helped someone enter the United States illegally? Apart from the fact that you'll be asked about this on the application form, USCIS may pick up other clues during your interview—for example, the USCIS officer may inquire about the immigration status of friends or family members.

Not all USCIS interviewers are nosy. In fact, USCIS interviewers often see cases where undocumented family members live in the same house as the applicant, and they let the issue pass. Again, as with all issues of moral character, see an immigration lawyer if in doubt.

4. You Lied to Gain U.S. Entry or Admission

If you lied to gain entry or admission to the U.S., you will not be granted U.S. citizenship. (See 8 C.F.R. § 316.10.) Admission means a lot more than just crossing the U.S. border; applying for a green card is a request for U.S. admission. For example, if you pretended to have a job offer in order to show USCIS that you wouldn't go on welfare or pretended to qualify for amnesty as a farm laborer when you really worked in a bank, these false statements—if discovered—could ruin your chances for citizenship. Even a relatively minor lie, which wouldn't have made a difference on your green card application, can be taken as a sign of bad moral character.

Because USCIS takes lying so seriously, it's better to be truthful about something you're ashamed about than to lie about it. Not all past lies will bar you from citizenship. (And if USCIS already "waived" this lie during the process of granting your green card, it should not present a problem.) After you've finished your required period of permanent residency, you may be able to overcome the problem with evidence of your recent good moral character. A lawyer can help and may also prevent you from losing your green card.

5. You Pretended to Be a U.S. Citizen or Voted Illegally

If you've told any government agency that you're a U.S. citizen, or if you have either registered to vote or actually voted illegally in a federal, state, or local U.S. election, you are barred from U.S. citizenship. A noncitizen who votes in a federal election can also be prosecuted criminally. (See 18 U.S.C. § 611.) You can also be deported or removed from the United States. (See I.N.A. § 237(a)(3)(D), (a)(6); 8 U.S.C. § 1227(a)(3)(D), (a)(6).)

This rule won't affect you if you told an employer or other private party that you were a citizen (although such lies could affect a determination as to your moral character or lead to criminal proceedings). And it's not a problem if you live in an area that allows noncitizens to vote in local elections, and you voted only on local candidates or ballot measures. But watch out for doing jury duty, which can in some circumstances be taken as a claim that you're a U.S. citizen.

Also, voting illegally will neither be considered a deportable offense nor a crime if the person's parents were or are U.S. citizens, the person permanently resided in the U.S. prior to age 16, and the person reasonably believed at the time of voting that he or she was a U.S. citizen.

CAUTION

Beware of state "Motor Voter" registration. Think back to when you got your driver's license—many states offer you a voter registration form at the same time, without checking to see whether you're actually eligible to vote. If you filled out the voter registration form, you may have disqualified yourself from U.S. citizenship.

If you registered to vote or voted illegally and didn't realize at the time that you weren't allowed to vote, get a lawyer's help. If you don't fit the exception described above, your lawyer can check whether your state punishes only those people who knew they were voting illegally, rather than punishing those who voted through a misunderstanding of their rights. That will help with your citizenship application.

6. You Obtained Government Assistance Through Fraud or Within Five Years of Any U.S. Entry

If you ever lied in order to get or keep welfare or disability benefits—for example, by pretending that a boyfriend or girlfriend was not supporting you, or by hiding a job or other source of income—you can run into problems. There are two ways in which your fraudulent receipt of government benefits can hurt your citizenship application:

- It can destroy your showing of good moral character.
- You can be found deportable and removed if it occured within five years of your U.S. entry.

If a small-scale fraud was committed—for example, you took a trip while on welfare but didn't realize your benefits program prohibited traveling—you can sometimes clear your name for citizenship purposes by arranging to pay back amounts you shouldn't have received. If you wait until your citizenship application to deal with this, the USCIS officer will probably refuse to approve your application until you've paid back the money and obtained a letter of proof that you can send to USCIS.

Under a little-noticed provision of the immigration laws, becoming a "public charge"—that is, receiving need-based government assistance— within five years of your last entry into the United States can make you deportable and therefore ineligible for citizenship. (See I.N.A. § 237(a) (5), 8 U.S.C. § 1227(a)(5).) In other words, you can be a green card holder for 20 years, leave the United States for a short vacation, then be at risk of deportation if you receive any government assistance during the next five years.

EXAMPLE 1: Jurgen has been a permanent resident since 2008. He worked until 2015, when his company ran out of customers. Jurgen has three children. In early 2016, he took a trip to see his parents in Scandinavia. He hoped they would help him out with some money, but they refused. Soon after Jurgen's return, he signed up for food stamps and other assistance. This makes Jurgen deportable—he should see an attorney before applying for citizenship.

Many citizenship manuals don't mention this—perhaps because USCIS rarely seems to invoke this part of the law. Also, many people can take advantage of an exception built into the law, stating that if the cause of needing the government assistance arose after your last entry, you're safe from removal.

7. You Haven't Paid Court-Ordered Child Support

If you have refused to pay court-ordered child support, you are barred from receiving U.S. citizenship and should consult with a lawyer before applying. (See 8 C.F.R. § 316.10.) The lawyer may be able to show that you didn't really "refuse" to pay child support, but simply couldn't pay for reasons beyond your control. If you made diligent, sincere efforts to support your children, your chances at citizenship are better.

A second possibility is for the lawyer to help you prove to USCIS that the good side of your character outweighs the bad. In that case, however, you'll have to wait for the same amount of time that you are required to have been a permanent resident before applying for citizenship (five years for most people), and the clock on those years won't start ticking until the date of your last failure to send a child support check.

8. You Haven't Paid Income Taxes

Unless you qualify under an exemption, you are required to pay U.S. income taxes. If you haven't paid them during any one of the required years of permanent residence leading up to your citizenship application, see a tax accountant or attorney before going any further. You'll need to pay any back taxes and clear your record with the Internal Revenue Service (IRS) before USCIS will grant your citizenship.

This is not in the immigration laws—it's a case of the IRS and USCIS working together to make sure you've paid your taxes. However, if you've actively committed tax evasion, that's a crime and a separate immigration law concern.

9. You Had a Drinking Problem

Your citizenship can be denied if you've been convicted of driving while under the influence of alcohol or drugs (commonly referred to as a "DUI" or "DWI") or if you are or have been a "habitual drunkard." (See 8 C.F.R. § 316.10.)

DUI is a crime, and the advice that we gave about crimes in Section D1, above, applies here too: Get a lawyer. The ordinary DUI case does not automatically bar someone from establishing good moral character, but since USCIS takes a very dim view of DUIs, you have to present strong evidence that you've reformed and have many positive character traits in order to convince USCIS that you deserve citizenship.

On top of this, a few additional circumstances can turn an ordinary DUI case into something far more serious. For example, in some parts of the United States, USCIS considers DUIs to be crimes of violence if committed recklessly or intentionally. In these situations, a DUI may escalate to an aggravated felony and become a permanent bar to citizenship.

It's not a crime to be a habitual drunkard, but if USCIS decides that you've made a lifestyle of heavy drinking—for example, based on arrests for disorderly conduct or domestic violence, or by asking for a doctor's report—you will have to demonstrate that you've gotten over your drinking problem in order to qualify for citizenship.

If you've had drinking problems but have gotten over them, wait from the date of your last drink until the number of years you're required to have held permanent residence have passed to apply for citizenship. Also, be prepared to show USCIS that you took steps to address the problem, such as consulting with a doctor or successfully completing a treatment program.

10. You Abused Drugs

If you have abused or been addicted to illegal drugs at any time since coming to the United States, you are barred from U.S. citizenship and could be removed. (See 8 C.F.R. § 316.10.) You do not have to have been arrested or convicted to fall into this category. In the eyes of USCIS, trying an illegal drug more than once is abuse. This hasn't been named as a permanent bar to citizenship, but its temporary nature won't help you much if you're placed in removal proceedings—so see a lawyer if you have a history of drug use or if you are addicted to drugs.

Of course, if you've been arrested for a drug crime, you've got a separate problem and should already be looking for a lawyer.

> ⓘ **CAUTION**
>
> **What about legal or medical use of marijuana?** Depending on which state you live in, marijuana use may be legal under certain circumstances. However, your immigration status is a federal matter, governed by federal law, which makes any marijuana use illegal. Green card holders convicted of a violation of a federal law relating to marijuana (other than a single offense involving possession for their own use of 30 grams or less) are deportable and will not be eligible for naturalization. You're also deportable if you are a "drug abuser or addict," and it's possible that the U.S. government will allege that even your legal use of marijuana constitutes abuse or addiction. This is a developing area of the law, however, so consult an immigration attorney for the latest.

11. You Believe in Polygamy

In certain cultures and religions, polygamy—the practice of taking multiple husbands or wives—is considered acceptable and normal. However, it is illegal in every U.S. state, and if you have committed or are practicing polygamy—even if only one pair within the web of household relationships is legally married—you are barred from showing the good moral character required for U.S. citizenship.

Even if you have only one spouse now, USCIS will deny citizenship if it believes you intend to enter into additional marriages later. USCIS will pay particularly close attention to applicants whose cultural or religious traditions recognize the custom of polygamy. The USCIS officer reviewing your N-400 form will scrutinize when and where your children were born, and whether you request a legal name change to match the name of an already married person with whom you live.

Also, for purposes of deciding whether you believe in polygamy, it doesn't matter whether you are the one with multiple spouses or partners, or whether you are just one of the many partners.

On the other hand, if you accidentally married a second person—for example, you incorrectly believed that your divorce was final when you remarried—you are not barred under this rule.

See an attorney if you have practiced polygamy or think USCIS might doubt your intentions, particularly if you come from a religion or culture in which polygamy is an accepted practice. You may be able to overcome past polygamy, but will first need to first terminate all but one of your spousal relationships and make sure your primary spouse or partner does the same. The safest course is wait to apply for naturalization until five years (or three years, if that's your good moral character period) have passed. Another possibility is to supply a (preferably written) explanation for why you got involved in the relationship and explain convincingly that you didn't intend to practice polygamy.

12. You've Committed Adultery

At one time, virtually any sexual act between a married person and an unmarried person was considered adultery, and constituted a crime. And in the past, this crime also barred people from U.S. citizenship. Because social standards have since changed, this is no longer an absolute bar. However, USCIS has stated that it will continue to deny naturalization based on a lack of good moral character in certain types of adultery cases, as follows:

"[W]here civil or criminal adultery . . . destroys a viable marriage, is grossly incestuous, as between parent and child, or brother and sister; or if it is commercialized, as where the petitioner prostitutes herself; or if it is flaunted openly with a willful disregard for the proprieties, causing publicized notoriety and public scandal; or if it is committed in the home under circumstances contributing to the delinquency of minor children; or if illegitimate children are begotten, and become public charges supported by public funds, or if the frequency of the adulterous acts, the number of different persons involved, the number of illegitimate children born and any other circumstances are such as to collectively indicate the petitioner's disregard for any standard of sexual morality."

(See USCIS Interpretation 316.1(g)(2)(viii).)

As a practical matter, USCIS reaction to an extramarital affair tends to depend on whether the applicant was living with his or her spouse at the time of the affair, and whether the spouse had full knowledge of the relationship. If you and your spouse were separated, or your spouse knew about and accepted the extramarital relationship, it shouldn't be considered evidence of bad moral character.

How does USCIS find out about applicants' adultery? A common tip-off is when an applicant has one or more children born or conceived with one person while having been married to someone else. This is not hard for USCIS to figure out. You are required to list ALL your children on your N-400 application, plus details about their birth dates and so forth. While Form N-400 does not ask you to name the other parent, USCIS officers are trained to ask clarifying questions; for instance, if you are the father of two children born less than nine months apart, or if the surname of your child is different from the surname of the man you were married to.

Another common way that USCIS catches on to an extramarital affair is when children were born during a marriage that ended in divorce, yet the divorce decree doesn't provide financial support for the child. Sometimes a divorce decree will state that a child born during the marriage is not the child of both parties; other times the divorce decree will simply fail to mention the child. In either case, USCIS examiners read through divorce decrees carefully, and may notice that the facts don't match up.

Finally, you will need to prove that you are current on all child support obligations. If, for example, you have been taken to court and required to pay child support for children born to one person while you were married to someone else, that too provides evidence of an extramarital affair.

13. You Fail to Register With the Selective Service

If you're a man who lived in the U.S. or got your green card at any time between the ages of 18 and 26, you were expected to register with the U.S. Selective Service System. The Selective Service collects the names of young men who are available to be called up in a military draft. The only exception likely to help you is if your entire time in the United States between ages 18 and 26 was spent in lawful, unexpired student, tourist, diplomatic, or other valid nonimmigrant status.

Notice, however, that no exception is made for undocumented or illegal aliens, including those who overstayed a visa. There are expected to register.

Another, less widely applicable exception is made for men born between March 29, 1957, and December 31, 1959—they were never under any obligation to register. For more information, see the Selective Service website at www.sss.gov.

Registering for Selective Service doesn't mean that you have to have actually joined the military. However, like all men who already are U.S. citizens, you are expected to be ready to join if a large-scale war or similar emergency arises.

If you knew about the requirement and refused to register, USCIS can deny your citizenship. But if you didn't know about this requirement, you're not alone. In fact, the average American is surprised to find out that noncitizens are on call to serve in our military. If you haven't registered, and you're younger than 26, see Subsection a, below. If you're between 26 and 31, see Subsection b, below. If you're older than 31, see Subsection c, below.

CAUTION
Don't assume that USCIS signed you up for Selective Service. If you filled out a Form I-485 for your green card (using the procedure known as "adjustment of status"), you may have noticed that you were, by signing the form, authorizing USCIS to provide your registration information to the Selective Service System. There's just one problem. USCIS takes the position that it never promised it would actually do this—and many people have found that it didn't.

a. You're Younger Than 26

If you didn't register for the Selective Service and you're not yet age 26, it's not too late—pick up the registration form at a U.S. post office, fill it out, and submit it.

b. You're Between 26 and 31

If you've passed age 26, it's too late for you to register for the Selective Service. Your chances of qualifying for U.S. citizenship depend on how many years have passed since you were supposed to register (after five years, you'll probably be okay) and how strict your local USCIS office is—they vary from sympathetic to unyielding. Nevertheless, many young men are able to show USCIS that they had no idea that registering was expected of them, and therefore didn't "willfully" fail to register, using a combination of:

- a Status Information Letter from the Selective Service System (Subsection i)
- a sworn declaration (Subsection ii), and
- where appropriate, sworn declarations from people who knew you (also discussed in Subsection ii).

i. Obtaining a Status Information Letter

A Status Information Letter from the Selective Service doesn't really help your case much—it simply states that you are over-age and therefore no longer required to register—but USCIS won't look at the rest of your materials without this letter.

In order to request the Status Information Letter, you'll need to visit the Selective Service System website (www.sss.gov). Click "Men 26 and older" and then "Status Information Letter Request Form." You can also get the request form by calling 847-688-6888.

After you receive the Status Information Letter, send the original to USCIS with your citizenship application and keep a copy for your records.

Sample Sworn Statement

I, Jean-Paul Mercredi, hereby say and declare as follows:

1. I am a French citizen and lawful permanent resident of the United States, residing at 432 Lake Place, Detroit, MI, 12345.

2. I was born on March 4, 1984. I was approved for permanent residence on April 10, 2008, when I was 24 years old.

3. I didn't register for Selective Service because I didn't know I was expected to. When I was approved for permanent residence, neither USCIS nor my lawyer said anything about my obligation to register—or if they did, I didn't understand it, because my English was rather weak then. Nor did I learn about the requirement independently.

4. I became a resident through marriage to a U.S. citizen. My wife did not know about the Selective Service requirement—she doesn't have any brothers, so registering for the draft is not something she has had to think about. Nor was Selective Service registration a topic of discussion among any of our friends. I have a few friends who have green cards, but they didn't say anything to me about this requirement—many of them are women or older than age 26, so they probably didn't know or remember.

5. Even when I first read about the Selective Service requirement in preparing my application for U.S. citizenship, I was surprised, thinking that someone would have contacted me if I was required to register. I was certainly never contacted by the U.S. military authorities or by anyone else.

6. I had no intention of avoiding my obligations, I was simply completely unaware that I was supposed to register for the Selective Service.

I swear, under penalty of perjury, that the contents of the foregoing statement are true and correct to the best of my knowledge.

Date: _March 12, 2016_____

Signed: _Jean-Paul Mercredi_____

ii. Writing a Sworn Declaration Explaining Your Failure to Register

Next, write a sworn statement explaining your failure to register. You'll find an example above. (Don't just copy the sample—insert facts that apply to your own life.)

Your sworn statement should offer reasons why you failed to learn about registration. If you attended high school in the United States—most U.S. high schools tell students about this requirement—explain why the information didn't prompt your registration. For example, you might have heard about the requirement but assumed it only applied to U.S. citizens. If possible, get letters from other people who knew you, such as a high school teacher, backing up your account of events.

CAUTION

You'll have trouble claiming ignorance of the registration requirement if you got your green card through the amnesty program in the 1980s, or if you got your green card more recently, during or after the year 2001. In both cases, participants were alerted as to the registration obligation.

PAPERWORK REMINDER

When explaining your failure to register, include your sworn statement and any additional letters with your citizenship application. Prepare these documents no matter how old you are now—even though USCIS is far more likely to deny your citizenship if only five years or fewer have passed since your failure to register.

c. You're Older Than 31

If you have passed the age of 31, it's a mathematical certainty that five years have passed since you were last required to register for Selective Service. And as you'll remember, it's the five years leading up to your citizenship application that are the most important in proving your good moral character. So, once these years have passed, even a knowing and willful failure to register for Selective Service is not an absolute bar to citizenship.

You can overcome any remaining concerns USCIS might have with other proof of your good moral character. However, if you want to be on the safe side, also provide documents showing that you didn't know about the Selective Service requirement, as described in Subsection b, above.

14. You Deserted or Avoided the U.S. Military During Wartime

If, during wartime, you deserted from the U.S. military, left the United States in order to evade the draft, or asked to be exempted from service based on being a noncitizen, you are permanently ineligible for U.S. citizenship. (See I.N.A. §§ 314, 315; 8 U.S.C. §§ 1425, 1426.)

If you believe you might fit into this category, see an immigration lawyer before going any farther with your application. Vietnam War draft dodgers who received amnesty from President Jimmy Carter do not fall into this category.

15. You've Been a Communist or Totalitarian or Opposed the U.S. Government

If, during the ten years before you apply for citizenship, you were involved in or advocated certain political activities, you are automatically (though not permanently) barred from receiving U.S. citizenship. More specifically, if you've shown support for activities involving anarchism (you oppose rule by government or law), world communism, totalitarianism, the overthrow of the U.S. government, or violence against the officers or property of the U.S. government, whether in the United States or abroad, you face a serious problem getting citizenship.

After ten years have passed from your date of involvement, this bar no longer applies—though if you committed any crimes based on your beliefs, separate bars may apply. (See I.N.A. § 313, 8 U.S.C. § 1424.)

There are exceptions—for example, you were too young to understand or your involvement was against your will or without your understanding of the group's true aims—but in general, you're facing an uphill battle if USCIS suspects you of support for, or involvement in, such a group.

SEE AN EXPERT

If you know you may be suspected of such involvement, get the help of an immigration attorney before you apply for citizenship. The attorney will help you draft an affidavit explaining your membership and activities.

16. You've Done Something That Society Frowns Upon

If you've done something that a USCIS officer might consider "bad," even if it's not listed in the law or mentioned in this book, you can still be denied citizenship on a discretionary basis. (See 8 C.F.R. § 316.10.) This vague standard is not commonly used to deny citizenship, and USCIS officers rarely ask prying personal questions.

In general, living with someone outside of marriage, having a child out of wedlock or with a person other than your spouse, or engaging in homosexual relationships are not a basis for denying citizenship. So don't be fearful about your personal life just because conservative members of society might frown on your actions. But keep in mind that when your personal behavior harms others—for example incest, prostitution, or having sex with minors—USCIS is more likely to find bad moral character.

For example, one immigration officer barred an applicant who sold liquor illegally in a restaurant. Another denied an applicant who had received a $152 ticket for collecting too many oysters along a beach, even though the man had promptly paid the fine.

In summary, you should primarily be concerned about antisocial behavior if a USCIS officer believes that your actions will harm others.

17. Showing Your Good Side

As your grandmother may have told you, everyone has some goodness inside of them. USCIS recognizes this, too. So, if you've done anything that you think a USCIS officer might take as a bad sign (and you've made sure the issue doesn't require a lawyer's help), get ready to show all your good deeds. Your goal is to show so many positive parts of your character that they outweigh the negative.

Here are some ideas to get you started:

- regular attendance at a church, temple, or mosque
- volunteer work
- caring for an ill or elderly friend or relative
- assisting with events at your child's school or with organized after-school activities, and
- winning community awards.

Sample Good Moral Character Letter

Bayshore Elementary P.T.A.
222 Bayshore Drive
Coasttown, CA 12345

November 9, 2016

To Whom It May Concern:

I am the president of the Bayshore Elementary P.T.A. It is my pleasure to write this letter in support of Marta Rivera's application for U.S. citizenship.

I have known Marta for four years. Our children both attend Bayshore Elementary. Marta has regularly attended P.T.A. meetings and enthusiastically participated in some special projects.

For the past two years, Marta has helped organize the holiday play, including helping supervise rehearsals and designing costumes. Everyone was amazed by her fir tree and elf costumes. She has also regularly baked cookies for our fundraising bake sales.

We particularly appreciate Marta's contributions since she, like many parents, works during the day. She obviously cares about her children a great deal. I never fail to see her at parent-teacher conference nights. Her children are lovely, always well dressed and well behaved.

Very truly yours,

Pat Pennyroyal
Pat Pennyroyal
P.T.A. President

Gather written materials to prove your activities—for example, a copy of your award certificate or a newspaper article discussing your achievements. Ask friends and community contacts to help. Once they hear that you're applying for U.S. citizenship, they may surprise you with their willingness to help. Show them a sample of the type of document you need (we provide one above) and ask them to make their letter personal to you, including your name, the dates you worked, volunteered, or attended services with the person, and anything else that you want USCIS to hear about.

PAPERWORK REMINDER
Once you've gathered these written materials, you should include copies of them with your citizenship application packet.

E. English Language Skills

To qualify for citizenship, you must have "an understanding of the English language, including an ability to read, write, and speak words in ordinary usage…." (I.N.A. § 312(a)(1), 8 U.S.C. § 1423(a)(1).) You'll need to demonstrate your English skills at your citizenship interview.

To more fully address this topic, and to help you prepare for the English exam, we've devoted a separate chapter to it—see Chapter 5. USCIS recognizes that age and physical disabilities can affect your ability to learn English and permits various waivers of the English requirement, discussed below.

1. Waiving the English Requirement for Advanced Age

Two separate rules allow older people to avoid the English requirement. If you're at least age 50 and have lived in the United States as a green card holder for at least 20 years, you can have the entire citizenship interview, including the history and government exam, conducted in your native language. (This is commonly known as the "50/20" waiver.) Your 20 years of residence do not need to have been continuous—if you've been away for short periods (fewer than six months at a time, to be safe), that's okay, so long as your total time living in the United States reaches 20 years.

The second rule—known as the "55/15" waiver—applies as follows. If you're at least age 55 and have lived in the United States as a green card holder for at least 15 years, you can have the citizenship interview and exam conducted in your native language. Your 15 years do not need to have been continuous.

To avoid delays, make sure the interviewer knows in advance that you are requesting a waiver. Mention this in your cover letter and write "50/20" or "55/15" in big letters at the top of your application form. (But don't use red ink, which USCIS's scanning equipment won't pick up.)

There will still be plenty of things to discuss at your interview. In Chapter 8, we discuss what happens at the interview.

> **CAUTION**
> **You may need to bring your own interpreter.** USCIS is not legally obligated to provide an interpreter for you, though some offices do so anyway. You can bring a friend or relative, or hire someone. The person must be age 18 or over, authorized to be in the United States, and able to translate all questions and answers accurately and literally.

2. Waiving the English Requirement for Disability

If you have a physical or mental disability that prevents you from learning English—for example, an ailment that requires regular medication that makes you severely drowsy, a developmental disability, or deafness—you may qualify for a waiver of the English requirement. In such a case, you would be allowed to have the citizenship interview done in your native language.

You can't just request this waiver; your doctor must fill out a form explaining your disability and why it prevents you from learning English. We cover the precise procedures for requesting this waiver in Chapter 7.

F. The U.S. History and Government Exam

In order to become a U.S. citizen, you must pass a test showing your "knowledge and understanding of the fundamentals of history, and of the principles and form of government, of the United States." (I.N.A. § 312(a) (2), 8 U.S.C. § 1423(a)(2).) As a practical matter, this means you'll have to memorize the answers to 100 potential questions. We give you all the possible questions, and help you prepare for them, in Chapter 6.

At your interview, the examiner will choose up to ten questions from the 100 to quiz you on. To pass, you'll need to answer six out of the ten questions correctly.

There are some people who, for reasons of age or disability, will find it nearly impossible to learn the answers to these questions. See Section F1, below, for information on age-related waivers and Section F2, below, for information on disability-related waivers of the history and government exam requirement.

1. The 65/20 Exception for Applicants of Advanced Age

If you are older than age 65 and have lived in the United States as a permanent resident for at least 20 years (these don't need to be continuous years) you can take an easier version of the history and government exam. This is commonly referred to as the "65/20 exception." You will have to study only 20 questions. You'll be asked ten of the questions and will need to answer six correctly in order to pass. For more information on these questions, see Chapter 6.

Your 20 years of U.S. residence don't need to have been continuous— if you've been out of the country for short periods (fewer than six months at a time, to be safe), that's okay—so long as your total time here reaches 20 years.

If you qualify for the easier exam, you automatically qualify to avoid the English language requirement as well. Alert USCIS in advance as to which waivers you are claiming in your cover letter, and write "65/20" in large numbers at the top of your N-400 application form.

2. Waiving the History and Government Exam for Disability

If you have a physical or mental disability that prevents you from learning the required concepts of U.S. history and government, you may qualify for a waiver. As we explained for people seeking to avoid the English requirement, you'll need to have your doctor fill out a form explaining exactly what your disability is and why it prevents you from learning concepts of U.S. civics and government.

Table Summarizing Available Language and U.S. History Waivers		
If you are:	**The USCIS can:**	**To request the waiver:**
Older than age 50, with 20 years' permanent residence	Allow you to take the citizenship test and interview in your own language	Alert USCIS in your cover letter and write "50/20" on top of your Form N-400
Older than age 55, with 15 years' permanent residence	Allow you to take the citizenship test and interview in your own language	Alert USCIS in your cover letter and write "55/15" on top of Form N-400
Older than age 65, with 20 years' permanent residence	Allow you to take a modified version of the citizenship test, with fewer possible questions; allow you to take the test and interview in your own language	Alert USCIS in your cover letter and write "65/20" on top of your Form N-400
Physically or mentally disabled	Make special accommodations for your interview, and/or allow you to avoid the citizenship test and/or have the interview done in your own language	Mention any needed accommodations in your cover letter. On Form N-400, fill out the appropriate box(es) on questions H and I. If requesting a waiver, have your doctor fill out Form N-648.

We cover the precise procedures for requesting a disability waiver in Chapter 7. This waiver may also qualify you to conduct the citizenship interview in your native language.

Using Past Exam Results

Some years ago, it was possible to take the U.S. history and government exam in advance, at a local adult school or community organization. Applicants could take the exam many times and wait until they had passed to submit their citizenship application. After allegations of fraud, the INS ended this program in the late 1990s. You now must wait until your naturalization interview to take the exam.

The only exception is an applicant who has obtained a green card through the legalization program (also called "1/1/82"). If you are one of these applicants and took the citizenship exam during Phase II of applying for your green card, you won't have to repeat the exam. If you have a certificate from the exam, include a copy with your application.

G. Loyalty to the U.S.

Several questions on the citizenship application reflect laws requiring that you be "attached" to the principles of the Constitution and be "favorably disposed to the good order and happiness" of the United States. (8 C.F.R. § 316.11(a).) This means that you should:

- not be hostile to the U.S. form of government
- believe in representative democracy
- believe in the ideals of liberty and equality among people that are described in the Bill of Rights portion of the Constitution, and
- believe that political change should be carried out only in a peaceful manner and in accordance with the law.

You can, however, still have a sentimental fondness for your home country.

You'll also be asked, on the application, whether you're willing to take the Oath of Allegiance to the United States (shown below) during the swearing-in ceremony that formally makes you a citizen. In addition, you'll be asked whether you're willing to serve in the U.S. Armed Forces (in a combat or noncombat role) or to perform "work of national importance under civilian direction when required by the law."

It's best if you can simply answer "yes" to all of these questions. However, if you have legitimate concerns over taking the Oath of Allegiance or serving in the U.S. military, review the sections below.

The Oath of Allegiance

I hereby declare, on oath,

that I absolutely and entirely renounce and abjure all allegiance and fidelity to any foreign prince, potentate, state or sovereignty, of whom or which I have heretofore been a subject or citizen;

that I will support and defend the Constitution and the laws of the United States against all enemies, foreign and domestic;

that I will bear true faith and allegiance to the same;

that I will bear arms on behalf of the United States when required by the law; and

that I take this obligation freely, without any mental reservation or purpose of evasion, so help me God.

1. Your Beliefs Forbid Taking Oaths

Some groups, most notably the Quakers and Jehovah's Witnesses, forbid their members to swear oaths. If you belong to such a group, USCIS will allow you to take a modified version of the Oath of Allegiance, substituting the words "and solemnly affirm" for the words "on oath" and leaving out the words "so help me God." For more on the swearing-in ceremony, see Chapter 11.

 PAPERWORK REMINDER

If you wish to modify the oath, advise USCIS when you submit your citizenship application. Include a letter from your pastor or religious leader indicating your religious affiliation.

2. Your Beliefs Forbid Serving in the Military

If your beliefs forbid you to carry or use weapons—that is, you are a "conscientious objector" or "CO"—you can still become a U.S. citizen. You do not have to be a member of a Christian or other organized religion, nor do you have to believe in God or a supreme being. However, you will need to show USCIS that:

- you are opposed to any type of military service
- you hold this objection based on religious, ethical, or moral principles, and
- you hold these beliefs deeply, sincerely, and meaningfully.

As a practical matter, however, USCIS tends to be most willing to recognize conscientious objectors who are formal members of religious communities with a tradition of pacifism, such as Buddhists, Quakers, and Mennonites.

Because you will answer "no" to certain questions on the citizenship application, you must send USCIS a sworn declaration explaining your beliefs. Make sure not to express your belief as opposition to a particular war, or you will not be viewed as a genuine CO. In your declaration, you should request permission to take a modified Oath of Allegiance. If your beliefs forbid you only to fight, then at your swearing-in ceremony, you will be allowed to leave out the words "I will bear arms on behalf of the United States when required by law."

If you can show USCIS that your beliefs also forbid you to serve in any military capacity, you'll also be able to leave out the words "I will perform noncombatant services in the Armed Forces of the United States when required by law." For more on the swearing-in ceremony, see Chapter 11.

PAPERWORK REMINDER

Explain your conscientious objector status in your application cover letter and include your sworn statement with your citizenship application packet. A letter from your pastor or religious leader might also help.

RESOURCE

For more information and support, contact the Center on Conscience & War (CCW), at www.centeronconscience.org, or 800-379-2679.

H. Overview: Are You Ready to Apply?

Use the list of questions below to confirm your citizenship eligibility. Check the box if your answer is "yes." For any unchecked boxes, review the appropriate section of this chapter and familiarize yourself with the rules. Once you are certain of your eligibility—that is, you have checked all the boxes—you're ready to prepare and submit your application.

Citizen Eligibility Checklist
☐ Have you had valid lawful permanent U.S. residence for the last five years (or less if you fall into an exception)? (See Section A.)
☐ Have you spent at least half of your required permanent residence period inside the United States (unless you qualify for an exception)? (See Section B1.)
☐ Has your U.S. stay been continuous—that is, unbroken by trips of six months or longer? (See Section B2.)
☐ Have you lived for at least three months in the state or USCIS district where you plan to submit your citizenship application? (See Section B3.)
☐ Are you at least 18 years of age? (See Section C.)
☐ Have you behaved in a way that shows your good moral character during your required years of permanent residence? (See Section D.)
☐ Can you speak, read, and write English (unless you fall into a group that can request a waiver of this requirement)? (See Section E.)
☐ Can you pass an exam in U.S. history and government (unless you fall into a group that can request a waiver of this requirement)? (See Section F.)
☐ Are you attached to the principles of the U.S. Constitution and willing to swear loyalty to the United States? (See Section G.)

Preparing and Submitting Your Application

Y ou'll find that applying for U.S. citizenship is far easier than getting your green card was. The application process involves only one form and very few accompanying materials. As with any application to USCIS, however, the form can be deceptive—a seemingly innocent question can be dangerously significant. And the USCIS bureaucracy is often frustrating. Officers who are new on the job, for example, may not have a complete understanding of the laws.

This chapter will show you how to get through the application process with the least possible frustration and difficulty. We explain to you:

- what goes into your application packet (see Section A)
- what to tell USCIS in your cover letter (see Section B)
- how to fill out Form N-400 (see Section C), and
- how to submit the application (see Section D).

Some time after submitting your citizenship application, you will be notified when to appear for a personal interview at your local USCIS office. During that interview, a USCIS officer will review your application and approve or deny your citizenship. However, you might wait a long time for this notification of your interview. What to do during this waiting period and during the interview itself is explained in Chapters 4 and 8, respectively.

CAUTION
Check for the latest forms and fees before you file. Although the USCIS sample forms and fee amounts included in this book were current on the date this book was published, both change regularly. If you submit an application with an old form or a fee that's too low, USCIS will eventually notify you, but you could lose weeks or months in the process. The USCIS website (www.uscis.gov/n-400) provides a handy way to check, or you can call USCIS at 800-375-5283.

A. What You'll Put in Your Application Packet

The most important part of your citizenship application is Form N-400. However, along with this form you'll need to prepare and assemble a few other items, listed below and summarized within the checklist in Section D1:

- **Cover letter.** (See Section B, below.)
- **Form N-400.** (See Section C, below.)
- **Fee payment.** Currently $595 for the application plus $85 for "biometrics" or fingerprints, for a total of $680. U.S. military personnel don't have to pay the fees. If you're age 75 or older, you don't have to be fingerprinted, and don't have to pay the $85 biometrics fee. See "Paying the Fee" in Section D2, below.
- **Two color photos, passport style.** It's too difficult to take a snapshot that meets USCIS's specifications, so find a shop that does passport photos. Gently write your name and your A-number (from your green card) on the back of each photo, in pencil or felt pen.
- **A photocopy of your green card.** (Both sides of the card, on two sheets of regular 8½" × 11" paper.) If your card has expired or you've lost it, see "How to Renew or Replace a Green Card," below.

If you plan to take advantage of one of the various exceptions described in Chapter 2, you may also need to include one or more of the following:

- If you've been married to a U.S. citizen for three years and you're applying after only three years of permanent residence on this basis, furnish proof of your eligibility for this exception—for example, copies of your spouse's citizenship certificate, your marriage certificate, proof that your or your spouse's previous marriages ended legally (certificate of death, divorce, or annulment), and copies of your tax returns for the last three years, as well as recent credit card bills in both your names and copies of your joint home title or rental receipts to show that you live together or share financial matters.

- If you've served in the U.S. military, include Form N-426, Request for Certification of Military or Naval Service. Follow USCIS's instructions, provided on the form and at the USCIS website (www.uscis.gov/n-426). Consult a lawyer if you need more help.

- If you are disabled and are asking for a waiver of the English and/or U.S. history and government exam requirements, furnish Form N-648, filled out by your doctor (see Chapter 7).

- Include any other items applicable to you as recommended elsewhere in this book and denoted by the Paperwork-Reminder icons—for example, a sworn explanatory statement if you're a male who forgot to register for the Selective Service, or a letter from your church if you're a Jehovah's Witness who can't swear the full Oath of Allegiance.

How to Renew or Replace a Green Card

It's possible your green card has expired or gotten lost. That doesn't mean that you've lost your permanent residence, but it's best to get a new green card before applying for U.S. citizenship. Some USCIS offices will allow you to apply without possession of a valid green card, but not all are so accommodating.

In any case, the law requires you to carry your green card with you at all times until you're a citizen. In these security-conscious times, it's likely that you'll be asked for your card by USCIS, the police, or airport authorities.

To renew or replace your green card, obtain Form I-90 from the USCIS website (www.uscis.gov/i-90) or by calling 800-870-3676. Follow the instructions that come with the form.

If a situation arises where you need proof of your permanent resident status more quickly, you can make an appointment with your local USCIS office through the INFOPASS system (online at www.uscis.gov). For instance, if you must take a trip outside the U.S. to help care for an ill family member, bring along a doctor's letter. They should give you an "I-551" stamp in your passport that proves your permanent residence and is good for one year.

> **CAUTION**
> **Always make your photocopies on one-sided, 8½" × 11" paper.**
> Don't create exact copies of small documents by making a copy on normal paper and cutting out the image—creating, for example, a tiny photocopied green card. The government doesn't appreciate "minicopies," which it will have to recopy onto a full-size sheet of paper. By the same token, 8½" × 14" paper (or larger) doesn't fit well into the government's files—if you have oversized documents, reduce them to 8½" × 11", if possible.

> **TIP**
> **Report stolen green cards to the police.** There is a hot market for illegal green cards. If yours is stolen, file a police report immediately. You may not get your card back, but when you apply for a replacement card, the police report will demonstrate your diligence and reduce suspicions regarding the loss.

B. Preparing Your Cover Letter

Including a cover letter with your citizenship application is not required, but it's a good idea. You can use the letter to list what's in your application, making it easier for USCIS to understand and organize your file. And the cover letter reminds you to include everything.

The cover letter is also a good place to advise USCIS of any special circumstances in your case—for example, that you're claiming a right to apply early based on an exception, or that you're requesting a waiver of the exam requirements based on age or disability.

The cover letter provided below covers the basic circumstances that apply to all applicants. Use it as a starting point, and if you determine that special circumstances exist in your case, mention these in the letter as well.

> **TIP**
>
> **You can't over-advise USCIS.** Even with a cover letter, USCIS frequently fails to notice important circumstances in applicants' cases—and therefore may not be adequately prepared for your interview. That's why it's important to follow any instructions we've given you in this book about writing things on the top of Form N-400. Bolding or highlighting important parts of your cover letter is also a good idea.

C. Filling Out USCIS Form N-400

Form N-400, Application for Naturalization, is the central and most important form that you will fill out in order to apply for U.S. citizenship. Everyone applying for citizenship through the naturalization process described in this book must fill out Form N-400. The form collects basic biographical information about you and asks questions to make sure that you meet all the citizenship eligibility requirements (discussed in Chapter 2).

> **RESOURCE**
>
> **Form N-400 is available by telephone at 800-870-3676, and on USCIS's website at www.uscis.gov/n-400.** The website version can be filled out on the computer—but it can't be submitted online. You can print out or photocopy the official version for your use.

Before you fill out the form, read the general tips in Section C1, below. Then, with a copy of Form N-400 in hand, follow the line-by-line instructions in Section C2 on how to fill it out. Also see the sample filled-out Form N-400 at the end of this chapter.

Cover Letter Template

[*Your address*]

[*Today's date*]

Re: A-number: [*Your eight- or nine-digit Alien number, from your green card*]

Application for Naturalization

[*Address of USCIS Service Center; see Section D4, below, for the one serving your geographic region.*]

Dear Sir or Madam:

Enclosed please find my application for naturalization, including the following items:

- Form N-400

- Application and biometrics fees, totaling $_____ [*or your request for a fee waiver*]

- Two photos

- A photocopy of my green card, front and back

- [*Any other needed documents as described elsewhere in this book*].

In addition, please note [*describe any exceptions or special circumstances in your case, and any accommodations that you need for disability, or any waivers of the English language, U.S. history and government exam, or oath-taking requirements that you're claiming based on age, disability, or religious convictions; see Chapter 7 for details*].

Thank you for your attention to this matter.

Very truly yours,

[*sign your name*]
[*print your name*]

1. Tips on Filling Out USCIS Forms

How clearly and carefully you prepare your paperwork can affect how your application is judged. This doesn't mean you have to hire someone to do it professionally—USCIS receives plenty of handwritten applications. But following these instructions will help avoid confusion and make your application stand out.

a. Typing or Ink?

This isn't the time to express your individuality with purple ink. Complete the form on a computer, as described below, or use a typewriter. If you cannot use a computer or typewriter, prepare it by hand, using black ink. Use all capital letters—that's right, CAPITAL LETTERS.

You can complete Form N-400 on your computer, using Adobe Acrobat. (If you don't have Adobe Acrobat, download a free copy from www.adobe.com.)

b. Inapplicable Questions

If you know that a question on Form N-400 doesn't fit your situation, write "N/A" (not applicable) rather than leaving the space blank. If you're not sure how or whether to answer a question, contact an attorney.

c. Tell the Truth

Lying to USCIS can get you in bigger trouble than the problem you are lying about. A USCIS officer who discovers that you've lied will not only become angry, but might have your citizenship application denied on moral character grounds, no matter how minor the lie. Even if undetected at your interview, a lie can result in your citizenship being revoked if USCIS finds out about it later—even many years later.

If you are torn between hiding and disclosing information on the form, now is the time to see a lawyer. An attorney can advise you how to complete the form honestly and protect your interests.

d. Be Consistent With Previous USCIS Applications

Pull out other applications or paperwork that you've submitted to USCIS and double-check that the information you're providing now matches what you've stated in previous applications. Failure to do this could lead to trouble.

> **EXAMPLE:** When Sarita applied for her green card, she was 17 and had a juvenile conviction for shoplifting. She mentioned the conviction on her green card application, but since USCIS doesn't ordinarily count juvenile arrests against applicants, Sarita got her green card. After becoming an adult, Sarita's juvenile record was sealed, and she figured the matter was far behind her. On Sarita's citizenship application, she answers "no" to the questions about whether she'd ever been arrested or convicted for a crime. The USCIS officer notices that this doesn't match the information on her green card application and because of her "lie," he denies Sarita's citizenship application on the grounds that she lacks good moral character. Sarita must wait for her full period of required permanent residence (in her case, five years) to rebuild her moral character before reapplying.

TIP

You can request a complete copy of your immigration file from USCIS. If you've misplaced copies of your previous immigration applications, this can be a handy option. The easiest way to make your FOIA request is to go through the Department of Homeland Security (DHS) website. It offers a "DHS FOIA Request Submission Form" (at www.dhs.gov/dhs-foia-request-submission-form), which allows you to choose USCIS (or another immigration-related agency) from a drop-down menu.

Of course, if you've found a harmless error in a previous application—such as a misspelled name or a wrong address—don't feel you have to stick to it. Insert the correct information on your citizenship application, but be prepared to explain the error and provide evidence of the true situation.

e. Use Extra Pages If Needed

In a few places on Form N-400, you may need more space for your response. In that case, attach a separate piece of paper and write "Please see attachment" in the appropriate space on the form. At the top of each attachment page, print your name, your A-number, and the words "Attachment to Form N-400." Then indicate which question(s) from which part(s) of the form you're answering. If you need more than one attachment page, add page numbers.

2. Line-by-Line Instructions for Form N-400

To follow the instructions in this section, you'll need to have a copy of Form N-400 in front of you. Below, we'll go through the form, question by question.

Notice that at the top of every page of the form, you'll need to fill in your A-number.

Part 1. Information About Your Eligibility

Check the box indicating your eligibility basis, usually depending on the number of years of permanent residency you need to have completed.

Most people check Box A (five years of permanent residence). However, spouses of U.S. citizens can check Box B (if they meet the conditions), spouses of people engaged in foreign employment for the U.S. government or military or other qualifying entities (described in Chapter 2) can check Box C, and people in military service can check Box D, indicating they qualify for an exception to the five-year rule. (These applicants must remember to provide proof that they fit in these alternative categories.)

TIP

What if you're the spouse of a U.S. citizen and have also held a green card for five years? Which box should you check? (This is the situation represented in the sample N-400 application shown later in this chapter.) In most cases, the choice makes no difference. But for some people, basing the application on a three-year period of eligibility offers an advantage, perhaps because an incident reflecting negatively on their good moral character happened during the two years before that. On the other hand, electing the three-year basis for eligibility will trigger a review of the marriage and the relations between the spouses at the time of the application; so if you want to avoid that, checking the box for five years would likely be better.

Refugees and those who obtained asylum should check Box A. Although they are permitted to credit some of their years as refugees or asylees toward the five-year requirement, they aren't exempt from the requirement itself, as discussed in Chapter 2, Section A3.

Date Permanent Residency Began

Old-Style Green Card (Back)   **New-Style Green Card (Front)**

Part 2. Information About You

Question 1. Your Current Legal Name. Enter your full name. If your name has changed during your life—for example, because of adoption, marriage, or a court-ordered name change—include legal documentation as proof.

Question 2. Your Name Exactly As It Appears on Your Permanent Resident Card. This question serves to match your application to your green card, so copy your name exactly as it appears on your green card, even if there are mistakes or your name has or will be changed.

Question 3. Other Names You Have Used Since Birth. Here you should provide alternate versions of your name (such as from past marriages) as well as names by which you've been commonly known. For example, if your legal name is Alexander but your nickname is Sasha and it appears on some of your personal records and documents, mention Sasha on this part of the application. If, however, only your mother or a few friends affectionately call you Sasha, then you don't need to enter it here. If you aren't sure, go ahead and include the nickname or alternate name, to be safe.

Question 4. Name Change. If you've wanted to change your legal name, this may be your chance. You can legally change it without any extra court procedures by simply filling in your chosen new name on the form. However, there's one catch. This service is available only at USCIS offices where the swearing-in ceremonies are held in a courtroom, presided over by a judge, not a USCIS officer. In some regions, ceremonies presided over by a judge are held only a few times per year, so asking for a name change will result in your waiting longer than most people to receive citizenship. Contact your local USCIS office and ask if a judge performs the ceremony, or wait until your USCIS interview and ask the officer who will preside. If you're in luck, the officer will have you fill out a form called a Petition for Name Change during your interview.

The judge will not approve your name change if:

- You changed your name for fraudulent reasons, such as to escape capture for a crime or to avoid paying a debt.
- Your new name interferes with someone else's right to a name, particularly a famous person, such as Bill Clinton or Cher, or of a company, such as Charles Schwab.

- Your name is intentionally confusing, such as "P.O. Box 2000" or "Boeing Jet."
- Your name is threatening, obscene, or likely to incite violence. "Beat U. Up," for example, is not likely to be allowed.

Most of the rest of this section is self-explanatory, but we'll discuss certain questions that may not be.

For Question 9, you can find the date you became a permanent resident on your green card. On the old-style green cards, the date begins with the year—so, for example, 870723 would be July 23, 1987, which you'd write 07/23/1987.

In Questions 12 and 13, and in **Part 3**, you have an opportunity to alert USCIS as to any physical or mental disabilities. USCIS wants to know two things: (1) whether you're seeking a reduction or waiver of the English language and/or U.S. history and government exam requirements because of your disability, and (2) whether there's anything USCIS can do to make your interview more comfortable, such as ensuring wheelchair access or providing a sign language interpreter. It's okay to say yes to both. Chapter 7 explains what it takes to qualify for a disability waiver or accommodation and what documents you'll need to add to your application.

In fact, there's a third issue regarding your disability that Form N-400 doesn't address here. Applicants whose conditions are particularly severe may, even after being approved for citizenship, be unable to understand or repeat the Oath of Allegiance that actually makes them a citizen. But, the applicant won't automatically be allowed to skip this oath—a separate waiver of the oath requirement must first be requested. Use Part 3 Question C to alert USCIS that the applicant is requesting this waiver. Then follow the instructions in Chapter 7 regarding writing a separate statement.

USCIS will conduct the interview in English unless you qualify to avoid the exam requirements based on disability (addressed above) or age combined with years of permanent residence (check the box that applies).

Part 4. Information to Contact You

This section asks for your phone numbers and email address. If you don't have a telephone or email address, answer "none." Alternatively, you could use a friend or neighbor's phone number—USCIS is unlikely to call you.

Part 5. Information About Your Residence

Question A. Enter your current home address. If you do not want to receive mail there, indicate where to send mail in the next section.

Question B. Current Mailing Address. Fill in this section only if you want someone else to receive your mail for you or you'd prefer that it be sent to a post office box or temporary address. (Even if you complete this section, you must enter your home address above.)

Questions C–E. If you didn't live at the first address you entered for a full five years, continue on by entering your previous addresses. If you can't remember an exact address from years past, enter as much information as you can remember.

Part 6. Information About Your Parents

Here, USCIS wants to find out whether your parents are U.S. citizens, in case they transmitted their citizenship to you. This may have happened automatically (by operation of law), but it depends on a variety of factors, such your date of birth, how long your parents lived in the U.S., and whether one or both of them were citizens.

For more information on the complex rules surrounding transmission of citizenship, see the articles in the Immigration section of www.nolo.com.

Part 7. Biographic Information

Fill in this information precisely and honestly. It's to help USCIS check on whether you have a criminal record. If you don't believe you fit into any of the categories, choose the one that is closest. Under "Race," people of Latin American or Hispanic background ordinarily check "White."

If you have a criminal history, you'll have a hard time hiding the truth — USCIS separately checks your fingerprints. If you are concerned about what USCIS may turn up in its check of your records, consult a lawyer.

Part 8. Information About Your Employment and Schools You Attended

Here, you must provide information about where you worked or went to school for the last five years.

If you had periods of unemployment, unpaid work, self-employment, or taking care of home or children, list these too. (Be specific—don't just write "none" in the employer box.) Include any time spent working in the U.S. illegally before you got your green card, if any (but make sure that it matches the information on your green card application forms).

Part 9. Time Outside the United States

As discussed in Chapter 2, Section B, you'll need to prove that you spent the required minimum amount of time in the United States in the years before your citizenship application and that your visits outside the United States didn't last too long.

For Question 3, copy the information from the box you filled out in Chapter 2, Section B, under "Tallying Up Your Time In and Out of the United States." If you cannot determine the information, put down as much as you can. For example, some people may write in the space (or on an attachment page) something like, "I crossed the border into Mexico to spend time with my mother approximately once a month for the last five years. Most of my visits were three days long, except for visits at Christmas, which usually lasted one week."

> **CAUTION**
>
> **Check your passport for travel notations—because USCIS will!**
> No matter how good you think your memory is, examine your passport and any other official documents concerning your travel in the last five years. At the interview, the USCIS examiner will open your passport. You don't want to hear the officer saying, "Hmm, there's a visa stamp showing that you traveled outside the U.S., but you didn't write those dates on your N-400!" The USCIS examiner is bound to become suspicious about the discrepancy, and you'll have a lot of explaining to do.

Part 10. Information About Your Marital History

Most of the questions about your marital history are self-explanatory. However, Question 8 may confuse you: It asks "How many times has your current spouse been married?" Many applicants wonder whether their current marriage counts in adding these up. The answer is yes. If, for example, your spouse has been married once before, you'll need to answer "two" here. (This makes sense when you realize that, if you didn't add your current marriage to the count, anyone whose spouse had not been married before would have to answer "zero.")

Information about marriages may not be relevant to all citizenship applications, but USCIS prefers to gather a wide range of information and decide what to do with it later. You may have one of three concerns:

- What happens if you've divorced the person who was the basis for getting your green card?
- What happens if you reveal that your spouse is living in the United States illegally?
- Why does USCIS need to know about your and your spouse's previous marriages?

Divorce. Some people worry that if they got their green card through marriage, but have since divorced, they won't qualify for citizenship. As long as your marriage wasn't a sham (meaning its main purpose was for you to get a green card), your divorce should not pose an obstacle to citizenship. However, USCIS may ask some additional questions to double-check that your marriage wasn't a sham.

To be ready for these questions, review the material in Chapter 1, Section A1.

Undocumented spouses. As you can see on the form, Question 7C specifically asks for your spouse's immigration status. If your spouse has no status at all, you can simply write "alien" in the "Other" box for Question 7C. If you have filed applications with USCIS to help your spouse immigrate, then you can write "pending" in the box (meaning that your spouse is awaiting his or her green card or other status). Historically, USCIS has not used this information to try to track down spouses living here illegally. The USCIS officer may, however, question you as to whether you helped smuggle your spouse into the country—see Chapter 8 for details.

Previous marriages. One of the main reasons that USCIS asks about previous marriages is to make sure that you aren't married to more than one person and that your current marriage is valid. Some people discover that their or their spouse's divorce wasn't legally final until after their current marriage took place—or even that they are married to two people at the same time.

Being intentionally married to more than one person may be viewed as bigamy or polygamy, which USCIS considers a sign of bad moral character. Even if the double marriage was an accident, it can create a problem if you got your green card as a result of your recent marriage. Applying for citizenship will give USCIS a chance to discover this problem and could result in the loss of your green card. If you find yourself in one of these situations, see a lawyer.

Part 11. Information About Your Children

As indicated in the N-400 instructions, you must list *all* of your children, whether they are:

- alive, missing, or dead
- born in other countries or in the United States
- younger or older than 18 years
- married or unmarried
- living with you or elsewhere
- stepsons or stepdaughters
- legally adopted, or
- born out of wedlock.

Carefully comply with this instruction, as it may help one of your children immigrate to the United States later. If you fail to mention a child on your citizenship application, then you come back later with a petition to immigrate that child, USCIS may suspect that you're just trying to help someone else's child immigrate.

Part 12. Additional Information About You

These questions relate to your eligibility for citizenship, focusing in particular on your moral character and the amount of time you've lived in the United States. (To review eligibility requirements, see Chapter 2.)

If your answer to any of the questions is "yes" (with the exception of Questions 9 and 46–51, discussed below), there's a risk that your application could be denied. See a lawyer before going further.

CAUTION

Don't guess! If you aren't sure how to answer one of these questions, see a lawyer. For example, if a department store once accused you of shoplifting and you went to court, but you don't remember whether you were convicted or not, and you didn't actually serve any jail time, a lawyer could help clarify matters. Incorrect answers on this set of questions can have devastating consequences, including denial of citizenship or deportation.

Question 9. Don't fear listing your membership in community organizations such as a social club, church group, P.T.A., volunteer corps, or other volunteer group. These memberships demonstrate you have good moral character. Not so, if you belong to a group that advocates world communism, violence, terrorism, or other perceived dangers to the United States, or if you were involved with Nazi activities in Germany (as also covered in Questions 10–21). If you belong to a controversial group, consult with a lawyer before going further. See Chapter 2, Section D15, for more on the effects of such group memberships on your citizenship eligibility.

Questions 22–32. Notice that the questions regarding your criminal history and moral character are very broad—so broad that you'll even need to disclose any traffic tickets that you've received (in Question 23), although traffic stops or tickets ordinarily will not disqualify you from citizenship. Also, USCIS does not (unlike with other crimes) require you to submit documentary evidence showing the outcome if you received only a traffic fine or if you were not arrested and the only penalty was a fine less than $500 and/or points on your driver's license. (Don't worry about parking tickets—it's the incidents that happened while you were behind the wheel that USCIS is worried about.)

On Question 30F, be aware that even paying for or helping a family member to enter (or try to enter) the U.S. illegally must be accounted for with a "yes" answer. See a lawyer if you've done this.

On Question 31, remember that the "U.S. Government" includes its immigration authorities, so if you have provided false information on an application for a green card, visa, or other immigration benefit, you need to answer "yes" here. (And see a lawyer)

Questions 33–36. If you've been placed into removal, exclusion, or deportation proceedings, applying for citizenship will not cure that. Your citizenship application will very likely be denied. See a lawyer for a full analysis.

Questions 37–46. These questions have to do with whether you have served in the U.S. Armed Forces. For the most part, military service may offer benefits in your quest for citizenship (as described in Chapter 2). Be careful with Question 44, however. If you are a male who was living in the U.S. or got your green card before or between the ages of 18 and 26, you were probably required to register for Selective Service, a list kept in preparation for a U.S. military draft. See the full discussion of this requirement in Chapter 2, Section D13, and on the Selective Service website at www.sss.gov. If you answer "yes" here, you must either register with the Selective Service now (which you can only do if you're younger than age 26) or attach a statement explaining why you didn't register. We provide a sample statement in Chapter 2.

Questions 45–50. Here, you must show that you're loyal to the United States and will fight for it if necessary.

If this application is being filled out for a person who is disabled and thus unable to understand the Oath Waiver, Question 46 provides a place to indicate that. (Also attach a letter of explanation, as described in Chapter 7.) If you are a conscientious objector, meaning that for religious or moral reasons you refuse to take up weapons or join in a war, answer "no" to Question 48, which asks whether you'll bear arms for the United States. If your beliefs would prohibit you from providing any support to a war effort, answer "no" to Question 49, which asks whether you're willing to provide noncombatant services. (As covered in Chapter 2, Section G, you'll need to attach proof of your conscientious objector status and ask to take a modified Oath of Allegiance.)

If you're a member of a religion that prohibits taking any sort of oath (for example, the Quakers and the Jehovah's Witnesses fall into this category), answer "no" to Question 47—but you must provide a letter from your church or other religious body confirming your membership. (Include this letter when you send in your citizenship application.)

Part 13. Applicant's Statement, Certification, and Signature

USCIS has a number of good reasons for asking whether you had help filling out this form. In Question 1, if you used an interpreter, this will cast doubt on whether you really speak and understand English, unless you are also requesting an age- or disability-related waiver of the English requirement.

Question 2 serves as a reminder to both you and anyone who prepared the N-400 application on your behalf that the person needs to have gotten all the information directly from you, not just filled out the form as he or she saw fit.

If possible, sign your name in cursive, not printed letters. Cursive means a flowing style, usually slanted to the right, where the letters are connected: it looks like this: *Vida Karalis*, rather than this: Vida Karalis.

If you're disabled and can't sign your own name (for example, because your hands don't work, or because of cognitive difficulties), you have two choices. You can either mark an "X" in place of your signature, or your legal guardian can sign for you. (After the signature, guardians should put in parentheses "signed by [*guardian's name*], designated representative.")

Part 14. Interpreter's Contact Information, Certification, and Signature

If you requested an age- or disability-related waiver of the English requirement, this is where your interpreter must sign.

Part 15. Contact Information, Declaration, and Signature of the Person Preparing This Application, if Other Than the Applicant

If a lawyer, paralegal, or other preparer (including the designated representative of a disabled person) completes this form for you, that person must sign this section. If you completed the form on your own, however, or if you merely received some advice from a friend, neither of you needs to complete this section.

Part 16. Signature at Interview

You won't fill these out until your interview.

Part 17. Renunciation of Foreign Titles

If you're allowed to go by a title such as "Princess," "Duke," or the like, you will have to give this up in order to become a U.S. citizen. (In fact, you will have to add language to your Oath of Allegiance formally renouncing your title.) Leave this blank for now—you will not fill in or sign this section until you are at your USCIS interview.

Part 18. Oath of Allegiance

You must also leave this blank and not sign it until your interview with a USCIS officer.

D. Submitting the Application

After you've filled out your Form N-400, obtained your photos, and assembled the materials described in Section A, you're almost ready to send your application.

Here are some final suggestions:

- See our checklist in Section D2, below, to ensure you have included everything in your application packet. Forgetting something probably won't disqualify you from citizenship, but it could delay the process.

- Double-check the USCIS website to make sure the fees haven't gone up.

- Check the USCIS website to see whether your interview is likely to take place within the next 90 days. If so, and you're applying 90 days before your actual eligibility date, you might want to wait to submit your application. What happens if you go ahead and submit the N-400 anyway and USCIS calls you in for an interview before the date you're eligible? USCIS will conduct the interview, but it won't approve you right away. Instead, it will hold onto your file until you reach your eligibility date—which could lead to further delays if the file gets buried in a pile of paperwork. To check on when USCIS is likely to hold your interview, go to www.uscis. gov and click "Check your Case Status," then "USCIS Processing Times Information." Select your local "Field Office" from the drop-down menu, and click the "Field Office Processing Dates" bar. Look on the row that says "N-400." The number of months shown means that people who submitted their applications that long ago are now being called in for interviews, so you can figure that you will wait approximately the same amount of time.

- Take precautions against your application being lost, as discussed in Section D4, below.

- Be careful about where you mail your application—not all USCIS offices are authorized to accept citizenship applications. Don't waste your time trying to walk it into the USCIS office in your city. You'll need to mail it to the USCIS lockbox listed in Section D5, below—and they never take walk-ins.

! CAUTION

Make double sure you're not applying too early. If you haven't already done so, read Chapter 2, Section A, to determine when you are eligible to file your citizenship application. Most applicants must wait four years and 275 days (five years minus 90 days) from when they were granted lawful permanent residency, but there are some exceptions (as discussed in Chapter 2). Calculate the days to avoid filing early. If you submit your application early—even one day too early—USCIS will send it back—sometimes waiting weeks or months before doing so.

1. Using the Checklist for Citizenship Packet

Use the checklist below when preparing your application. Attach a copy to the file folder or envelope in which you're collecting the various items, and mark off each box as you add the item. That way, you'll ensure that nothing is left out.

2. Paying the Fee

To pay the fees, a personal check works well, because after it's cashed, the USCIS stamp on the back can be used to trace your application if it's lost. A cashier's check or money order is okay, but harder to trace. Or, you can make a credit card payment, by including a Form G-1450, Authorization for Credit Card Transactions, with your N-400 packet (one form per packet if several people file together). The form is available at www.uscis. gov/g-1450. Do not send cash. Make checks or money orders payable to Department of Homeland Security. (Or if you live in one of these places, either "Treasurer, Guam," or "Commissioner of Finance of the Virgin Islands.") To make sure they see your check, paperclip or staple it to the upper left-hand corner of your Form N-400. If you're living overseas, don't send the $85 for fingerprints—you can have your fingerprints done at a local U.S. consulate or USCIS office.

> CAUTION
> **By the time you read this, the N-400 fees may have changed.**
> In May of 2016, USCIS proposed various changes to immigration application fees, with a final decision to be made months later. One of the major proposed changes was to the N-400 application fee, for which USCIS planned to create a three-tier system. If it goes through, the new fee structure will be $640 for most applicants; no fee to applicants who meet military-service criteria and those approved for fee waivers based on low income; and $320 for applicants whose family income is above 150% of the Federal Poverty Guidelines but below 200%.

Checklist for Citizenship Packet
☐ Cover letter
☐ Form N-400
☐ Fees for application and biometrics (unless you're in the U.S. military or have requested a fee waiver)
☐ Two photos, passport style
☐ Photocopy of your green card
☐ If your name has changed since you got your green card, copies of the appropriate documents legalizing the change, such as a marriage certificate, divorce decree, or court order
☐ If you're applying earlier than five years on the basis of an exception, proof that you're eligible
☐ If you've been in the U.S. military, Form N-426, Request for Certification of Military or Naval Service
☐ If you've been married before, proof that all marriages were legally ended
☐ If you're requesting a waiver of the testing requirements based on disability, Form N-648, filled out by your doctor
☐ Any other items applicable to you as recommended elsewhere in this book or in USCIS's *Guide to Naturalization*.

Whichever form of payment you choose, be sure to keep all receipts, copies, or other records, and make a photocopy before you send it. This will help trace your application and your money if either is lost—and perhaps help you avoid paying twice.

TIP

Are you a member of the U.S. military filing for naturalization on the basis of your service? If so, you need not pay the fee.

3. Asking for a Fee Waiver If Necessary

No question about it, applying for citizenship is expensive: When this book went to print, it was $595 for the application and $85 for fingerprints (unless you're 75 or older). (By the time you're reading this, however, USCIS may have implemented a proposed change to have a reduced-fee option for all low-income applicants.) If your income is below the federally established poverty guidelines and you can't come up with the required amount, USCIS offers an alternative: You can make a written request to be excused from paying the application fee (to receive a "fee waiver") using USCIS Form I-912. (You can also request a fee waiver without using this form and instead submit a written request of your own drafting, but it's more work to make sure you include all the required information.)

RESOURCE

The poverty guidelines are updated annually. For the most recent version, go to www.uscis.gov/i-912p. The 2016 version is reprinted below.

There is nothing automatic about which cases USCIS will approve for the fee waiver. They consider each case individually, taking into account such factors as:

- whether you have received public benefits such as food stamps, Medicaid, or Supplemental Security Income (SSI)
- your age, particularly if you're elderly (65 or over)
- whether you're disabled
- the age and number of dependents in your household, and
- humanitarian or other reasons.

Most attorneys recommend against using the waiver at all unless it's absolutely necessary. The paperwork is lengthy and complicated. You must prepare a monthly budget of all your income and expenses, an explanation of your living arrangements, a list of your assets, and more—all with supporting documents.

After all your trouble, USCIS may deny your request if the agency is convinced that your expenses are inflated or unrealistic, or that you're spending money on so-called luxuries (items not necessary for your survival). In these cases, USCIS may advise economizing and saving up for a few more months to pay the fee. After all, no one is forcing you to apply for citizenship right now. Also keep in mind that a little mistake could raise suspicions of lying—which could destroy your chances of obtaining citizenship.

Even if USCIS grants your fee waiver, the time that it takes to make this decision may add to the time that you wait for your interview. If USCIS denies your fee waiver, it will send you back your entire N-400 package for refiling with the appropriate fee.

CAUTION

If requesting a fee waiver, don't attach a check as a "backup." In hopes of saving time, some people have tried sending both a fee waiver and a check, with instructions to use the check only if the fee waiver is denied. However, this approach doesn't work. As soon as USCIS sees the check, its policy is to cash it and pay no attention to the fee waiver request.

As if these reasons aren't enough, when you later attend your naturalization interview, your case may be reviewed by a USCIS officer who, consciously or subconsciously, judges people based on their income. USCIS cannot use poverty as the basis for a bad moral character judgment—but an officer may ask unpleasant questions if, for example, he or she believes that you're refusing to get out and find a job.

If you must apply for a fee waiver, go to the USCIS website at www.uscis.gov/i-912 to obtain the form and instructions.

2016 HHS Poverty Guidelines for Fee Waiver Request

2016 HHS Poverty Guidelines for Fee Waiver Request Department of Homeland Security U.S. Citizenship and Immigration Services		**USCIS** **Form I-912P** Supplement

2016 HHS Poverty Guidelines*

For the 48 Contiguous States, the District of Columbia, Puerto Rico, the U.S. Virgin Islands, Guam, and the Commonwealth of the Northern Mariana Islands:

Household Size	150% of HHS Poverty Guidelines*
1	$17,820
2	$24,030
3	$30,240
4	$36,450
5	$42,660
6	$48,870
7	$55,095
8	$61,335
	Add $6,240 for each additional person.

For Alaska:

Household Size	150% of HHS Poverty Guidelines*
1	$22,260
2	$30,030
3	$37,800
4	$45,570
5	$53,340
6	$61,110
7	$68,880
8	$76,680
	Add $7,800 for each additional person.

For Hawaii:

Household Size	150% of HHS Poverty Guidelines*
1	$20,505
2	$27,645
3	$34,785
4	$41,925
5	$49,065
6	$56,205
7	$63,345
8	$70,515
	Add $7,170 for each additional person.

* These poverty guidelines remain in effect for use with Form I-912, Request for Fee Waiver, from January 28, 2016 until new guidelines go into effect in 2017.

> **TIP**
> **Write "Fee Waiver Requested" on the top of your Form N-400 and all attachments, as well as on the outside of your mailing envelope.** This helps to alert USCIS as to your waiver request and may prevent your application from getting bounced back with USCIS claiming you forgot to pay. But don't use red ink—their document scanners won't pick it up.

4. Protecting Your Application Against Loss

You must prepare for the very real possibility that you will send in your application and hear nothing back, ever, even after writing many letters and trying to make contact in every other way possible. Here are three tips to help you avoid a USCIS disaster:

- Make copies of everything you send.
- Use a traceable method when mailing your application.
- Don't give USCIS anything you can't replace.

We'll explain the reasons for these maxims—and how to follow them.

a. Make Complete Copies

When you've finished preparing your citizenship application, don't mail it until you've made photocopies. Copy every page of the application form, as well as photos, documents, checks, and money orders. This will help you recreate these pages and items if they're lost in the mail or in the overstuffed files of a USCIS office. It may also help convince USCIS to take another look for the lost items.

b. Mail by a Traceable Method

It's not uncommon for applications to be misplaced when they arrive in the USCIS mailroom. If this happens to your application, you'll need proof that you mailed it. For that reason, if you use the U.S. Postal Service, use Priority Mail or certified mail with a return receipt. You can use the tracking information to convince USCIS to look for your misplaced application. Mailing by a service such as FedEx is also a good option.

By taking these steps, you'll have the evidence you need to show USCIS that it was its fault that a file was delayed or mislaid. In some cases, USCIS will rely on your own photocopies to proceed with your application.

c. Don't Send Anything That You'd Want Back

You may have to include personal documents with your application. Don't send originals of important documents such as marriage certificates or green cards to USCIS. You run a serious risk of losing them. USCIS refuses to give any assurance that you'll get your originals back.

Photocopy any document (as long as the original is the official version), and send the copy. Bring the originals to your interview so the USCIS examiner will have a chance to view them. (If USCIS makes a special request that you mail the original, comply with the demand, but make copies for yourself first!) Add the following text on the front of the copy, if there's room:

> Copies of documents submitted are exact photocopies of unaltered original documents, and I understand that I may be required to submit original documents to an immigration official at a later date.

> _Signature_

> _Typed or printed name_

> _Date_

d. Form G-1145

Including this optional form with your citizenship application packet is a smart way to help track its progress through the system. The form itself is simple to fill out, requiring only your name and contact information. You can choose to enter your email address, your mobile phone number, or both. By doing this, you will trigger USCIS to notify you electronically (via email or text message) when it has received your N-400 application. Clip Form G-1145 to the top of your packet when mailing it to USCIS.

RESOURCE

Form G-1145 is available by telephone at 800-870-3696, or on USCIS's website at www.uscis.gov/g-1145. See the sample below.

e-Notification of Application/Petition Acceptance
Department of Homeland Security
U.S. Citizenship and Immigration Services

USCIS
Form G-1145
OMB No. 1615-0109
Expires 09/30/2016

What Is the Purpose of This Form?

Use this form to request an electronic notification (e-Notification) when U.S. Citizenship and Immigration Services accepts your immigration application. This service is available for applications filed at a USCIS Lockbox facility.

General Information

Complete the information below and clip this form to the first page of your application package. You will receive one e-mail and/or text message for each form you are filing.

We will send the e-Notification within 24 hours after we accept your application. Domestic customers will receive an e-mail and/or text message; overseas customers will only receive an e-mail. Undeliverable e-Notifications cannot be resent.

The e-mail or text message will display your receipt number and tell you how to get updated case status information. It will not include any personal information. The e-Notification does not grant any type of status or benefit; rather it is provided as a convenience to customers.

USCIS will also mail you a receipt notice (I-797C), which you will receive within 10 days after your application has been accepted; use this notice as proof of your pending application or petition.

USCIS Privacy Act Statement

AUTHORITIES: The information requested on this form is collected pursuant to section 103(a) of the Immigration and Nationality Act, as amended INA section 101, et seq.

PURPOSE: The primary purpose for providing the information on this form is to request an electronic notification when USCIS accepts immigration form. The information you provide will be used to send you a text and/or email message.

DISCLOSURE: The information you provide is voluntary. However, failure to provide the requested information may prevent USCIS from providing you a text and/or email message receipting your immigration form.

ROUTINE USES: The information provide on this form will be used by and disclosed to DHS personnel and contractors in accordance with approved routine uses, as described in the associated published system of records notices [**DHS-USCIS-007 - Benefits Information System and DHS-USCIS-001 - Alien File (A-File) and Central Index System (CIS),** which can be found at **www.dhs.gov/privacy**]. The information may also be made available, as appropriate for law enforcement purposes or in the interest of national security.

Paperwork Reduction Act

An agency may not conduct or sponsor an information collection and a person is not required to respond to a collection of information unless it displays a currently valid OMB control number. The public reporting burden for this collection of information is estimated at 3 minutes per response, including the time for reviewing instructions and completing and submitting the form. Send comments regarding this burden estimate or any other aspect of this collection of information, including suggestions for reducing this burden, to: U.S. Citizenship and Immigration Services, Regulatory Coordination Division, Office of Policy and Strategy, 20 Massachusetts Avenue, NW, Washington, DC 20529-2140. OMB No. 1615-0109. **Do not mail your completed Form G-1145 to this address.**

Complete this form and clip it on top of the first page of your immigration form(s).

Applicant/Petitioner Full Last Name	Applicant/Petitioner Full First Name	Applicant/Petitioner Full Middle Name
Mancini	Terese	Maria

E-mail Address	Mobile Phone Number (Text Message)
tmancini@email.com	

Form G-1145 09/15/14 Y

Page 1 of 1

5. Where to Mail Your Application

You are required to mail your application to a USCIS "lockbox"—a large processing facility that will handle your file until it's turned over to a USCIS office near you for your interview. The table below lists the addresses. Find the one serving the state where you live and send your application there.

USCIS Lockboxes for N-400	
If you live in:	**Send your citizenship application to:**
Alaska, Arizona, California, Colorado, Hawaii, Idaho, Illinois, Indiana, Iowa, Kansas, Michigan, Minnesota, Missouri, Montana, Nebraska, Nevada, North Dakota, Ohio, Oregon, South Dakota, Utah, Washington, Wisconsin, Wyoming, Guam, or the Commonwealth of the Northern Mariana Islands	USCIS P.O. Box 21251 Phoenix, AZ 85036 **For express/courier deliveries, use:** USCIS Attn: N-400 1820 E. Skyharbor Circle S Suite 100 Phoenix, AZ 85034
Alabama, Arkansas, Connecticut, Delaware, District of Columbia, Florida, Georgia, Kentucky, Louisiana, Maine, Maryland, Massachusetts, Mississippi, New Hampshire, New Jersey, New Mexico, New York, North Carolina, Oklahoma, Pennsylvania, Rhode Island, South Carolina, Tennessee, Texas, Vermont, Virginia, West Virginia, Puerto Rico, or the U.S. Virgin Islands	USCIS P.O. Box 660060 Dallas, TX 75266 **For express/courier deliveries, use:** USCIS Attn: N-400 2501 S. State Hwy 121 Business Suite 400 Lewisville, TX 75067

CAUTION

The addresses above are only for citizenship applications. If you want to submit other applications to USCIS, such as visa petitions for family members, you can find the correct addresses and post office boxes for those applications at the USCIS website or by calling USCIS at 800-375-5283.

TIP

People applying while on active duty with the U.S. Armed Forces and their spouses must use a different address. Your application should go to: USCIS Nebraska Service Center, P.O. Box 87426, Lincoln, Nebraska, 68501-7426. Or if you're using express or courier service (such as FedEx or UPS), send it to Nebraska Service Center, 850 S. Street, Lincoln, NE 68508.

Sample N-400 Application for Naturalization—Page 1

Application for Naturalization

Department of Homeland Security
U.S. Citizenship and Immigration Services

USCIS
Form N-400
OMB No. 1615-0052
Expires 03/31/2019

For USCIS Use Only	Date Stamp	Receipt	Action Block

Remarks	

▶ **START HERE - Type or print in black ink.** Type or print "N/A" if an item is not applicable or the answer is none, unless otherwise indicated. Failure to answer all of the questions may delay U.S. Citizenship and Immigration Services (USCIS) processing your Form N-400. **NOTE: You must complete Parts 1. - 15.**

If your biological or legal adoptive mother or father is a U.S. citizen by birth, or was naturalized before you reached your 18th birthday, you may already be a U.S. citizen. Before you consider filing this application, please visit the USCIS Website at www.uscis.gov for more information on this topic and to review the instructions for Form N-600, Application for Certificate of Citizenship, and Form N-600K, Application for Citizenship and Issuance of Certificate Under Section 322.

NOTE: Are either of your parents a United States citizen? If you answer "Yes," then complete **Part 6. Information About Your Parents** as part of this application. If you answer "No," then skip **Part 6.** and go to **Part 7. Biographic Information.**

Part 1. Information About Your Eligibility (Select only one box or your Form N-400 may be delayed)

Enter Your 9 Digit A-Number:
▶ A- | 1 | 2 | 3 | 4 | 1 | 2 | 3 | 4 | 1 |

1. You are at least 18 years of age **and:**

   A. ☒ Have been a lawful permanent resident of the United States for at least 5 years.

   B. ☐ Have been a lawful permanent resident of the United States for at least 3 years. In addition, you have been married to and living with the same U.S. citizen spouse for the last 3 years, **and** your spouse has been a U.S. citizen for the last 3 years at the time you filed your Form N-400.

   C. ☐ Are a lawful permanent resident of the United States **and** you are the spouse of a U.S. citizen **and** your U.S. citizen spouse is regularly engaged in specified employment abroad. (See the Immigration and Nationality Act (INA) section 319(b).) If your residential address is outside the United States and you are filing under Section 319(b), select the USCIS Field Office from the list below where you would like to have your naturalization interview:

   D. ☐ Are applying on the basis of qualifying military service.

   E. ☐ Other (Explain):

Part 2. Information About You (Person applying for naturalization)

1. Your Current Legal Name (**do not** provide a nickname)

Family Name (Last Name)	Given Name (First Name)	Middle Name (if applicable)
MANCINI	Terese	Maria

2. Your Name Exactly As It Appears on Your Permanent Resident Card (if applicable)

Family Name (Last Name)	Given Name (First Name)	Middle Name (if applicable)
MANCINI	Terese	Maria

Sample N-400 Application for Naturalization—Page 2

Part 2. Information About You (Person applying for naturalization) (continued) A- 1 2 3 4 1 2 3 4 1

3. Other Names You Have Used Since Birth (include nicknames, aliases, and maiden name, if applicable)

Family Name (Last Name)
Brabantio

Given Name (First Name)
Terese

Middle Name (if applicable)
Maria

4. Name Change (Optional)

Read the Form N-400 Instructions before you decide whether or not you would like to legally change your name.

Would you like to legally change your name? ☐ Yes ☒ No

If you answered "Yes," type or print the new name you would like to use in the spaces provided below.

Family Name (Last Name)

Given Name (First Name)

Middle Name (if applicable)

5. U.S. Social Security Number (if applicable) ▶ 1 2 3 4 5 6 7 8 9

6. USCIS Online Account Number (if any) ▶

7. Gender ☐ Male ☒ Female

8. Date of Birth (mm/dd/yyyy) **02/02/1982**

9. Date You Became a Lawful Permanent Resident (mm/dd/yyyy) **04/05/2011**

10. Country of Birth **Italy**

11. Country of Citizenship or Nationality **Italy**

12. Do you have a physical or developmental disability or mental impairment that prevents you from demonstrating your knowledge and understanding of the English language and/or civics requirements for naturalization? ☐ Yes ☒ No

If you answered "Yes," submit a completed Form N-648, Medical Certification for Disability Exceptions, when you file your Form N-400.

13. Exemptions from the English Language Test

A. Are you **50** years of age or older **and** have you lived in the United States as a lawful permanent resident for periods totaling at least **20** years at the time you file your Form N-400? ☐ Yes ☒ No

B. Are you **55** years of age or older **and** have you lived in the United States as a lawful permanent resident for periods totaling at least **15** years at the time you file your Form N-400? ☐ Yes ☒ No

C. Are you **65** years of age or older **and** have you lived in the United States as a lawful permanent resident for periods totaling at least **20** years at the time you file your Form N-400? (If you meet this requirement, you will also be given a simplified version of the civics test.) ☐ Yes ☒ No

Part 3. Accommodations for Individuals With Disabilities and/or Impairments

NOTE: Read the information in the Form N-400 Instructions before completing this part.

1. Are you requesting an accommodation because of your disabilities and/or impairments? ☐ Yes ☒ No

If you answered "Yes," select any applicable box.

A. ☐ I am deaf or hard of hearing and request the following accommodation. (If you are requesting a sign-language interpreter, indicate for which language (for example, American Sign Language).)

B. ☐ I am blind or have low vision and request the following accommodation:

Sample N-400 Application for Naturalization—Page 3

Part 3. Accommodations for Individuals With Disabilities and/or Impairments (continued)

A- 1 2 3 4 1 2 3 4 1

C. ☐ I have another type of disability and/or impairment (for example, use a wheelchair). (Describe the nature of your disability and/or impairment and the accommodation you are requesting.)

Part 4. Information to Contact You

1. Daytime Telephone Number
   212-222-9822

2. Work Telephone Number (if any)
   212-876-5432

3. Evening Telephone Number
   212-522-1212

4. Mobile Telephone Number (if any)
   212-987-6543

5. Email Address (if any)
   teresanatz@yahoo.com

Part 5. Information About Your Residence

1. Where have you lived during the last five years? Provide your most recent residence and then list every location where you have lived during the last five years. If you need extra space, use additional sheets of paper.

   A. Current Physical Address

   Street Number and Name
   800 Broadway

   Apt. ☒ Ste. ☐ Flr. ☐ Number A

   City or Town: Lindenhurst

   County: Suffolk

   State: NY

   ZIP Code + 4: 11757 - 1234

   Province or Region (foreign address only)

   Postal Code (foreign address only)

   Country (foreign address only)

   Dates of Residence
   From (mm/dd/yyyy): 04/05/2011
   To (mm/dd/yyyy): Present

   B. Current Mailing Address (if different from the address above)

   In Care Of Name (if any)

   Street Number and Name

   Apt. ☐ Ste. ☐ Flr. ☐ Number

   City or Town

   County

   State

   ZIP Code + 4: -

   Province or Region (foreign address only)

   Postal Code (foreign address only)

   Country (foreign address only)

Sample N-400 Application for Naturalization—Page 4

Part 5. Information About Your Residence (continued) A- 1 2 3 4 1 2 3 4 1

C. Physical Address 2

Street Number and Name

Apt. ☐ Ste. ☐ Flr. ☐ Number ☐

City or Town   County   State   ZIP Code + 4
☐ - ☐

Province or Region
(foreign address only)   Postal Code
(foreign address only)   Country
(foreign address only)

Dates of
Residence   From (mm/dd/yyyy)   To (mm/dd/yyyy)

D. Physical Address 3

Street Number and Name

Apt. ☐ Ste. ☐ Flr. ☐ Number ☐

City or Town   County   State   ZIP Code + 4
☐ - ☐

Province or Region
(foreign address only)   Postal Code
(foreign address only)   Country
(foreign address only)

Dates of
Residence   From (mm/dd/yyyy)   To (mm/dd/yyyy)

E. Physical Address 4

Street Number and Name

Apt. ☐ Ste. ☐ Flr. ☐ Number ☐

City or Town   County   State   ZIP Code + 4
☐ - ☐

Province or Region
(foreign address only)   Postal Code
(foreign address only)   Country
(foreign address only)

Dates of
Residence   From (mm/dd/yyyy)   To (mm/dd/yyyy)

Part 6. Information About Your Parents

If neither one of your parents is a United States citizen, then skip this part and go to Part 7.

1. Were your parents married before your 18th birthday?   ☐ Yes ☒ No

Information About Your Mother

2. Is your mother a U.S. citizen?   ☐ Yes ☒ No

If you answered "Yes," complete the following information. If you answered "No," go to **Item Number 3.**

Sample N-400 Application for Naturalization—Page 5

Part 6. Information About Your Parents (continued)	A- |1|2|3|4|1|2|3|4|

A. Current Legal Name of U.S. Citizen Mother

Family Name (Last Name)   Given Name (First Name)   Middle Name (if applicable)

B. Mother's Country of Birth   **C.** Mother's Date of Birth (mm/dd/yyyy)

D. Date Mother Became a U.S. Citizen   **E.** Mother's A-Number
(if known) (mm/dd/yyyy)   (if any)
► A-

Information About Your Father

3. Is your father a U.S. citizen?   ☐ Yes ☒ No

If you answered "Yes," complete the information below. If you answered "No," go to **Part 7.**

A. Current Legal Name of U.S. Citizen Father

Family Name (Last Name)   Given Name (First Name)   Middle Name (if applicable)

B. Father's Country of Birth   **C.** Father's Date of Birth (mm/dd/yyyy)

D. Date Father Became a U.S. Citizen   **E.** Father's A-Number
(if known) (mm/dd/yyyy)   (if any)
► A-

Part 7. Biographic Information

NOTE: USCIS requires you to complete the categories below to conduct background checks. (See the Form N-400 Instructions for more information.)

1. Ethnicity (Select **only one** box)
☐ Hispanic or Latino   ☒ Not Hispanic or Latino

2. Race (Select **all applicable** boxes)
☒ White ☐ Asian ☐ Black or African American ☐ American Indian or Alaska Native ☐ Native Hawaiian or Other Pacific Islander

3. Height Feet [5] Inches [4]   **4.** Weight Pounds [1][3][5]

5. Eye color (Select **only one** box)
☐ Black ☐ Blue ☒ Brown ☐ Gray ☐ Green ☐ Hazel ☐ Maroon ☐ Pink ☐ Unknown/Other

6. Hair color (Select **only one** box)
☐ Bald (No hair) ☐ Black ☐ Blond ☐ Brown ☐ Gray ☐ Red ☐ Sandy ☐ White ☐ Unknown/Other

Sample N-400 Application for Naturalization—Page 6

Part 8. Information About Your Employment and Schools You Attended A-|1|2|3|4|1|2|3|4|

List where you have worked or attended school full time or part time during the last five years. Provide information for the complete time period. Include all military, police, and/or intelligence service. Begin by providing information about your most recent or current employment, studies, or unemployment (if applicable). Provide the locations and dates where you worked, were self-employed, were unemployed, or have studied for the last five years. If you worked for yourself, type or print "self-employed." If you were unemployed, type or print "unemployed." If you need extra space, use additional sheets of paper.

1. Employer or School Name

Moon Technosystems

Street Number and Name | Apt. ☐ Ste. ☐ Flr. ☐ Number ☐

123 Center St.

City or Town | State | ZIP Code + 4

Lindenhurst | NY | 11758 - 1111

Province or Region (foreign address only) | Postal Code (foreign address only) | Country (foreign address only)

Date From (mm/dd/yyyy) | Date To (mm/dd/yyyy) | Your Occupation

06/02/2011 | present | Marketing Copywriter

2. Employer or School Name

Self-employed

Street Number and Name | Apt. ☐ Ste. ☐ Flr. ☐ Number ☐

108 Piazza D'Azeglio

City or Town | State | ZIP Code + 4

Venice

Province or Region (foreign address only) | Postal Code (foreign address only) | Country (foreign address only)

Veneto | 30122 | Italy

Date From (mm/dd/yyyy) | Date To (mm/dd/yyyy) | Your Occupation

08/01/2003 | 04/05/2011 | Freelance writer

3. Employer or School Name

Street Number and Name | Apt. ☐ Ste. ☐ Flr. ☐ Number ☐

City or Town | State | ZIP Code + 4

Province or Region (foreign address only) | Postal Code (foreign address only) | Country (foreign address only)

Date From (mm/dd/yyyy) | Date To (mm/dd/yyyy) | Your Occupation

Sample N-400 Application for Naturalization—Page 7

| Part 9. Time Outside the United States | | | | A- | 1 2 3 4 1 2 3 4 1 |

1. How many **total days (24 hours or longer)** did you spend outside the United States during the last 5 years? **30** days

2. How many trips of **24 hours or longer** have you taken outside the United States during the last 5 years? **3** trips

3. List below all the trips of **24 hours or longer** that you have taken outside the United States during the last 5 years. Start with your most recent trip and work backwards. If you need extra space, use additional sheets of paper.

Date You Left the United States (mm/dd/yyyy)	Date You Returned to the United States (mm/dd/yyyy)	Did Trip Last 6 Months or More?	Countries to Which You Traveled	Total Days Outside the United States
03/05/2014	03/09/2014	☐ Yes ☒ No	Canada	5
06/12/2013	06/22/2013	☐ Yes ☒ No	Italy	10
07/15/2012	07/30/2012	☐ Yes ☒ No	Italy, France	15
		☐ Yes ☐ No		
		☐ Yes ☐ No		
		☐ Yes ☐ No		

| Part 10. Information About Your Marital History |

1. What is your current marital status?

   ☐ Single, Never Married ☒ Married ☐ Divorced ☐ Widowed ☐ Separated ☐ Marriage Annulled

   If you are single and have **never** married, go to **Part 11.**

2. If you are married, is your spouse a current member of the U.S. armed forces? ☐ Yes ☒ No

3. How many times have you been married (including annulled marriages, marriages to other people, and marriages to the same person)? **2**

4. If you are married now, provide the following information about your current spouse.

   A. Current Spouse's Legal Name

Family Name (Last Name)	Given Name (First Name)	Middle Name (if applicable)
MANCINI	Alberto	Ilario

   B. Current Spouse's Previous Legal Name

Family Name (Last Name)	Given Name (First Name)	Middle Name (if applicable)

   C. Other Names Used by Current Spouse (include nicknames, aliases, and maiden name, if applicable)

Family Name (Last Name)	Given Name (First Name)	Middle Name (if applicable)

   D. Current Spouse's Date of Birth (mm/dd/yyyy) **03/30/1982**

   E. Date You Entered into Marriage with Current Spouse (mm/dd/yyyy) **01/01/2010**

Sample N-400 Application for Naturalization—Page 8

Part 10. Information About Your Marital History (continued)   A- |1|2|3|4|1|2|3|4|1|

F. Current Spouse's Present Home Address

Street Number and Name   Apt. Ste. Flr. Number

800 Broadway   ☒   ☐   ☐   **A**

City or Town   County   State   ZIP Code + 4

Lindenhurst   **Suffolk**   **NY**   **11757** - **1234**

Province or Region   Postal Code   Country
(foreign address only)   (foreign address only) (foreign address only)

G. Current Spouse's Current Employer or Company

Techno Industries, Inc.

5. Is your current spouse a U.S. citizen?   ☒ Yes ☐ No

If you answered "Yes," answer **Item Number 6.** If you answered "No," go to **Item Number 7.**

6. If your current spouse is a U.S. citizen, complete the following information.

    A. When did your current spouse become a U.S. citizen?

    ☒ At Birth - Go to **Item Number 8.**   ☐ Other - Complete the following information.

    B. Date Your Current Spouse Became
    a U.S. Citizen (mm/dd/yyyy)

7. If your current spouse is not a U.S. citizen, complete the following information.

    A. Current Spouse's Country of Citizenship or Nationality   B. Current Spouse's A-Number (if any)

                                              ▶ A-

    C. Current Spouse's Immigration Status
    ☐ Lawful Permanent Resident   ☐ Other (Explain):

8. How many times has your current spouse been married (including annulled marriages, marriages to
other people, and marriages to the same person)? If your current spouse has been married before,
provide the following information about your current spouse's prior spouse. |1|

If your current spouse has had more than one previous marriage, provide that information on additional sheets of paper.

    A. Legal Name of My Current Spouse's Prior Spouse

    Family Name (Last Name)   Given Name (First Name)   Middle Name (if applicable)

    B. Immigration Status of My Current Spouse's Prior Spouse (if known)
    ☐ U.S. Citizen   ☐ Lawful Permanent Resident   ☐ Other (Explain):

    C. Date of Birth of My Current Spouse's   D. Country of Birth of My Current Spouse's
    Prior Spouse (mm/dd/yyyy)   Prior Spouse

    E. Country of Citizenship or Nationality of My Current
    Spouse's Prior Spouse

Sample N-400 Application for Naturalization—Page 9

Part 10. Information About Your Marital History (continued)	A- 1 2 3 4 1 2 3 4 1

F. My Current Spouse's Date of Marriage with Prior Spouse (mm/dd/yyyy)

G. Date My Current Spouse's Marriage Ended with Prior Spouse (mm/dd/yyyy)

H. How My Current Spouse's Marriage Ended with Prior Spouse

☐ Annulled ☐ Divorced ☐ Spouse Deceased ☐ Other (Explain):

9. If you were married before, provide the following information about your prior spouse. If you have more than one previous marriage, provide that information on additional sheets of paper.

A. My Prior Spouse's Legal Name

Family Name (Last Name)	Given Name (First Name)	Middle Name (if applicable)
MORENO	Giovanni	Paolo

B. My Prior Spouse's Immigration Status When My Marriage Ended (if known)

☐ U.S. Citizen ☐ Lawful Permanent Resident ☒ Other (Explain): Citizen and resident of Italy

C. My Prior Spouse's Date of Birth (mm/dd/yyyy)
05/22/1970

D. My Prior Spouse's Country of Birth
Italy

E. My Prior Spouse's Country of Citizenship or Nationality
Italy

F. Date of Marriage with My Prior Spouse (mm/dd/yyyy)
08/05/2002

G. Date Marriage Ended with My Prior Spouse (mm/dd/yyyy)
07/10/2004

H. How Marriage Ended with My Prior Spouse

☐ Annulled ☒ Divorced ☐ Spouse Deceased ☐ Other (Explain):

Part 11. Information About Your Children

1. Indicate your total number of children. (You must indicate **ALL** children, including: children who are alive, missing, or deceased; children born in the United States or in other countries; children under 18 years of age or older; children who are currently married or unmarried; children living with you or elsewhere; current stepchildren; legally adopted children; **and** children born when you were not married.)

2. Provide the following information about all your children (sons and daughters) listed in **Item Number 1.**, regardless of age. To list any additional children, use additional sheets of paper.

A. Child 1

Current Legal Name

Family Name (Last Name)	Given Name (First Name)	Middle Name (if applicable)
MORENO	Maria	Giovanna

A-Number (if any)
► A-

Date of Birth (mm/dd/yyyy)
12/11/2003

Country of Birth
Italy

Sample N-400 Application for Naturalization—Page 10

| Part 11. Information About Your Children (continued) | A- | 1 | 2 | 3 | 4 | 1 | 2 | 3 | 4 | 1 |

Current Address

Street Number and Name | Apt. Ste. Flr. Number

800 Broadway ☒ ☐ ☐ | A

| City or Town | County | State | ZIP Code + 4 |
| _Lindenhurst_ | _Suffolk_ | _NY_ | _11757_ - _1234_ |

| Province or Region (foreign address only) | Postal Code (foreign address only) | Country (foreign address only) |

What is your child's relationship to you? (for example, biological child, stepchild, legally adopted child)

Biological child

B. Child 2

Current Legal Name

| Family Name (Last Name) | Given Name (First Name) | Middle Name (if applicable) |

A-Number (if any)

▶ A-

Date of Birth (mm/dd/yyyy) Country of Birth

Current Address

Street Number and Name | Apt. Ste. Flr. Number

| City or Town | County | State | ZIP Code + 4 |

| Province or Region (foreign address only) | Postal Code (foreign address only) | Country (foreign address only) |

What is your child's relationship to you? (for example, biological child, stepchild, legally adopted child)

C. Child 3

Current Legal Name

| Family Name (Last Name) | Given Name (First Name) | Middle Name (if applicable) |

A-Number (if any)

▶ A-

Date of Birth (mm/dd/yyyy) Country of Birth

Sample N-400 Application for Naturalization—Page 11

Part 11. Information About Your Children (continued)   A- | 1 | 2 | 3 | 4 | 1 | 2 | 3 | 4 | 1 |

Current Address

Street Number and Name   Apt. Ste. Flr. Number

☐ ☐ ☐

City or Town   County   State   ZIP Code + 4

-

Province or Region   Postal Code   Country
(foreign address only)   (foreign address only)   (foreign address only)

What is your child's relationship to you? (for example, biological child,
stepchild, legally adopted child)

D. **Child 4**

Current Legal Name

Family Name (Last Name)   Given Name (First Name)   Middle Name (if applicable)

A-Number (if any)   Date of Birth (mm/dd/yyyy) Country of Birth

▶ A-

Current Address

Street Number and Name   Apt. Ste. Flr. Number

☐ ☐ ☐

City or Town   County   State   ZIP Code + 4

-

Province or Region   Postal Code   Country
(foreign address only)   (foreign address only)   (foreign address only)

What is your child's relationship to you? (for example, biological child,
stepchild, legally adopted child)

Part 12. Additional Information About You (Person Applying for Naturalization)

Answer **Item Numbers 1. - 21.** If you answer "Yes" to any of these questions, include a typed or printed explanation on additional
sheets of paper.

1. Have you **EVER** claimed to be a U.S. citizen (in writing or any other way)?   ☐ Yes ☒ No

2. Have you **EVER** registered to vote in any Federal, state, or local election in the United States?   ☐ Yes ☒ No

3. Have you **EVER** voted in any Federal, state, or local election in the United States?   ☐ Yes ☒ No

4. A. Do you now have, or did you **EVER** have, a hereditary title or an order of nobility in any foreign   ☐ Yes ☒ No
      country?

   B. If you answered "Yes," are you willing to give up any inherited titles or orders of nobility that you ☐ Yes ☒ No
      have in a foreign country at your naturalization ceremony?

5. Have you **EVER** been declared legally incompetent or been confined to a mental institution?   ☐ Yes ☒ No

Sample N-400 Application for Naturalization—Page 12

Part 12. Additional Information About You (Person Applying for Naturalization) (continued)

A- 1 2 3 4 1 2 3 4 1

6. Do you owe any overdue Federal, state, or local taxes? ☐ Yes ☒ No

7. A. Have you **EVER** not filed a Federal, state, or local tax return since you became a lawful permanent resident? ☐ Yes ☒ No

    B. If you answered "Yes," did you consider yourself to be a "non-U.S. resident"? ☐ Yes ☒ No

8. Have you called yourself a "non-U.S. resident" on a Federal, state, or local tax return since you became a lawful permanent resident? ☐ Yes ☒ No

9. A. Have you **EVER** been a member of, involved in, or in any way associated with, any organization, association, fund, foundation, party, club, society, or similar group in the United States or in any other location in the world? ☒ Yes ☐ No

    B. If you answered "Yes," provide the information below. If you need extra space, attach the names of the other groups on additional sheets of paper and provide any evidence to support your answers.

Name of the Group	Purpose of the Group	Dates of Membership	
		From (mm/dd/yyyy)	To (mm/dd/yyyy)
Lindenhurst Parent-Teacher Association	Support local public school	09/11/2015	present
Society of Technical Writers	Professional association	10/01/2003	present
Amnesty International	Human rights promotion	03/12/1990	07/28/1999

10. Have you **EVER** been a member of, or in any way associated (either directly or indirectly) with:

    A. The Communist Party? ☐ Yes ☒ No

    B. Any other totalitarian party? ☐ Yes ☒ No

    C. A terrorist organization? ☐ Yes ☒ No

11. Have you **EVER** advocated (either directly or indirectly) the overthrow of any government by force or violence? ☐ Yes ☒ No

12. Have you **EVER** persecuted (either directly or indirectly) any person because of race, religion, national origin, membership in a particular social group, or political opinion? ☐ Yes ☒ No

13. Between March 23, 1933 and May 8, 1945, did you work for or associate in any way (either directly or indirectly) with:

    A. The Nazi government of Germany? ☐ Yes ☒ No

    B. Any government in any area occupied by, allied with, or established with the help of the Nazi government of Germany? ☐ Yes ☒ No

    C. Any German, Nazi, or S.S. military unit, paramilitary unit, self-defense unit, vigilante unit, citizen unit, police unit, government agency or office, extermination camp, concentration camp, prisoner of war camp, prison, labor camp, or transit camp? ☐ Yes ☒ No

Sample N-400 Application for Naturalization—Page 13

Part 12. **Additional Information About You** (Person Applying for Naturalization) (continued)	A- |1|2|3|4|1|2|3|4|1|

14. Were you **EVER** involved in any way with any of the following:

   A. Genocide? ☐ Yes ☒ No

   B. Torture? ☐ Yes ☒ No

   C. Killing, or trying to kill, someone? ☐ Yes ☒ No

   D. Badly hurting, or trying to hurt, a person on purpose? ☐ Yes ☒ No

   E. Forcing, or trying to force, someone to have any kind of sexual contact or relations? ☐ Yes ☒ No

   F. Not letting someone practice his or her religion? ☐ Yes ☒ No

15. Were you **EVER** a member of, or did you **EVER** serve in, help, or otherwise participate in, any of the following groups:

   A. Military unit? ☐ Yes ☒ No

   B. Paramilitary unit (a group of people who act like a military group but are not part of the official military)? ☐ Yes ☒ No

   C. Police unit? ☐ Yes ☒ No

   D. Self-defense unit? ☐ Yes ☒ No

   E. Vigilante unit (a group of people who act like the police, but are not part of the official police)? ☐ Yes ☒ No

   F. Rebel group? ☐ Yes ☒ No

   G. Guerrilla group (a group of people who use weapons against or otherwise physically attack the military, police, government, or other people)? ☐ Yes ☒ No

   H. Militia (an army of people, not part of the official military)? ☐ Yes ☒ No

   I. Insurgent organization (a group that uses weapons and fights against a government)? ☐ Yes ☒ No

16. Were you **EVER** a worker, volunteer, or soldier, or did you otherwise **EVER** serve in any of the following:

   A. Prison or jail? ☐ Yes ☒ No

   B. Prison camp? ☐ Yes ☒ No

   C. Detention facility (a place where people are forced to stay)? ☐ Yes ☒ No

   D. Labor camp (a place where people are forced to work)? ☐ Yes ☒ No

   E. Any other place where people were forced to stay? ☐ Yes ☒ No

17. Were you **EVER** a part of any group, or did you **EVER** help any group, unit, or organization that used a weapon against any person, or threatened to do so? ☐ Yes ☒ No

   A. If you answered "Yes," when you were part of this group, or when you helped this group, did you ever use a weapon against another person? ☐ Yes ☐ No

   B. If you answered "Yes," when you were part of this group, or when you helped this group, did you ever tell another person that you would use a weapon against that person? ☐ Yes ☐ No

18. Did you **EVER** sell, give, or provide weapons to any person, or help another person sell, give, or provide weapons to any person? ☐ Yes ☐ No

   A. If you answered "Yes," did you know that this person was going to use the weapons against another person? ☐ Yes ☐ No

   B. If you answered "Yes," did you know that this person was going to sell or give the weapons to someone who was going to use them against another person? ☐ Yes ☐ No

Form N-400 03/26/16 N

Sample N-400 Application for Naturalization—Page 14

Part 12. Additional Information About You (Person Applying for Naturalization) (continued)

A- |1|2|3|4|1|2|3|4|1|

19. Did you **EVER** receive any type of military, paramilitary (a group of people who act like a military group but are not part of the official military), or weapons training? ☐ Yes ☒ No

20. Did you **EVER** recruit (ask), enlist (sign up), conscript (require), or use any person under 15 years of age to serve in or help an armed force or group? ☐ Yes ☒ No

21. Did you **EVER** use any person under 15 years of age to do anything that helped or supported people in combat? ☐ Yes ☒ No

If any of Item Numbers 22. - 28. apply to you, you must answer "Yes" even if your records have been sealed, expunged, or otherwise cleared. You must disclose this information even if someone, including a judge, law enforcement officer, or attorney, told you that it no longer constitutes a record or told you that you do not have to disclose the information.

22. Have you **EVER** committed, assisted in committing, or attempted to commit, a crime or offense for which you were **NOT** arrested? ☐ Yes ☒ No

23. Have you **EVER** been arrested, cited, or detained by any law enforcement officer (including any immigration official or any official of the U.S. armed forces) for any reason? ☐ Yes ☒ No

24. Have you **EVER** been charged with committing, attempting to commit, or assisting in committing a crime or offense? ☐ Yes ☒ No

25. Have you **EVER** been convicted of a crime or offense? ☐ Yes ☒ No

26. Have you **EVER** been placed in an alternative sentencing or a rehabilitative program (for example, diversion, deferred prosecution, withheld adjudication, deferred adjudication)? ☐ Yes ☒ No

27. A. Have you **EVER** received a suspended sentence, been placed on probation, or been paroled? ☐ Yes ☒ No

    B. If you answered "Yes," have you completed the probation or parole? ☐ Yes ☐ No

28. A. Have you **EVER** been in jail or prison? ☐ Yes ☒ No

    B. If you answered "Yes," how long were you in jail or prison? Years ☐ Months ☐ Days ☐

29. If you answered "No" to **ALL** questions in **Item Numbers 23. - 28.**, then skip this item and go to **Item Number 30.**

    If you answered "Yes" to any question in **Item Numbers 23. - 28.**, then complete this table. If you need extra space, use additional sheets of paper and provide any evidence to support your answers.

Why were you arrested, cited, detained, or charged?	Date arrested, cited, detained, or charged. (mm/dd/yyyy)	Where were you arrested, cited, detained, or charged? (City or Town, State, Country)	Outcome or disposition of the arrest, citation, detention, or charge (no charges filed, charges dismissed, jail, probation, etc.)

Form N-400 03/26/16 N

Sample N-400 Application for Naturalization—Page 15

Part 12. Additional Information About You (Person Applying for Naturalization) (continued)

A- 1 2 3 4 1 2 3 4 1

Answer **Item Numbers 30. - 46.** If you answer "Yes" to any of these questions, except **Item Numbers** 37. and 38., include a typed or printed explanation on additional sheets of paper and provide any evidence to support your answers.

30. Have you **EVER**:

A. Been a habitual drunkard? ☐ Yes ☒ No

B. Been a prostitute, or procured anyone for prostitution? ☐ Yes ☒ No

C. Sold or smuggled controlled substances, illegal drugs, or narcotics? ☐ Yes ☒ No

D. Been married to more than one person at the same time? ☐ Yes ☒ No

E. Married someone in order to obtain an immigration benefit? ☐ Yes ☒ No

F. Helped anyone to enter, or try to enter, the United States illegally? ☐ Yes ☒ No

G. Gambled illegally or received income from illegal gambling? ☐ Yes ☒ No

H. Failed to support your dependents or to pay alimony? ☐ Yes ☒ No

I. Made any misrepresentation to obtain any public benefit in the United States? ☐ Yes ☒ No

31. Have you **EVER** given any U.S. Government officials **any** information or documentation that was false, fraudulent, or misleading? ☐ Yes ☒ No

32. Have you **EVER** lied to any U.S. Government officials to gain entry or admission into the United States or to gain immigration benefits while in the United States? ☐ Yes ☒ No

33. Have you **EVER** been removed, excluded, or deported from the United States? ☐ Yes ☒ No

34. Have you **EVER** been ordered removed, excluded, or deported from the United States? ☐ Yes ☒ No

35. Have you **EVER** been placed in removal, exclusion, rescission, or deportation proceedings? ☐ Yes ☒ No

36. Are removal, exclusion, rescission, or deportation proceedings (including administratively closed proceedings) **currently** pending against you? ☐ Yes ☒ No

37. Have you **EVER** served in the U.S. armed forces? ☐ Yes ☒ No

38. A. Are you **currently** a member of the U.S. armed forces? ☐ Yes ☒ No

B. If you answered "Yes," are you scheduled to deploy overseas, including to a vessel, within the next three months? (Refer to the **Address Change** section in the Instructions on how to notify USCIS if you learn of your deployment plans after you file your Form N-400.) ☐ Yes ☐ No

C. If you answered "Yes," are you **currently** stationed overseas? ☐ Yes ☐ No

39. Have you **EVER** been court-martialed, administratively separated, or disciplined, or have you received an other than honorable discharge, while in the U.S. armed forces? ☐ Yes ☒ No

40. Have you **EVER** been discharged from training or service in the U.S. armed forces because you were an alien? ☐ Yes ☒ No

41. Have you **EVER** left the United States to avoid being drafted in the U.S. armed forces? ☐ Yes ☒ No

42. Have you **EVER** applied for any kind of exemption from military service in the U.S. armed forces? ☐ Yes ☒ No

43. Have you **EVER** deserted from the U.S. armed forces? ☐ Yes ☒ No

Sample N-400 Application for Naturalization—Page 16

Part 12. Additional Information About You (Person Applying for Naturalization) (continued)

A- 1 2 3 4 1 2 3 4 1

44. **A.** Are you a male who lived in the United States at any time between your 18th and 26th birthdays? ☐ Yes ☒ No
(This does not include living in the United States as a lawful nonimmigrant.)

    B. If you answered "Yes," when did you register for the Selective Service? Provide the information below.

    Date Registered   Selective Service
    (mm/dd/yyyy)   Number

    C. If you answered "Yes," but you **did not register** with the Selective Service System and you are:

       1. Still under 26 years of age, you must register before you apply for naturalization, and complete the Selective Service information above; **OR**

       2. Now 26 to 31 years of age (29 years of age if you are filing under INA section 319(a)), but you did not register with the Selective Service, you must attach a statement explaining why you did not register, and provide a status information letter from the Selective Service.

Answer **Item Numbers 45. - 50.** If you answer "No" to any of these questions, include a typed or printed explanation on additional sheets of paper and provide any evidence to support your answers.

45. Do you support the Constitution and form of Government of the United States? ☒ Yes ☐ No

46. Do you understand the full Oath of Allegiance to the United States? ☒ Yes ☐ No

47. Are you willing to take the full Oath of Allegiance to the United States? ☒ Yes ☐ No

48. If the law requires it, are you willing to bear arms on behalf of the United States? ☒ Yes ☐ No

49. If the law requires it, are you willing to perform noncombatant services in the U.S. armed forces? ☒ Yes ☐ No

50. If the law requires it, are you willing to perform work of national importance under civilian direction? ☒ Yes ☐ No

Part 13. Applicant's Statement, Certification, and Signature

NOTE: Read the **Penalties** section of the Form N-400 Instructions before completing this part.

Applicant's Statement

NOTE: Select the box for either **Item A.** or **B.** in **Item Number 1.** If applicable, select the box for **Item Number 2.**

1. Applicant's Statement Regarding the Interpreter

    A. ☒ I can read and understand English, and I have read and understand every question and instruction on this application and my answer to every question.

    B. ☐ The interpreter named in **Part 14.** read to me every question and instruction on this application and my answer to every question in _____ , a language in which I am fluent, and I understood everything.

2. Applicant's Statement Regarding the Preparer

    ☐ At my request, the preparer named in **Part 15.,** _____ , prepared this application for me based only upon information I provided or authorized.

Sample N-400 Application for Naturalization—Page 17

| Part 13. Applicant's Statement, Certification, and Signature (continued) | A- 1 2 3 4 1 2 3 4 1 |

Applicant's Certification

Copies of any documents I have submitted are exact photocopies of unaltered, original documents, and I understand that USCIS may require that I submit original documents to USCIS at a later date. Furthermore, I authorize the release of any information from any of my records that USCIS may need to determine my eligibility for the immigration benefit that I seek.

I further authorize release of information contained in this application, in supporting documents, and in my USCIS records to other entities and persons where necessary for the administration and enforcement of U.S. immigration laws.

I understand that USCIS will require me to appear for an appointment to take my biometrics (fingerprints, photograph, and/or signature) and, at that time, I will be required to sign an oath reaffirming that:

1) I reviewed and provided or authorized all of the information in my application;

2) I understood all of the information contained in, and submitted with, my application; and

3) All of this information was complete, true, and correct at the time of filing.

I certify, under penalty of perjury, that I provided or authorized all of the information in my application, I understand all of the information contained in, and submitted with, my application, and that all of this information is complete, true, and correct.

Applicant's Signature

3. Applicant's Signature
   Terese Maria Mancini

   Date of Signature (mm/dd/yyyy)
   08/14/2016

NOTE TO ALL APPLICANTS: If you do not completely fill out this application or fail to submit required documents listed in the Instructions, USCIS may deny your application.

| Part 14. Interpreter's Contact Information, Certification, and Signature |

Provide the following information about the interpreter.

Interpreter's Full Name

1. Interpreter's Family Name (Last Name)   Interpreter's Given Name (First Name)

2. Interpreter's Business or Organization Name (if any)

Interpreter's Mailing Address

3. Street Number and Name   Apt. Ste. Flr. Number
   ☐ ☐ ☐

   City or Town   State   ZIP Code + 4
                                                      -

   Province   Postal Code   Country

Sample N-400 Application for Naturalization—Page 18

Part 14. Interpreter's Contact Information, Certification, and Signature (continued)

A- | 1 | 2 | 3 | 4 | 1 | 2 | 3 | 4 | 1 |

Interpreter's Contact Information

4. Interpreter's Daytime Telephone Number

5. Interpreter's Mobile Telephone Number (if any)

6. Interpreter's Email Address (if any)

Interpreter's Certification

I certify, under penalty of perjury, that:

I am fluent in English and _____, which is the same language specified in **Part 13., Item B.** in **Item Number 1.**, and I have read to this applicant in the identified language every question and instruction on this application and his or her answer to every question. The applicant informed me that he or she understands every instruction, question and answer on the application, including the **Applicant's Certification** and has verified the accuracy of every answer.

Interpreter's Signature

7. Interpreter's Signature

➡

Date of Signature (mm/dd/yyyy)

Part 15. Contact Information, Declaration, and Signature of the Person Preparing This Application, if Other Than the Applicant

Provide the following information about the preparer.

Preparer's Full Name

1. Preparer's Family Name (Last Name)

Preparer's Given Name (First Name)

2. Preparer's Business or Organization Name (if any)

Preparer's Mailing Address

3. Street Number and Name

Apt. Ste. Flr. Number

☐ ☐ ☐

City or Town

State

ZIP Code + 4

-

Province

Postal Code

Country

Sample N-400 Application for Naturalization—Page 19

Part 15. Contact Information, Declaration, and Signature of the Person Preparing This Application, if Other Than the Applicant (continued)

A- |1|2|3|4|1|2|3|4|1|

Preparer's Contact Information

4. Preparer's Daytime Telephone Number

5. Preparer's Mobile Telephone Number (if any)

6. Preparer's Email Address (if any)

Preparer's Statement

7. **A.** ☐ I am not an attorney or accredited representative but have prepared this application on behalf of the applicant and with the applicant's consent.

    B. ☐ I am an attorney or accredited representative and my representation of the applicant in this case ☐ extends ☐ does not extend beyond the preparation of this application.

    NOTE: If you are an attorney or accredited representative whose representation extends beyond preparation of this application, you may be obliged to submit a completed Form G-28, Notice of Entry of Appearance as Attorney or Accredited Representative, with this application.

Preparer's Certification

By my signature, I certify, under penalty of perjury, that I prepared this application at the request of the applicant. The applicant then reviewed this completed application and informed me that he or she understands all of the information contained in, and submitted with, his or her application, including the **Applicant's Certification**, and that all of this information is complete, true, and correct. I completed this application based only on information that the applicant provided to me or authorized me to obtain or use.

Preparer's Signature

8. Preparer's Signature

   Date of Signature (mm/dd/yyyy)

NOTE: Do not complete Parts 16., 17., or 18. until the USCIS Officer instructs you to do so at the interview.

Part 16. Signature at Interview

I swear (affirm) and certify under penalty of perjury under the laws of the United States of America that I know that the contents of this Form N-400, Application for Naturalization, subscribed by me, including corrections number 1 through _____, are complete, true, and correct. The evidence submitted by me on numbered pages 1 through _____ are complete, true, and correct.

Subscribed to and sworn to (affirmed) before me

USCIS Officer's Printed Name or Stamp

Date of Signature (mm/dd/yyyy)

Applicant's Signature

USCIS Officer's Signature

Sample N-400 Application for Naturalization—Page 20

Part 17. Renunciation of Foreign Titles	A- 1 2 3 4 1 2 3 4 1

If you answered "Yes" to **Part 12.**, **Items A.** and **B.** in **Item Number 4.**, then you must affirm the following before a USCIS officer:

I further renounce the title of _____ **which I have heretofore held; or**
(list titles)

I further renounce the order of nobility of _____ **to which I have heretofore belonged.**
(list order of nobility)

Applicant's Printed Name

Applicant's Signature

USCIS Officer's Printed Name

USCIS Officer's Signature

Date of Signature (mm/dd/yyyy)

Part 18. Oath of Allegiance

If your application is approved, you will be scheduled for a public oath ceremony at which time you will be required to take the following Oath of Allegiance immediately prior to becoming a naturalized citizen. By signing below you acknowledge your willingness and ability to take this oath:

I hereby declare on oath, that I absolutely and entirely renounce and abjure all allegiance and fidelity to any foreign prince, potentate, state, or sovereignty, of whom or which I have heretofore been a subject or citizen;

that I will support and defend the Constitution and laws of the United States of America against all enemies, foreign, and domestic;

that I will bear true faith and allegiance to the same;

that I will bear arms on behalf of the United States when required by the law;

that I will perform noncombatant service in the armed forces of the United States when required by the law;

that I will perform work of national importance under civilian direction when required by the law; and

that I take this obligation freely, without any mental reservation or purpose of evasion; so help me God.

Applicant's Printed Name

Family Name (Last Name)

Given Name (First Name)

Middle Name (if applicable)

Applicant's Signature

Date of **Signature** (mm/dd/yyyy)

Between Filing and Interview: Dealing With the Wait

The period between the time you submit your citizenship application and the time you obtain your USCIS interview could be several weeks or months. During this period, you should:

- improve your eligibility by working on your English language skills and knowledge of American history (see Section A), and

- monitor the processing of your application (to be sure it isn't lost, misplaced, or ignored) (see Section B).

In this chapter, we'll discuss these activities and what you should do if:

- you move or go on vacation (see Section C), or

- you need to request emergency attention from USCIS (see Section D).

A. Improving Your Eligibility for Citizenship

Submitting your citizenship application is not like turning in a final paper in school—you can't just go celebrate and forget everything you've learned. Use this time wisely! Try to improve your chances for citizenship by expanding your understanding of the English language (unless you're already fluent) and U.S. history and government.

Don't put off studying—and then fly into a panic when you receive your interview appointment notice, which may arrive sooner than you were expecting. Two weeks is not enough time to cram an entire language and more than two hundred years of history into your head. Review Chapters 5 and 6 on preparing for the exam portions of your citizenship interview.

Also, keep in mind that all of the factors that affect eligibility described in Chapter 2—from avoiding long trips outside the United States to staying out of legal trouble—also apply during the months leading up to your citizenship interview. In fact, they continue to apply after your interview and until the day you are sworn in as a U.S. citizen. (See 8 C.F.R. § 316(a)(2).)

B. Tracking Your Application and Dealing With Delays

After you file your application, you will want to know:

- whether it successfully made it into the USCIS system (discussed in Subsections a and b, below), and
- whether there has been an unreasonable delay getting your interview or fingerprinting appointments (see Section B2, below).

How Long Does It Take to Become a U.S. Citizen?

The chart below will give you an idea of how long you might wait between the time you file your application and your interview. But don't make any decisions based solely on this chart, since the average wait may change by the time you read this. You can find the latest information at www.uscis.gov by clicking "Check your Case Status" on the home page then, "USCIS Processing Information Times." Choose your field office from the drop-down menus. Then click "Field Office Processing Dates." Look for "N-400" in the left column. In the right column, you may see the length of time that applicants currently being interviewed waited first, such as "5 months." Or you may see a date, such as "January 5, 2016." That would mean that USCIS is currently scheduling interviews for applicants who submitted their N-400s around that date.

1. Your Application's First Stop: The USCIS Lockbox

To be certain that your application got to USCIS and was appropriately logged in at their mailroom, and to protect yourself against its being lost later, collect all of the following:

- any email or text response USCIS sent you (in response to your having filed a Form G-1145 requesting e-notification of USCIS having received your application)

Reported Time Between Filing and Interview: April 2016

USCIS office (by U.S. city)	Average wait (in months)	USCIS office (by U.S. city)	Average wait (in months)	USCIS office (by U.S. city)	Average wait (in months)
Agana, GU	7	Hartford, CT	5	Phoenix, AZ	7
Albany, NY	7	Helena, MT	5	Pittsburgh, PA	8
Albuquerque, NM	8	Hialeah, FL	5	Portland, ME	7
Anchorage, AK	8	Honolulu, HI	5	Portland, OR	7
Atlanta, GA	7	Houston, TX	8	Providence, RI	5
Baltimore, MD	8	Imperial, CA	5	Raleigh, NC	5
Boise, ID	5	Indianapolis, IN	5	Reno, NV	5
Boston, MA	7	Jacksonville, FL	9	Sacramento, CA	7
Buffalo, NY	7	Kendall, FL	5	St. Albans, VT	7
Casper, WY	7	Kansas City, MO	5	St. Louis, MO	10
Charleston, SC	7	Las Vegas, NV	8	St. Paul, MN	9
Charleston, WV	7	Long Island, NY	9	Salt Lake City, UT	5
Charlotte Amalie, VI	8	Los Angeles, CA	5	San Antonio, TX	8
Charlotte, NC	5	L.A. County	7	San Bernardino, CA	5
Chicago, IL	8	Louisville, KY	7	San Fernando Valley, CA	7
Christiansted, VI	8	Manchester, NH	5	San Diego, CA	5
Cincinnati, OH	10	Memphis, TN	8	San Francisco, CA	8
Cleveland, OH	5	Miami, FL	8	San Jose, CA	7
Columbus, OH	5	Milwaukee, WI	5	San Juan, PR	7
Dallas, TX	9	Mt. Laurel, NJ	7	Santa Ana, CA	7
Denver, CO	7	New Orleans, LA	7	Seattle, WA	7
Des Moines, IA	9	New York City, NY	8	Spokane, WA	5
Detroit, MI	5	Newark, NJ	7	Tampa, FL	7
El Paso, TX	7	Norfolk, VA	8	Tucson, AZ	5
Fort Smith, AR	7	Oklahoma City, OK	7	Washington, DC	9
Fresno, CA	5	Omaha, NE	5	West Palm Beach, FL	7
Greer, SC	7	Orlando, FL	7	Wichita, KS	7
Harlington, TX	7	Philadelphia, PA	7	Yakima, WA	5

- any mailing confirmation that you received, such as a certified mail receipt, if you used the U.S. Postal Service (see Chapter 3, Section D)

- your canceled check or credit card statement showing the DHS charge, and

- an official receipt notice on Form I-797C, which confirms that your application has been logged into the USCIS system. USCIS usually sends the receipt within six weeks of receiving your application. (A sample receipt notice is shown below.)

It's important to get your hands on the postal or delivery receipt so that you can later show it to USCIS if it loses your application.

Next, keep an eye on your bank or credit card statements to see when your check has been cashed or a charge made against your account. Then make a copy of the check or bank record and put it in your personal citizenship file—it will also be useful if USCIS loses your application.

If you paid by check, and you're lucky, your bank may provide copies of your canceled checks. This is handy, because USCIS may (but doesn't always) print the case number on the canceled check. This gives you a way to verify whether your case made it into the system, and you can use this tracer number to track your application using the USCIS website. However, many banks no longer return canceled checks, or they destroy them.

If weeks or months go by and the bank or credit card company doesn't indicate that USCIS has charged you, it may not be a problem— sometimes USCIS is slow to act. However, if you don't also get a USCIS receipt notice, this will help confirm your suspicion that USCIS has lost your application. Below we discuss what to do if USCIS takes an unusually long time to send you your receipt notice and what to do if USCIS says that elements of your application are missing.

a. Delayed Receipt Notices

If you don't get your USCIS Form I-797C receipt notice within two months of mailing, we recommend that you follow up.

Unfortunately, USCIS lockboxes and Service Centers are like walled fortresses. You can't visit or call them. Your best option would normally

Sample N-400 Receipt Notice

Department of Homeland Security
U.S. Citizenship and Immigration Services

I-797C, Notice of Action

THE UNITED STATES OF AMERICA

Receipt	NOTICE DATE March 16, 2016
CASE TYPE N-400 Application For Naturalization	USCIS A# A075 123 456

APPLICATION NUMBER NBC*001634567	RECEIVED DATE March 09, 2016	PRIORITY DATE March 09, 2016	PAGE 1 of 1

APPLICANT NAME AND MAILING ADDRESS

5   1111

PATRICK LEUNG CHAN
c/o ILONA BRAY
950 PARKER ST.
BERKELEY, CA 94710

PAYMENT INFORMATION:

Single Application Fee: $680.00

Total Balance Due: $0.00

The above application has been received by our office and is in process. Our records indicate your personal information is as follows:

Date of Birth: August 30, 1972
Address Where You Live: 1234 COURT AVE.
BURLINGAME. CA 94010

Please verify your personal information listed above and immediately notify our office at the address or phone number listed below if there are any changes.

Upon receipt of all required Record Checks, you will be scheduled to appear for an interview at your local USCIS field office.

For more information about the naturalization process and eligibility requirements, please read *A Guide to Naturalization* (M-476). USCIS also has a free booklet to help study for the naturalization test. Ask about *Learn About the United States: Quick Civics Lessons* when you go to have your fingerprints taken at the Application Support Center.

You can get a copy of the Guide, the Quick Civics Lessons booklet, and other civics and citizenship study materials from the USCIS website (www.uscis.gov). You can also visit the USCIS website to find valuable information about forms and filing instructions, and about general immigration services and benefits.

If you have additional questions about possible immigration benefits and services, filing information, or USCIS forms, please call the USCIS National Customer Service Center (NCSC) at 1-800-375-5283. If you are hearing impaired, please call the NCSC TDD at 1-800-767-1833.

If you have any questions or comments regarding this notice or the status of your case, please contact our office at the below address or customer service number. You will be notified separately about any other case you may have filed.

USCIS Office Address:

USCIS - National Benefits Center
P. O. Box 648005
Lee's Summit, MO 64002
Attention: N-400 Naturalization Applications
NBC$000814578

USCIS Customer Service Number:

(800)375-5283
ATTORNEY COPY

Form I-797C (Rev. 01/31/05) N

be to check the status of your application online, at www.uscis.gov. But to use this, you would need the processing number from your USCIS receipt notice. If USCIS has failed to send you a receipt notice and hasn't canceled your check, you won't get very far with this.

In the end, you may have to resort to calling 800-375-5283 or making an INFOPASS appointment at www.uscis.gov and visiting a local USCIS office in person to inquire about a missing receipt notice.

If your visit does not produce results, consult an attorney (Chapter 10 has tips on finding a good one) or call a U.S. Congressperson's office for help, as described below in Section E.

Eventually, you will get a receipt notice from USCIS, whether in response to your inquiry or in the normal course of processing. Sometime after that—when your case is ready for interview—your file will be transferred to your local USCIS office.

b. Incomplete or Lost Portions of Your Application

If you receive a USCIS request for more documentation or evidence— such as photos or a missing document—gather whatever was asked for in the "RFE" and get it in the mail as soon as possible. Use the same precautions detailed in the beginning of Section B1, above—include the notification form as a cover sheet—and make a copy for yourself.

USCIS will routinely give you a 12-week time limit on returning the requested information. However, many applicants find that that's too little time, particularly if they're supposed to come up with documents held in government offices. If you can't meet the deadline, you have three options:

- You can "partially respond" by providing some of the evidence that was requested, which will alert USCIS that you would like a decision to be made based on that information alone.

- You can withdraw your application.

- You can request an extension, by sending USCIS a letter explaining why you need more time.

Sending separate mailings with portions of the requested documents in each is NOT an option. USCIS regulations require that you submit all requested materials at the same time. Sending a partial response might be your best bet if you are unable to locate certain documents and the deadline for your reply is looming.

Withdrawing your application is a last resort, but could be a useful option if you realize that you've got a problem you'd rather not bring to USCIS's attention, such as having committed a crime that might make you deportable. Consult an attorney in a situation like this.

Request an extension only if you can't come up with the most significant evidence within the 30 days, but feel certain you can get it soon after. Also include any proof of your reason for needing more time, such as an acknowledgment and a copy of a written time estimate from the government office of which you're requesting a document.

What should you do if you're asked for something that you know you've already sent? This is surprisingly common.

If it's something inexpensive or easy to produce, don't waste time arguing—even if you have photocopies proving that you already sent the item. Assume it has been lost and send another one.

Lost checks or money orders are a different matter. Do not send USCIS another check or money order until you find out what happened to the first payment. If you sent a check and haven't received information about it with your monthly bank statement, ask your bank to determine whether the check has been cashed. If it has been cashed, get the check and, if it shows a USCIS stamp and processing number, send USCIS a copy of both sides.

If the check hasn't been cashed, send a new check, but make sure to stop payment on the old check first. (Of course, USCIS has been known to relocate lost checks even after new checks have been sent, then attempt to cash the old ones and demand yet another set of checks from applicants when the old checks bounce. If avoiding delays is extremely important to you, go ahead and give USCIS an opportunity to double-charge you by not stopping payment on the first check—but we think this is a case where it's worth arguing it out with USCIS.)

If you sent a money order and kept the receipt with the tracer number, call the company that issued the money order to find out whether it has been cashed. Ask the company to send you a copy of the cashed money order to prove to USCIS that it did indeed receive your money. If you can't get a copy of the cashed money order, send USCIS a copy of your receipt and an explanation. Hopefully, USCIS will stop bugging you for the money.

Some applicants receive USCIS RFE requests for things that don't exist—proof of having paid child support, for example, even though the applicant has no children. This usually results from a processing error—for example, the USCIS officer issued a form letter and forgot to cross off an item, or a USCIS officer didn't have an applicant's complete immigration history available. If you receive one of these requests, write a polite letter explaining why it is impossible to comply with this request.

And if you simply don't understand the request—for example, it cites a provision of immigration law and asks you to provide evidence that it does or doesn't affect you—see an attorney.

c. Important Information on Your Receipt Notice

Carefully examine your I-797C receipt notice from USCIS. It contains some important pieces of information, namely your file's application number. It's in one of the boxes near the top of the receipt notice, and is used to identify your application throughout USCIS processing. In the sample, the application number starts with "NBC"—for "National Benefits Center." Include your application number in any follow-up correspondence.

If you requested a fee waiver, the receipt notice is also your indication that it was accepted, and it will show that the payment received was $0. When fee waivers are rejected, the applicant receives a "Reject" notice explaining the denial.

2. Your Application's Second Stop: A USCIS Field Office

After you get your receipt notice from USCIS, your case file will be transferred to your local USCIS Field Office. Unfortunately, USCIS won't notify you when this transfer happens. If your fingerprints or interview aren't scheduled by the normal time in your district, correspond with both the lockbox and the Field Office.

Usually within a couple of months of your receipt notice, you will get your fingerprint appointment notice. Getting this notice is probably a sign that your case has been transferred to the Field Office—but it's not a sure sign. For more on the fingerprint appointment notice, see Subsection a, below.

Don't count on just "checking in" with USCIS to monitor your application's progress (other than by using its website, which will probably tell you that your case is "pending"). No matter which office has your file, USCIS generally refuses to respond to inquiries until you've waited past the normal processing time. Among the factors that can affect your waiting period are the number of people in line ahead of you and how well USCIS is doing at getting those people through the application process. You can get an up-to-date estimate of how long it takes to get a fingerprint appointment by talking to the staff of local nonprofit agencies serving immigrants. (This is not information that you can get by contacting USCIS.)

Even if you're sure that your application is at the USCIS Field Office, it's still a challenge to track it. USCIS Field Offices do not accept phone calls from applicants, period. If you've waited too long (we describe average waiting periods in Subsections a and b) for your fingerprints or interview, you should contact USCIS at 800-375-5283, where a live person will take your question, typically from 8 a.m. until 6 p.m. local time. Although the person you speak with will most likely not be able to tell you anything useful during that phone call, he or she will start an inquiry for you and tell you when to expect a response.

Another approach is to make an appointment at your local USCIS office using the online INFOPASS system (at https://infopass.uscis.gov). At your appointment, ask the officer what can be done to get your application back on track. Local officers sometimes have more information than the people at the 800 number, although they too will probably just start an inquiry and tell you when to expect a response. Unfortunately, writing a letter to USCIS is not likely to produce a response, other than a boilerplate letter telling you to call the 800 number or to make an INFOPASS appointment.

Sample Fingerprint Notice

Department of Homeland Security.
U.S. Citizenship and Immigration Ser{

I-797C, Notice of Action

THE UNITED STATES OF AMERICA

Fingerprint Notification		NOTICE DATE April 02, 2016
CASE/TYPE N400 Application For Naturalization		USCIS A# A 075 123 456
APPLICATION NUMBER NBC*001634567	RECEIVED DATE March 09, 2016	PRIORITY DATE March 09, 2016	PAGE 1 of 1

APPLICANT NAME AND MAILING ADDRESS

PATRICK LEUNG CHAN
c/o ILONA BRAY
950 PARKER ST
BERKELEY CA 94710

To process your application, USCIS must take your fingerprints and have them cleared by the FBI. **PLEASE APPEAR AT THE BELOW APPLICATION SUPPORT CENTER AT THE APPOINTED DATE AND TIME TO HAVE YOUR FINGERPRINTS TAKEN.** If you are unable to appear at this time, you may go on any **following** Wednesday at the same time noted below, as long as you appear before 07/22/2010. If you do not have your fingerprints taken by that date, your application will be considered abandoned.

APPLICATION SUPPORT CENTER USCIS OAKLAND 2040 TELEGRAPH AVE. OAKLAND CA 946122306	DATE AND TIME OF APPOINTMENT 04/29/2016 08:00 AM

WHEN YOU GO TO THE APPLICATION SUPPORT CENTER TO HAVE YOUR FINGERPRINTS TAKEN, YOU MUST BRING:

1. THIS APPOINTMENT NOTICE and
2. PHOTO IDENTIFICATION. Naturalization applicants must bring their Alien Registration Card. All other applicants must bring a passport, driver's license, national ID, military ID, or State-issued photo ID. If you appear without proper identification, you will not be fingerprinted.

PLEASE DISREGARD THIS NOTICE IF YOUR APPLICATION HAS ALREADY BEEN GRANTED.

WARNING!

Due to limited seating availability in our lobby areas, only persons who are necessary to assist with transportation or completing the fingerprint worksheet should accompany you.

NO CELL PHONES, CAMERAS, OR OTHER RECORDING DEVICES PERMITTED.

USCIS has a free booklet to help you study for the naturalization test. Ask about 'Learn About the United States: Quick Civics Lessons' when you go to have your fingerprints taken at the Application Support Center.

If you have any questions regarding this notice, please feel free to call 1-800-375-5283.

REPRESENTATIVE COPY

Form I-797C (Rev. 01/31/05) N

a. Your Fingerprint Appointment

Within a few weeks or months after you've submitted your application, USCIS should send you an appointment notice to have your fingerprints (also called "biometrics") taken. (A sample biometrics appointment notice is shown below.) You cannot submit a card with your fingerprints on it (as your friends may have done in past years); USCIS must fingerprint you in person. Your fingerprints will be sent to the FBI, which will summarize any criminal or immigration charges or convictions on your record, and will be checked against various security databases.

Every applicant older than 14 and younger than 75 must be fingerprinted. If your fingerprints can't be taken, perhaps because of skin conditions or physical deformities, the USCIS officer may waive this requirement and ask you to supply local police clearance statements instead. You'll have to go to the appointment and let the officer figure this out at that time—advance correspondence with USCIS isn't likely to get you very far.

The fingerprint notice instructs you to bring your green card with you as photo identification. The reason is obvious—USCIS doesn't want people with criminal records to send someone with a clean record in their place.

Since any delay in the process increases the chances that USCIS will delay or misplace your application, we recommend that you try your best to attend your fingerprint appointment. If you really can't make it on the appointed day, check the box near the bottom of your appointment notice indicating when you'd like your next appointment, copy the notice for your records, and send the original to the Field Office address listed on the notice. You should receive a new appointment notice.

If you don't receive a fingerprint appointment notice within six months or your local USCIS district's expected time, you should follow up as described earlier in this chapter.

b. Your Interview Appointment

Within a few months or more after your fingerprints are taken (and after USCIS has received the results from the FBI), you'll receive your

Sample Interview Notice

Department of Homeland Security
U.S. Citizenship and Immigration Services

I-797, Notice of Action

THE UNITED STATES OF AMERICA

Request for Applicant to Appear for Naturalization Initial Interview		NOTICE DATE September 03, 2016
CASE TYPE N400 Application For Naturalization		USCIS A# A075 123 456
APPLICATION NUMBER WSC*001634567	RECEIVED DATE March 09, 2016	PRIORITY DATE March 09, 2016	PAGE 1 of 1

APPLICANT NAME AND MAILING ADDRESS

PATRICK LEUNG CHAN
c/o ILONA BRAY
950 PARKER ST
BERKELEY CA 94710

Ihlmlulullmullull

Please come to:
USCIS SAN FRANCISCO FIELD OFFICE
630 SANSOME ST
2ND FLOOR RECEPTION
CITIZENSHIP
SAN FRANCISCO CA 94111
On (Date): Tuesday, October 25, 2016
At (Time): 08:20 AM

You are hereby notified to appear for an interview on your Application for Naturalization at the date, time, and place indicated above. **Waiting room capacity is limited. Please do not arrive any earlier than 30 minutes before your scheduled appointment time.** The proceeding will take about two hours. If for any reason you cannot keep this appointment, return this letter immediately to the USCIS office address listed below with your explanation and a request for a new appointment; otherwise, no further action will be taken on your application.

If you are applying for citizenship for yourself, you will be tested on your knowledge of the government and history of the United States. You will also be tested on reading, writing, and speaking English, unless on the day you filed your application, you have been living in the United States for a total of at least 20 years as a lawful permanent resident and are over 50 years old, or you have been living in the United States for a total of 15 years as a lawful permanent resident and are over 55 years old, or unless you have a medically determinable disability (you must have filed form N648 Medical Certification for Disability Exception, with your N400 Application for Naturalization).

You MUST BRING the following with you to the interview:
- This letter.
- Your Alien Registration Card (green card).
- Any evidence of Selective Service Registration.
- Your passport and/or any other documents you used in connection with any entries into the United States.
- Those items noted below which are applicable to you:

If applying for NATURALIZATION AS THE SPOUSE of a United States Citizen;
- Your marriage certificate.
- Proof of death or divorce for each prior marriage of yourself or spouse.
- Your spouse's birth or naturalization certificate or certificate of citizenship.

If applying for NATURALIZATION as a member of the United States Armed Forces;
- Your discharge certificate, or form DD 214.

If copies of a document were submitted as evidence with your N400 application, the originals of those documents should be brought to the interview.

PLEASE keep this appointment, even if you do not have all the items indicated above.

If you have any questions or comments regarding this notice or the status of your case, please contact our office at the below address or customer service number. You will be notified separately about any other cases you may have filed

USCIS has a free booklet to help you study for the naturalization test. Ask about 'Learn About the United States: Quick Civics Lessons' when you go to have your fingerprints taken at the Application Support Center.

USCIS Office Address:

U.S. CITIZENSHIP AND IMMIGRATION SERVICES
630 SANSOME ST
SAN FRANCISCO CA 94111-

USCIS Customer Service Number:
(800) 375-5283

APPLICANT COPY

Form I-797 (Rev. 01/31/05) N

naturalization interview notice and a list of documents to bring. (A sample notice, on USCIS Form I-797, is provided below.) Usually, you have about two weeks' warning before your interview—so avoid taking any long vacations while you're waiting. If you miss a naturalization interview, you'll find that rescheduling leads to long delays. (The interview process is discussed in more detail in Chapter 8.)

If you've waited longer than the estimate given when you use the "Processing Times" function at www.uscis.gov, it's wise to either visit your local USCIS office in person (via an INFOPASS appointment) or call 800-375-5283 to make an inquiry. If visiting in person, give USCIS a copy of your receipt notice and point out that the predicted time has passed.

CAUTION

If more than 15 months pass between your fingerprint appointment and your interview appointment, you'll probably get another fingerprint appointment notice. This isn't a mistake. Your case won't go forward until the FBI has run a new check on your record, because USCIS figures that after 15 months you had time to get into some new trouble. You won't, however, have to pay a second fingerprinting fee.

Lawyers Get Special Access for Case Inquiries

Immigration lawyers sometimes receive special email addresses for making inquiries—and even supervisors' phone numbers. Unfortunately, these email addresses and phone numbers are not available to the general public—and probably never will be, given the number of inquiries that USCIS would then have to deal with. If you're getting nowhere with your personal inquiries, this might be the time to hire a lawyer. Don't expect miracles, however—sometimes even the lawyers are told nothing more than that an applicant's case is "pending" or still in line.

See Chapter 10 for information on how to find an immigration attorney.

C. If You Move or Go on Vacation

If you're waiting for USCIS to act on your application, we advise you not to go anywhere! Missing an appointment notice can result in long delays in getting your application back on track. Worse yet, USCIS doesn't always pay attention to your changes of address. To top it off, transferring a file from one USCIS office to another seems to put it at risk of disappearing forever.

That said, some people will have no choice but to move—or simply can't tolerate spending months, and even years, waiting for an appointment without taking a vacation. If you do go on vacation, have a friend check your mail. Leave a number where you can be reached if your fingerprint or interview notice arrives. If the scheduled date occurs while you're vacationing, write to the office whose address is on the notice, requesting a new appointment. Do this before, not after, the scheduled appointment. If you've already missed one appointment, however, come back from your vacation early. USCIS rarely gives third chances.

If you move to a different city, you'll need to do two things:

- Advise USCIS of your change of address.
- Figure out whether you're still within the same USCIS district.

Advising USCIS of your change of address is not the same as advising the U.S. post office. You are required to send notice of your change of address to USCIS, using Form AR-11. It's best to file the AR-11 online, by going to www.uscis.gov/ar-11 and, from the right-hand column, clicking "Online Change of Address." When finished, click "Signature" to e-file the form. Print a copy for your records. It will show the date and time the form was filed, and will contain a USCIS confirmation number. There is no fee for this form. One advantage to e-filing your AR-11 is that you will be asked whether you have applications pending, so that the office that will interview you will automatically be informed of your address change (a big improvement over the old system, in which you had to separately advise each office handling your application).

If you prefer to file your AR-11 by regular mail, print out the form from the USCIS website and mail it to the address shown on the form. It's best to file by certified or Priority mail and keep copies of the filed forms and proof of mailing. Realize, however, that if you mail your AR-11, you will still have to separately advise the USCIS office that will hold your naturalization interview of your address change. Do this either using the online change of address system or by calling USCIS at 800-375-5283.

In addition, check in regularly with the new occupants of your former home, if possible—just in case the local USCIS office doesn't succeed in entering your address change into its records. You'll also probably want to advise the post office, because it will forward your mail to you after you move—but only for a limited time, and without advising the senders. That's why it's important to use the USCIS procedure described above.

Depending on how far you're moving, you may end up in a different USCIS district. USCIS has many districts within most states, and only the one serving your address can help you. So, for example, if you applied for citizenship while you were living in or near San Francisco, the San Francisco USCIS Office would have your case file. But if you moved to Sacramento before your interview, the San Francisco office would no longer have the authority to hear your case. Only the Sacramento USCIS Office could handle it. As a general rule, if you've moved to a different state, you're more than likely in a new USCIS district.

To find out if you're in a new district, make an INFOPASS appointment at the USCIS office that has your case, and tell the officer where you're moving to. If the officer determines that it's a new district, ask to transfer your file—then follow up in writing to your local office with the same request. Be prepared for a long wait—asking USCIS to transfer files often produces delays.

If you're moving to a new state, there's an added complication. You have to have lived in the new state for three months before your application can be considered. Fortunately, because of the delays involved in transferring your file, this will probably not affect your citizenship eligibility. If, however, you receive a notice scheduling you for an interview before three months in your new home have passed, write back asking that USCIS reschedule the interview for a date after the three-month period. If you don't get a response, go to the interview anyway—USCIS can reschedule you at that time.

D. Requesting Emergency Attention

If there is a pressing reason that your application should be put ahead of all the other waiting applications so that your interview is scheduled early—USCIS calls this expediting a case—you'll need to request this in a letter. However, such a letter cannot be included with your citizenship application. You must send it separately to the local USCIS office handling your interview. Limit your cries for help to true emergencies, such as:

- you are about to have surgery and will be unable to leave your hospital bed to attend a USCIS interview for several months
- you have been selected for an important federal job that requires U.S. citizenship, or
- you have a terminal illness and want to become a U.S. citizen before you die.

If your emergency is a medical one, include a letter from your doctor explaining the situation. For other types of emergencies, try to find an equivalent form of proof to include with your request—for example, a letter from a government official indicating your federal job offer.

E. When All Else Fails, Call Your U.S. Congressperson

If you feel your case has turned into a true bureaucratic nightmare or a genuine miscarriage of justice, ask your U.S. Congressperson for help. Some congressional offices have a staff person dedicated to helping constituents who have immigration-related problems. You will soon be a member of their voting public, so they have every interest in gaining your support now.

A simple inquiry by a U.S. Congressperson can end months of USCIS stonewalling or inaction. In rare cases, the Congressperson's office might be willing to put some actual pressure on USCIS.

EXAMPLE: Kyllikki applies for citizenship in December 2015. She attends her fingerprint appointment in June 2016, and that is the last she hears from USCIS. She fills out an inquiry form in person at a USCIS District Office in January 2017. USCIS promises to respond to her inquiry—but no reply comes. In March, Kyllikki visits USCIS again and is told that all people who applied at the same time as she did have already been called in for interviews. Again, USCIS promises to look into the delay—but by May, she has still heard nothing. She then writes a letter to her U.S. Congresswoman, outlining the problem. The Congresswoman contacts USCIS to ask what's going on, and Kyllikki receives an interview notice within three weeks.

Your Congressperson probably won't be surprised to hear from you. Complaints about USCIS delays are all too common ●

Preparing for the English Exam

n order to pass the U.S. citizenship test, you will need to demonstrate basic skills in reading, writing, and speaking English. If you're reading this book by yourself, you're already doing quite well. If—like many applicants—someone is assisting you through the process, that's okay, too. Ask your friend to keep reading!

This chapter won't teach you English but it will provide:

- an idea of how much English you'll need to know (Section A)
- a description of the exam you're preparing for (Section B), and
- resources for learning English (Section C).

TIP

If you're older than age 50 or disabled, you may be able to avoid trying to learn English. For details on whether you qualify to have your citizenship interview conducted in your native language, see Chapter 2, Section E.

A. How Much English You'll Need to Know

USCIS does not expect you to sound like a college professor or to win public-speaking awards. The object of testing your English language skills is to determine whether you can have a basic conversation in English—that is, whether you can speak at the same level as "ordinary" U.S. citizens. USCIS is not allowed to impose any "extraordinary or unreasonable condition" on you when testing your English. (See I.N.A. § 312, 8 U.S.C. § 1423.) So, don't worry that the officer will intentionally speak too quickly or use long or obscure words.

That said, we encourage you to put as much effort into learning English as you can. Being comfortable in English will reduce the chances of unpleasant surprises at the interview. For example, many applicants are thrown off when the USCIS interviewer asks a question using different words than they were expecting (such as "Do you have any previous spouses?" instead of "How many times have you been married?"). And some interviewers were simply born with speaking voices that are unclear, too quick, or otherwise difficult to understand. Speaking English will also help you actively participate in U.S. society.

Should You Submit Your Application Before You Can Speak English?

USCIS doesn't require you to be conversant in English at the time you submit your citizenship application—only that you have learned it by the time your interview rolls around. That gives you the opportunity to take a calculated risk—turn in your citizenship application while your English is still weak, then spend the months leading up to your interview studying intensively. (We discuss study methods in Section C, below.)

Thanks to USCIS delays, this works pretty well for some people. But USCIS can sometimes surprise you with how fast it calls people in for interviews, so the risk is real. Plus, if you are not diligent or if your life is full of unpredictable crises and obligations, even a long wait might not be enough to get yourself ready. To be safe, don't submit your application until you're comfortable in English. If you submit it without knowledge of English, you will fail the English exam and will have to reapply for citizenship.

B. How USCIS Tests Your English

For some applicants, the English exam can be one of the most difficult parts of the citizenship process. Others have been speaking English for years, and may not even realize that parts of the exam are happening. During the citizenship interview, you will be tested on your ability to:

- speak English (see Section B1, below)
- read English (see Section B2, below), and
- write in English (see Section B3, below).

1. Testing Your Ability to Speak English

In order to pass the spoken part of the English exam, you must understand what the USCIS interviewing officer says and make yourself understood during the citizenship interview. There is no formal test of your spoken English apart from the requirement that you speak English during the interview.

Much of the interview will involve reviewing your Form N-400, so learning the vocabulary on this form is critical. You may find a number of words on the form difficult to comprehend. Some aren't commonly used. For example, the average American rarely discusses his willingness to "bear arms on behalf of the United States" (translated: defend the United States by joining the military).

Review the language in Form N-400—with a dictionary in hand—and then have a friend read all the questions aloud to you. The USCIS interviewer probably won't ask you every question on the form—but will ask you a good number of them. Since it's impossible to predict which ones the officer will choose, be prepared for all of them. You'll be much more comfortable at the interview if you prepare!

TIP

You don't need to know every word of the English language. During the interview, there may be some words you don't know or recognize. Admitting your lack of knowledge as to a word will not be a deadly strike against you. If you can't comprehend something, say to the interviewer, "I don't know that word. Can you repeat what you said in another way?"

You'll impress your interviewer if, instead of answering a question with "yes" or "no" (or nodding your head affirmatively or negatively), you respond in a complete sentence. This may require repeating part of the question back to the interviewer—for example, if he or she asks you "What is your name?," practice answering "My name is Charles Olisadebe" rather than just "Charles Olisadebe." Say your answers clearly and firmly.

Ask an English-speaking friend to rephrase the questions from Form N-400 in different ways. For example, USCIS interviewers often shorten the questions or put them into different words. So, for example, the form reads "If you are married now, provide the following information about your current spouse; Current Spouse's Legal Name." However, the USCIS interviewer is more likely to ask, "What's your husband's name?" or "Are you currently single, married, divorced, or widowed?"

> **TIP**
>
> **An audio recorder can be your friend, too.** If you need practice with the questions but don't want to impose too much on friends and family, ask one of them to read all the questions on the N-400 application into a recorder. Then play it back to yourself as many times as you need.

Another, less obvious way in which USCIS tests your English ability is by watching your response to the interviewer's instructions. For example, the officer may say things like, "Follow me," "Please remain standing," "Raise your right hand," "Take a seat," or "Show me any documents that you've brought with you." We know of one case in which the applicant failed to take a seat when asked twice by the officer. He was told to go home. In another case, an applicant failed the interview because she sat down before the officer told her to!

The lesson here is to listen very carefully to the interviewer's instructions and, if you really don't understand, to ask the interviewer to rephrase the sentence so you won't be left standing when you should be in your chair.

2. Testing Your Reading of English

In order to test your reading ability, the USCIS officer will give you something to read out loud. If you're clearly doing well, the officer may stop you after one sentence—otherwise you may have to read two or three sentences. You'll need to get one out of the three sentences right.

Reading Vocabulary for the Naturalization Exam

People	Civics	Places	Holidays
Abraham Lincoln George Washington	American flag Bill of Rights capital citizen city Congress country Father of Our Country government President right Senators state/states White House	America United States U.S.	Presidents' Day Memorial Day Flag Day Independence Day Labor Day Columbus Day Thanksgiving
Question Words	**Verbs**	**Other (Function)**	**Other (Content)**
how what when where who why	can come do/does elects have/has is/are/was/be lives/lived meet name pay vote want	a for here in of on the to we	colors dollar bill first largest many most north one people second south

Reading correctly means getting through a whole sentence without pausing for a long time, leaving out important words, or pronouncing words so badly that they lose their meaning. And you'll need to sound like you know what you're saying, for example by putting the emphasis in the right place. It's okay, however, if you still have an accent from another language or make minor mispronunciations or skip over an unimportant word or two.

USCIS hasn't specified what types of materials it will ask you to read from. However, it says you should expect to see some of the vocabulary words on the list above.

As you learn English, however, remember that reading out loud is a separate skill from reading quietly to yourself. Some people can understand words on a page without understanding how the sentence flows or how the words are pronounced. So, practice reading out loud—not only will it help you on this portion of the exam, but you'll find that it improves your ability to remember English words.

3. Testing Your Ability to Write English

To test your ability to write English, the USCIS interviewer will give you up to three chances to correctly write down a sentence that he or she dictates (says out loud). These sentences are, for the most part, not difficult. They are created from the USCIS's list of vocabulary, reproduced at the end of this section.

Spelling and punctuation—things like periods and commas—are important, but getting the right meaning is the key to success. If the USCIS officer can figure out what you're trying to write—that is, it's understandable to the average person despite minor errors of spelling, grammar, capitalization, or punctuation—you'll pass. Still, your chances are better if you spell everything perfectly.

> **EXAMPLE 1:** The USCIS officer asks Benjiro to write "The sky is blue."
> He writes "The Sky iz blu." He may pass the writing portion of the exam, because the USCIS officer can understand what he has written. (However, some USCIS officers are stricter than others.)

EXAMPLE 2: The USCIS officer asks Junko to write "The sky is blue." Junko writes "The sky is blew." She fails the writing portion of the exam, because "blew"—though it's an actual word—has a different meaning than "blue," turning the sentence into nonsense.

Also, make sure you write legibly. If the officer can't read your writing, you'll fail.

C. Study Resources

Children learn languages by listening, but for adults it's not so easy. Fortunately, many communities have a wonderful resource called "adult schools" or "adult education programs," which offer classes in "ESL" (English as a Second Language) as well as citizenship exam preparation. These programs are held on the campuses of local schools, community centers, or community colleges, usually on evenings or weekends. The class term is typically six weeks to two months long, and the tuition is usually fairly low or even free.

To find an adult school or program near you, ask at your local library, community center, public school district, or community college. Also ask your friends, immigrant or American, whether they've taken any evening classes nearby. Look for a program that fits your schedule and needs. In California, at least, most ESL and citizenship classes are offered through local public school districts and are free.

If you can't find an adult school near you, your local library or bookstore will likely have English-language study CDs or access to online study resources. They're not as effective as studying with a live teacher, but are usually better than trying to learn English from a book.

Often, classroom or other formal study isn't enough when it comes to learning a language. If you've been shy about using your English up until now, it's time to come out of your shell. Practice on your children, the bus driver, and the local store clerk. You'll find that many Americans are eager to help you learn, once they see that you're making an effort. You may find it helpful to listen to talk-radio shows or to watch television. The more you speak and listen, the more you'll remember.

The USCIS website also contains resources such as flashcards to help you study for the English language portion of the exam. Go to www.uscis.gov, and under "Citizenship" click "Citizenship Through Naturalization." Next, click "Naturalization Test" and then "Study Materials for the English Test."

Writing Vocabulary for the Naturalization Exam

People	Civics	Places	Months
Adams	American Indians	Alaska	February
Lincoln	capital	California	May
Washington	citizens	Canada	June
	Civil War	Delaware	July
	Congress	Mexico	September
	Father of Our Country	New York City	October
	flag	United States	November
	free	Washington	
	freedom of speech	Washington, DC	
	President		
	right		
	Senators		
	state/states		
	White House		

Holidays	Verbs	Other (Function)	Other (Content)
Presidents' Day	can	and	blue
Memorial Day	come	during	dollar bill
Flag Day	elect	for	fifty/50
Independence Day	have/has	here	first
Labor Day	is/was/be	in	largest
Columbus Day	lives/lived	of	most
Thanksgiving	meets	on	north
	pay	the	one
	vote	to	one hundred/100
	want	we	people
			red
			second
			south
			taxes
			white

Preparing for the U.S. History and Government Exam

n order to become a U.S. citizen, you must pass an exam covering U.S. history and government. You will take this exam during your citizenship interview. The officer will, somewhere in the course of interviewing you, simply ask you up to ten questions chosen from a list of 100, and you must answer six correctly in order to pass. If you're older than 65 and have been a permanent resident for 20 years or more, your ten questions will be chosen from a smaller pool of 20 potential questions.

For the average applicant, the questions will be chosen randomly. However, USCIS officers are supposed to select easier questions if your studying would have been hampered by such factors as advanced age or lack of education.

After studying this chapter, you should be able to pass the exam. First, we'll give you a strategy for preparing (Section A), then help you review the pool of 100 potential questions and answers (Section B). (The list for people older than 65 who can take the shorter exam is in Section C, toward the end of this chapter.)

A. Your Exam Preparation Strategy

This may be the only exam you ever take where you receive all the possible questions and answers ahead of time. But having the answers doesn't mean you are guaranteed to pass. Like any exam, if you don't prepare, you'll flunk.

You could simply memorize the answers to all of the questions. That may work for some applicants—though probably not if they wait until the night before the interview to attempt it. Generally, however, relying solely on memorization makes your task harder, not easier. For example, consider the question, "Name one branch or part of the government." If you don't have any idea what the words "legislative," "executive," or "judicial" mean, you may run into trouble naming any of these three. For that reason, it's best to understand at least a little bit about the background and meaning of all 100 questions.

That said, we're not advocating that you immerse yourself in all 400-plus years of American history. After all, the USCIS officer expects you to give only the answer that appears on the official USCIS list—in the same or similar words, with no added information.

Instead, we recommend a combination of memorization and background study. First, develop some understanding of the background behind each question and answer, and then launch into memorizing the answers on the USCIS list.

> **EXAMPLE:** During Matilde's citizenship exam, the USCIS interviewer asked her "What did Martin Luther King, Jr., do?" Matilde started giving a long answer—she was working on her Ph.D. dissertation in modern U.S. history at a prestigious university and she knew quite a bit about Dr. King. But the answer that the officer was looking for was on the list: Either that he "fought for civil rights" or "worked for equality of all Americans." The officer counted Matilde's answer as wrong.

You'll see that some of the sample questions are difficult and some are surprisingly easy. For example, remembering how many voting members are in the House of Representatives can be tough, but remembering that the Pacific Ocean is on the West Coast of the U.S. should be easy.

Also, USCIS officers are not supposed to just throw all the hardest questions at you, no matter how cranky they're feeling that day. In fact, if you are elderly or have a limited education, they're supposed to limit their questions to the easier ones. In all likelihood, you will get a mix of easy and difficult questions in your interview.

Should you still do your best to memorize every answer? Probably yes. Keep in mind that you will have only ten questions in which to prove yourself. If the officer asks you the few questions that you decided not to learn (or you happen to forget a few answers on top of the few you avoided), you will fail the exam.

RESOURCE

USCIS's list of questions is a superficial history lesson focusing on basic, not controversial facts. Don't expect to find out much about free speech, civil rights, or other important issues. If you're interested in learning more about what really happened during the many centuries of American history, we recommend easy-to-understand history texts such as *Don't Know Much About History: Everything You Need to Know About American History but Never Learned*, by Kenneth C. Davis (Avon), and *A People's History of the United States: 1492 to Present*, by Howard Zinn (Harper Perennial).

B. Learning the Answers to the 100 Questions

In this section, we've summarized the material you'll need to know, and followed that with questions from the official USCIS list. At the end of this chapter, we give you all the questions followed by the answers, so that you'll have a chance to test yourself by choosing questions in random order.

Also check the USCIS website, www.uscis.gov, for study materials (under "Citizenship," click "Citizenship Through Naturalization." Then "Study Materials for the Civics Test"). You'll find videos, flash cards, and more.

TIP

Don't try to memorize every choice of answer. You'll notice that many of the answers to the 100 questions are in list form, giving you several options. But read carefully, because they usually ask you to provide only one or two items off the list as your answer. You might as well choose the one or two you want to memorize, and not bother with the rest. In fact, if you try to supply more answers than are asked for, you may be marked as wrong.

The questions and answers are grouped into the following categories:
- Principles of American Democracy (discussed in Section B1, below)
- System of Government (see Section B2)

- Rights and Responsibilities (see Section B3)
- American History: Colonial Period and Independence (see Section B4)
- American History: 1800s (see Section B5)
- Recent American History and Other Important Historical Information (see Section B6).
- Geography (see Section B7)
- Symbols (see Section B8)
- Holidays (see Section B9).

> **TIP**
>
> **Age 65 or over?** Look for the asterisk. You'll notice that some of the questions are marked with an asterisk (which looks like "*"). These are the ones that people age 65 or older who've had a green card for more than 20 years will need to remember. We've also made a separate list of these questions in Section C, below.

1. Principles of American Democracy

The first set of questions is primarily concerned with two of the most important documents in U.S. history: the Constitution (including the First Amendment) and the Declaration of Independence.

The Constitution is the "supreme law of the land"—meaning, according to USCIS, that it:

- sets up the government
- defines the government, and
- protects basic rights of all Americans.

However, the Constitution was written so as to make clear that it represents self-government by the people of America. In fact, the first three words of the Constitution are "We the People."

TIP

If you want to read the full text of the Constitution: Ask at your local library or go to www.archives.gov. Under "I want to," click "View Online Exhibits," then "The Charters of Freedom," then "Constitution of the United States."

The Constitution is not fixed in stone. Through a process called "amendment," it can either be changed or added to. Today, there are a total of 27 amendments.

The first ten amendments to the Constitution are called the Bill of Rights. And the first one of these ten is particularly important. Here is what the First Amendment says:

Congress shall make no law respecting an establishment of religion, or prohibiting the free exercise thereof; or abridging the freedom of speech, or of the press; or the right of the people peaceably to assemble, and to petition the Government for a redress of grievances.

From this, you'll need to remember that people in the U.S. are guaranteed rights to freedom:

- of speech
- of religion
- of assembly
- of the press, and
- to petition the government.

Here's a little more explanation if you're having trouble remembering these. Freedom of the "press" means of the media (like newspapers and television), which the government is not supposed to interfere with or censor. Freedom of assembly means the right to meet and gather (which might include holding demonstrations).

The U.S. Constitution

Freedom to "petition the government for a redress of grievances" means to ask it to fix things that it has done wrong. And you may be asked to explain freedom of religion, which means, "You can practice any religion, or not practice a religion."

The second important document for you to learn about is the Declaration of Independence. This is where the first colonists announced that the United States is free from Great Britain. They also declared that people have the right to life, liberty, and the pursuit of happiness. (You'll need to remember at least two of those.)

> **TIP**
>
> **To see the full text of the Declaration of Independence:** Ask at your local law library or go to the website of the National Archives and Records Administration (www.archives.gov). Under "I want to," click "View Online Exhibits," then "The Charters of Freedom," then "Declaration of Independence."

Another question in this section concerns the U.S. economic system. You're expected to know that it is a capitalist, or market economy. (That means that goods and services can be privately owned and traded.)

And the final question asks you to define the "rule of law." This is an important question, because the U.S.—and the very immigration system that will allow you to become a citizen—runs according to previously written laws. In other words, no one monarch or dictator can make up the rules as he goes along. Your possible answers include:

- Everyone must follow the law.
- Leaders must obey the law.
- Government must obey the law.
- No one is above the law.

Now let's see if you can answer the first 12 questions on USCIS's list.

1. What is the supreme law of the land?
2. What does the Constitution do?
3. The idea of self-government is in the first three words of the Constitution. What are these words?

4. What is an amendment?

5. What do we call the first ten amendments to the Constitution?

6. What is *one* right or freedom from the First Amendment?*

7. How many amendments does the Constitution have?

8. What did the Declaration of Independence do?

9. What are *two* rights in the Declaration of Independence?

10. What is freedom of religion?

11. What is the economic system in the United States?*

12. What is the "rule of law?"

You'll find the answers (along with a full list of the questions) at the end of this chapter.

2. System of Government

In this set of questions, you're asked to provide information about how the U.S. government is set up. Once you understand the government's basic structure, these questions are not as hard as they look. In any case, this information will be important once you become a citizen because it will help you understand what the federal government is doing.

The federal (national) government is divided into three branches: executive (also known as the President and those who directly serve him or her), legislative (also known as Congress), and judicial (also known as the courts). The idea of having these three branches is to create checks and balances, or a separation of powers, so that no one branch of government becomes too powerful. Look at the diagram below.

The executive branch is run by the President, with some help from the Vice President. It also includes the Cabinet, which advises the President. Each Cabinet adviser also leads a department. The Cabinet-level positions include the following (and you'll need to remember at least two of them):

- Secretary of Agriculture
- Secretary of Commerce
- Secretary of Defense
- Secretary of Education

- Secretary of Energy
- Secretary of Health and Human Services
- Secretary of Homeland Security
- Secretary of Housing and Urban Development
- Secretary of the Interior
- Secretary of State
- Secretary of Transportation
- Secretary of the Treasury
- Secretary of Veterans Affairs
- Secretary of Labor
- Attorney General.

The President's duties include leading the country, serving as Commander in Chief of the military, signing bills passed by Congress so that they become laws (or instead choosing to veto these bills), and much more.

U.S. citizens vote for a new President (and Vice President) every four years, in November. Traditionally, the President comes from one of the United States' two major political parties, the Democratic and Republican Party. We won't try to describe the differences in philosophy between the two parties. You'll develop your own sense of this by following the news and the words of various politicians. USCIS won't ask you to describe the parties' philosophies or differences.

Executive   **Legislative**   **Judicial**

Three Branches of Government

The name of the U.S. President when this book went to print was Barack Obama, from the Democratic Party. The name of the Vice President was Joseph R. Biden, Jr., or "Joe Biden."

If the President can no longer serve (for example, dies, becomes ill, or is impeached), the Vice President steps in and becomes President. If neither of them is able to serve, the Speaker of the House of Representatives becomes President. At the time this book went to print, the Speaker of the House of Representatives was Paul Ryan.

The legislative branch of the U.S. government, also known as the U.S. Congress, is made up of two parts: the Senate and the House of Representatives. Together, their main job is to make federal laws.

The Senate is made up of 100 U.S. Senators (two for each U.S. state). Their job is to represent all the people of your state. We elect U.S. Senators for six years. You may be asked to name one of your state's U.S. Senators, so you'll need to look that up in advance. You can find this information on www.senate.gov (click "Senators," then choose your state from the drop-down menu). However, if you live in Washington, DC, or a U.S. territory such as Guam or Puerto Rico, you'll need to answer that you have no U.S. Senator representing you.

Members of the House of Representatives are elected every two years. The number of Representatives per state depends on how many people live in that state. Some states have more Representatives than others. The more people in your state (the higher the population), the more Representatives you are allowed to send to Congress. At this time, there are a total of 435 Representatives.

You may be asked to name your U.S. Representative. (Although your state may have many Representatives, you have only one, representing your region of the state.) You can find this person's name by going to www.house.gov and entering your zip code where it says "Find Your Representative."

The judicial branch of the federal government is primarily made up of the Supreme Court, which is the highest court in the United States. The job of the judicial branch can be described in any one of four ways; it either:

- reviews laws
- explains laws
- resolves disputes (disagreements), or
- decides if a law goes against the Constitution.

Nine justices serve on the Supreme Court. The current Chief Justice is John Roberts (or John G. Roberts, Jr.).

As you can see, the federal government has a great deal of power. Among its most important powers include:

- to print money
- to declare war
- to create an army, and
- to make treaties.

However, U.S. states also have powers of their own, as laid out in the U.S. Constitution. These powers include:

- provide schooling and education
- provide protection (police)
- provide safety (fire departments)
- give a driver's license, and
- approve zoning and land use.

You may be asked to name one of these powers.

At the head of your state's government is a person called the Governor. You may be asked, on the exam, who the Governor of your state is. You can find this out on your state's website, or by asking a local librarian. However, if you live in Washington, DC, or a U.S. territory, you'll need to answer, "We don't have a Governor."

Your state Governor's office will be in a city within your state known as the "capital." For example, Sacramento is the capital of California, and Albany is the capital of New York. You'll need to know your own state's capital—don't just assume that it's the biggest or most well-known city. If you live in Washington, DC, you should answer that it is not a state and does not have a capital. If you live in a U.S. territory, name the capital of your territory.

Now you're ready to try answering the next set of questions on the citizenship exam:

13. Name *one* branch or part of the government.*

14. What stops *one* branch of government from becoming too powerful?

15. Who is in charge of the executive branch?

16. Who makes federal laws?

17. What are the *two* parts of the U.S. Congress?*

18. How many U.S. Senators are there?

19. We elect a U.S. Senator for how many years?

20. Who is *one* of your state's U.S. Senators?*

21. The House of Representatives has how many voting members?

22. We elect a U.S. Representative for how many years?

23. Name your U.S. Representative.

24. Who does a U.S. Senator represent?

25. Why do some states have more Representatives than other states?

26. We elect a President for how many years?

27. In what month do we vote for President?*

28. What is the name of the President of the United States now?*

29. What is the name of the Vice President of the United States now?

30. If the President can no longer serve, who becomes President?

31. If both the President and the Vice President can no longer serve, who becomes President?

32. Who is the Commander in Chief of the military?

33. Who signs bills to become laws?

34. Who vetoes bills?

35. What does the President's Cabinet do?

36. What are *two* Cabinet-level positions?

37. What does the judicial branch do?

38. What is the highest court in the United States?

39. How many justices are on the Supreme Court?

40. Who is the Chief Justice of the United States?

41. Under our Constitution, some powers belong to the federal government. What is *one* power of the federal government?

42. Under our Constitution, some powers belong to the states. What is *one* power of the states?

43. Who is the Governor of your state?

44. What is the capital of your state?*

45. What are the *two* major political parties in the United States?*

46. What is the political party of the President now?

47. What is the name of the Speaker of the House of Representatives now?

You'll find the answers (along with a full list of the questions) at the end of this chapter.

3. Rights and Responsibilities

The next set of questions addresses the rights and responsibilities that you will have as a U.S. citizen, and that other people living in the United States have as well.

After you become a U.S. citizen, you will earn the rights to apply for a federal job, vote, run for office, and carry a U.S. passport. You may be asked, during your citizenship exam, to name two of these rights.

Only U.S. citizens are allowed to do these things. However, your rights will come with some new responsibilities, including to serve on a jury and to vote. (Notice that voting is considered both a right and responsibility.) You may be asked, during the citizenship exam, to name one of these rights.

Here are some more things you need to know about voting. Citizens need to be at least 18 years of age or older in order to vote for President. The U.S. Constitution contains four amendments that talk about who can vote. They say that:

- Citizens eighteen (18) and older can vote.
- You don't have to pay (a poll tax) to vote.
- Any citizen can vote. (In other words, women and men can vote.)
- A male citizen of any race can vote.

You may be asked, during your citizenship exam, to provide one of these descriptions of the voting amendments.

As you may remember from filling out Form N-400, you will need to make certain promises when you become a United States citizen. These include:

- give up loyalty to other countries
- defend the Constitution and laws of the United States
- obey the laws of the United States
- serve in the U.S. military (if needed)
- serve (do important work for) the nation (if needed), and
- be loyal to the United States.

You may be asked, during the citizenship exam, to name one of these promises. One way that people show loyalty to the United States (or its flag) is to recite the Pledge of Allegiance.

At the moment, the U.S. does not have a military draft or mandatory military service. However, as you know from filling out Form N-400, all men between the ages of 18 and 26 must register for what's called the Selective Service. This means that their names are on record in case circumstances change and a draft must be started.

Whether or not someone is a U.S. citizen, that person enjoys certain rights while living in the United States. These include freedom of expression, of speech, of assembly, and of worship, to petition the government, as well as the right to bear arms. You may be asked, during the citizenship exam, to name two of these rights.

Everyone working in the United States must also pay taxes on their income. You'll need to remember, for the exam, that the last day you can send in federal tax forms is April 15. (You'll also need to remember it every year, if you don't want to get into trouble with the Internal Revenue Service (IRS).)

Finally, the exam asks you to name two ways that Americans can participate in their democracy, from the following list:

- vote
- join a political party
- help with a campaign
- join a civic group
- join a community group
- give an elected official your opinion on an issue
- call Senators and Representatives
- publicly support or oppose an issue or policy
- run for office, and
- write to a newspaper.

Now you're ready to try answering the next set of questions on the citizenship exam:

48. There are four amendments to the Constitution about who can vote. Describe one of them.

49. What is one responsibility that is only for United States citizens?*

50. What are two rights only for United States citizens?

51. What are two rights of everyone living in the United States?

52. What do we show loyalty to when we say the Pledge of Allegiance?

53. What is one promise you make when you become a United States citizen?

54. How old do citizens have to be to vote for President?*

55. What are two ways that Americans can participate in their democracy?

56. When is the last day you can send in federal income tax forms?*

57. When must all men register for the Selective Service?

You'll find the answers at the end of this chapter.

4. American History: Colonial Period and Independence

The next section of questions has to do with the United States' founding and early history.

Colonists meet Native Americans

A number of the questions concern the "colonists," or the first people who came to the United States from Europe. They came for a variety of reasons, such as for freedom, political liberty, religious freedom, economic opportunity, to practice their religion, and to escape persecution. You'll need to remember at least one of these reasons.

The U.S. was not, however, empty of people when the colonists arrived. The Native Americans (or American Indians) already lived here. (If you have children, you've probably seen pictures of the colonists, also called Pilgrims, with the American Indians helping them plant corn.) And the Europeans were not the only new people to arrive in America. The early settlers also brought in people from Africa. The Africans had been captured and sold as slaves.

By the mid-1700s, the American colonies were mostly under the protection and control of England. However, the colonists became unhappy with this, and began trying to fight off this control (during the Revolutionary War), for three main reasons:

- because of high taxes (taxation without representation)
- because the British army stayed in their houses (boarding, quartering), and
- because they (the colonists) didn't have self-government.

You'll need to remember all three of these reasons.

Thomas Jefferson

The U.S. began on July 4, 1776 when the Declaration of Independence was adopted. This document was written by Thomas Jefferson.

The new United States was not as big as it is today, and had only 13 original states. You'll recognize their names as present-day U.S. states nonetheless: Connecticut, New Hampshire, New York, New Jersey, Massachusetts, Pennsylvania, Delaware, Virginia, North Carolina, South Carolina, Georgia, Rhode Island, and Maryland. Locate these on the map below. (Maryland is shortened to "MD.") With your pencil, put a star on each of the 13 original colonies. On the exam, you may be asked to name three of them.

The U.S. Constitution (which we've already talked about) was written not long after, in 1787. It was a group effort by several men we call the "Founding Fathers," who met at the Constitutional Convention.

However, before the Constitution could become U.S. law, it needed to be passed by the U.S. Congress. Three men wrote something called the "Federalist Papers" in support of its passage. These men included James Madison, Alexander Hamilton, and John Jay. However, they published the Federalist papers under a false name: "Publius." You may be asked to give at least one of these four names on the citizenship exam.

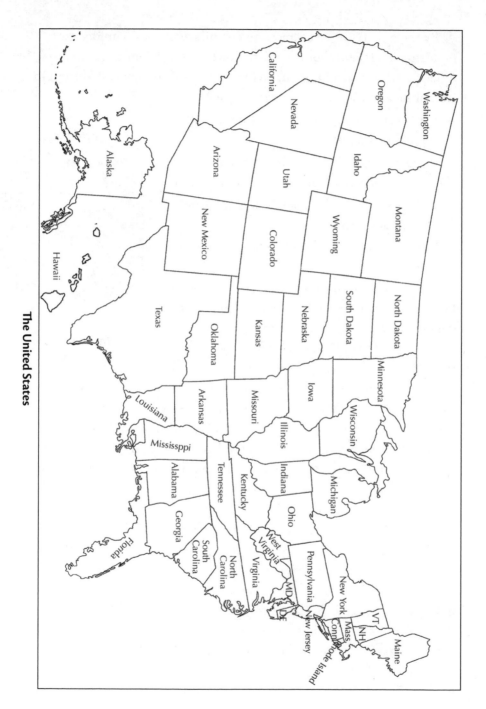

The United States

The first President of the United States was George Washington. He is known as the "Father of Our Country."

Another active person in early U.S. history was Benjamin Franklin. Among other things, he is famous for being a U.S. diplomat, the oldest member of the Constitutional Convention, the first Postmaster General of the United States, writer of "Poor Richard's Almanac," and the man who started the first free libraries. You may be asked to name one of these things.

Now you're ready to try answering the next set of questions on the citizenship exam:

58. What is *one* reason colonists came to America?

59. Who lived in America before the Europeans arrived?

60. What group of people was taken to America and sold as slaves?

61. Why did the colonists fight the British?

62. Who wrote the Declaration of Independence?

63. When was the Declaration of Independence adopted?

64. There were 13 original states. Name *three*.

65. What happened at the Constitutional Convention?

66. When was the Constitution written?

67. The Federalist Papers supported the passage of the U.S. Constitution. Name one of the writers.

68. What is *one* thing Benjamin Franklin is famous for?

69. Who is the "Father of Our Country"?

70. Who was the first President?*

You'll find a list of answers at the end of this chapter.

5. American History: 1800s

Now we'll move forward a bit, to the 1800s. This period is often remembered for war and territorial expansion. In 1803, the U.S. bought a large area known as the Louisiana territory, from France.

The U.S. fought four wars during the 1800s, including the War of 1812 (mostly fought against Britain), the Mexican-American war, the Civil War, and the Spanish-American war. (You may be asked to name at least one of these.)

**Abraham Lincoln—
16th President of the U.S.**

The Civil War, also known as the "War between the States," was between the North and the South. The reasons for the war were slavery, economic matters, and disputes over states' rights. (You may be asked to name one of these.) President Abraham Lincoln led the United States during the Civil War. During these years, he issued the Emancipation Proclamation, which declared that all the slaves in the rebellious southern states were now free. He is credited with having saved (or preserved) the Union.

Another person who was active during the 1800s was Susan B. Anthony, who fought for women's rights and civil rights.

Now try answering the next set of questions on the citizenship exam:

71. What territory did the United States buy from France in 1803?

72. Name *one* war fought by the United States in the 1800s.

73. Name the U.S. war between the North and South.

74. Name *one* problem that led to the Civil War.

75. What was *one* important thing that Abraham Lincoln did?*

76. What did the Emancipation Proclamation do?

77. What did Susan B. Anthony do?

You'll find a list of answers at the end of this chapter.

6. Recent American History and Other Important Historical Information

Moving right along, the exam questions turn to the 1900s and more recent American history.

Unfortunately, the United States participated in a number of wars during the 1900s, including World War I, World War II (against Japan, Germany, and Italy), the Korean War, the Vietnam War, and the Persian Gulf War. You may be asked to name one of these.

The President during World War I was Woodrow Wilson.

The President during World War II, as well as the Great Depression, was Franklin Roosevelt. Eisenhower served as a general in World War II, and later became U.S. President.

Another so-called war (although it was fought without battles) is known as the "Cold War." This refers to the United States' efforts to make sure that Communism did not spread, particularly from the Soviet Union.

In approximately the mid-1950s, the movement known as the civil rights movement began. Its purpose was to end racial discrimination. A key participant was Martin Luther King, Jr., who fought for civil rights and worked for the equality of all Americans.

Franklin D. Roosevelt—
32nd President of the U.S.

You may be asked to name one American Indian tribe; your choices include Cherokee, Navajo, Sioux, Chippewa, Choctaw, Pueblo, Apache, Iroquois, Creek, Blackfeet, Seminole, Cheyenne, Arawak, Shawnee, Mohegan, Huron, Oneida, Lakota, Crow, Teton, Hopi, and Inuit.

Since the turn of the century in 2000, one defining event was September 11, 2001, when terrorists attacked the United States.

Are you ready to try answering the related questions?

78. Name *one* war fought by the United States in the 1900s.*

79. Who was President during World War I?

80. Who was President during the Great Depression and World War II?

81. Who did the United States fight in World War II?

82. Before he was President, Eisenhower was a general. What war was he in?

83. During the Cold War, what was the main concern of the United States?

84. What movement tried to end racial discrimination?

85. What did Martin Luther King, Jr. do?*

86. What major event happened on September 11, 2001 in the United States?

87. Name *one* Indian tribe in the United States.

You'll find a list of answers at the end of this chapter.

7. Geography

Next, you will need to learn a little bit about the geography, or physical landscape and important features, of the United States.

U.S. and Border Countries

The United States is bordered by two other countries, Canada and Mexico. The U.S. states that fall along the Canadian border include Maine, New Hampshire, Vermont, New York, Pennsylvania, Ohio, Michigan, Minnesota, North Dakota, Montana, Idaho, Washington, and Alaska. You'll need to be ready to name one of these.

The U.S. states that are found along the border with Mexico include California, Arizona, New Mexico, and Texas. You'll need to be ready to name one of these.

On the western and eastern sides of the United States are two oceans: the Pacific Ocean on the West Coast, and the Atlantic Ocean on the East Coast.

A number of major rivers run through the United States. Two of the longest ones are the Missouri River and the Mississippi River. You may be asked to name one of those.

The United States includes land beyond its 50 states, including the territories of Puerto Rico, the U.S. Virgin Islands, American Samoa, Northern Mariana Islands, and Guam. Be ready to name one of those.

The capital of the United States is in Washington, DC. And one of the most important U.S. symbols is the Statue of Liberty, in New York Harbor (or Liberty Island).

Here are the questions for this section.

88. Name *one* of the two longest rivers in the United States.

89. What ocean is on the West Coast of the United States?

Statue of Liberty

90. What ocean is on the East Coast of the United States?

91. Name *one* U.S. territory.

92. Name *one* state that borders Canada.

93. Name *one* state that borders Mexico.

94. What is the capital of the United States?*

95. Where is the Statue of Liberty?*

You will find a list of answers at the end of this chapter.

8. Symbols

You have no doubt seen the American flag, shown below. The 13 stripes represent the original 13 colonies (now called "states") that formed the United States when it was first founded. The 50 white stars on the flag represent the 50 states in the United States today, also shown on our map.

The American flag is an important symbol. That's why our national song (or "national anthem") was written about it. The title of our national anthem is "The Star-Spangled Banner." The title is a poetic name for "the flag with stars all over it" (which would not have sounded as nice). Spanish speakers won't have much trouble remembering the word "banner," because it's related to the Spanish word for flag, "bandera."

United States Flag

Now try answering a few questions for this section:

96. Why does the flag have 13 stripes?

97. Why does the flag have 50 stars?*

98. What is the name of the national anthem?

You'll find the answers at the end of this chapter.

9. Holidays

Only two questions left!

Martin Luther King

In recognition of the Declaration of Independence, July 4 is now celebrated, with fireworks and parties and a day off work for many, as Independence Day.

Other national U.S. holidays include New Year's Day, Martin Luther King, Jr. Day, Presidents' Day, Memorial Day, Independence Day, Labor Day, Columbus Day, Veterans' Day, Thanksgiving, and Christmas. You may be asked to name two of these. You won't be asked to describe what they symbolize. (In fact, for many Americans, many of these holidays' most important meaning is that people get the day off work!)

Here are your last two questions:

99. When do we celebrate Independence Day?*

100. Name two national U.S. holidays.

C. The 20 Questions for Applicants Age 65 and Older

As we explained, this easier version of the exam is only for applicants age 65 and older who have spent 20 or more years as U.S. permanent residents. You'll need to study the following 20 questions and answer at least six out of ten of them correctly to pass your citizenship exam.

The questions that you'll have to study and remember include the ones listed below. We don't give a narrative to explain them, but they are drawn from the list of 100 questions that everyone else studies, so you can find the background information in the sections above. And to help you find the answers on the official USCIS list at the end of this chapter, we've put the original question number in brackets on the list below.

The List of 20 Questions

1. [#6] What is *one* right or freedom from the First Amendment?
2. [#11] What is the economic system in the United States?
3. [#13] Name one branch or part of the government.
4. [#17] What are the *two* parts of the U.S. Congress?
5. [#20] Who is one of your state's U.S. Senators?
6. [#27] In what month do we vote for President?
7. [#28] What is the name of the President of the United States now?
8. [#44] What is the capital of your state?
9. [#45] What are the *two* major political parties in the United States?
10. [#49] What is one responsibility that is only for United States citizens?
11. [#54] How old do citizens have to be to vote for president?
12. [#56] When is the last day you can send in federal income tax forms?

13. [#70] Who was the first President?

14. [#75] What was *one* important thing that Abraham Lincoln did?

15. [#78] Name *one* war fought by the United States in the 1900s.

16. [#85] What did Martin Luther King, Jr. do?

17. [#94] What is the capital of the United States?

18. [#95] Where is the Statue of Liberty?

19. [#97] Why does the flag have 50 stars?

20. [#99] When do we celebrate Independence Day?

Independence Day Fireworks

USCIS List of 100 Questions and Answers

(rev. 02/16)

U.S. Citizenship and Immigration Services

Civics (History and Government) Questions for the Naturalization Test

The 100 civics (history and government) questions and answers for the naturalization test are listed below. The civics test is an oral test and the USCIS Officer will ask the applicant up to 10 of the 100 civics questions. An applicant must answer 6 out of 10 questions correctly to pass the civics portion of the naturalization test.

On the naturalization test, some answers may change because of elections or appointments. As you study for the test, make sure that you know the most current answers to these questions. Answer these questions with the name of the official who is serving at the time of your eligibility interview with USCIS. The USCIS Officer will not accept an incorrect answer.

Although USCIS is aware that there may be additional correct answers to the 100 civics questions, applicants are encouraged to respond to the civics questions using the answers provided below.

AMERICAN GOVERNMENT

A: Principles of American Democracy

1.   **What is the supreme law of the land?**
   - *the Constitution*

2.   **What does the Constitution do?**
   - *sets up the government*
   - *defines the government*
   - *protects basic rights of Americans*

3.   **The idea of self-government is in the first three words of the Constitution. What are these words?**
   - *We the People*

4.   **What is an amendment?**
   - *a change (to the Constitution)*
   - *an addition (to the Constitution)*

5.   **What do we call the first ten amendments to the Constitution?**
   - *the Bill of Rights*

6.   **What is <u>one</u> right or freedom from the First Amendment?***
   - *speech*
   - *religion*
   - *assembly*
   - *press*
   - *petition the government*

7.   **How many amendments does the Constitution have?**
   - *twenty-seven (27)*

* If you are 65 years old or older and have been a legal permanent resident of the United States for 20 or more years, you may study just the questions that have been marked with an asterisk.

www.uscis.gov

USCIS List of 100 Questions and Answers (continued)

8. **What did the Declaration of Independence do?**
   - *announced our independence (from Great Britain)*
   - *declared our independence (from Great Britain)*
   - *said that the United States is free (from Great Britain)*

9. **What are <u>two</u> rights in the Declaration of Independence?**
   - *life*
   - *liberty*
   - *pursuit of happiness*

10. **What is freedom of religion?**
    - *You can practice any religion, or not practice a religion.*

11. **What is the economic system in the United States?***
    - *capitalist economy*
    - *market economy*

12. **What is the "rule of law"?**
    - *Everyone must follow the law.*
    - *Leaders must obey the law.*
    - *Government must obey the law.*
    - *No one is above the law.*

B: System of Government

13. **Name <u>one</u> branch or part of the government.***
    - *Congress*
    - *legislative*
    - *President*
    - *executive*
    - *the courts*
    - *judicial*

14. **What stops <u>one</u> branch of government from becoming too powerful?**
    - *checks and balances*
    - *separation of powers*

15. **Who is in charge of the executive branch?**
    - *the President*

16. **Who makes federal laws?**
    - *Congress*
    - *Senate and House (of Representatives)*
    - *(U.S. or national) legislature*

17. **What are the <u>two</u> parts of the U.S. Congress?***
    - *the Senate and House (of Representatives)*

18. **How many U.S. Senators are there?**
    - *one hundred (100)*

---

* If you are 65 years old or older and have been a legal permanent resident of the United States for 20 or more years, you may study just the questions that have been marked with an asterisk.

www.uscis.gov

USCIS List of 100 Questions and Answers (continued)

19. **We elect a U.S. Senator for how many years?**
    - *six (6)*

20. **Who is <u>one</u> of your state's U.S. Senators now?***
    - *Answers will vary. [District of Columbia residents and residents of U.S. territories should answer that D.C. (or the territory where the applicant lives) has no U.S. Senators.]*

21. **The House of Representatives has how many voting members?**
    - *four hundred thirty-five (435)*

22. **We elect a U.S. Representative for how many years?**
    - *two (2)*

23. **Name your U.S. Representative.**
    - *Answers will vary. [Residents of territories with nonvoting Delegates or Resident Commissioners may provide the name of that Delegate or Commissioner. Also acceptable is any statement that the territory has no (voting) Representatives in Congress.]*

24. **Who does a U.S. Senator represent?**
    - *all people of the state*

25. **Why do some states have more Representatives than other states?**
    - *(because of) the state's population*
    - *(because) they have more people*
    - *(because) some states have more people*

26. **We elect a President for how many years?**
    - *four (4)*

27. **In what month do we vote for President?***
    - *November*

28. **What is the name of the President of the United States now?***
    - *Barack Obama*
    - *Obama*

29. **What is the name of the Vice President of the United States now?**
    - *Joseph R. Biden, Jr.*
    - *Joe Biden*
    - *Biden*

30. **If the President can no longer serve, who becomes President?**
    - *the Vice President*

31. **If both the President and the Vice President can no longer serve, who becomes President?**
    - *the Speaker of the House*

32. **Who is the Commander in Chief of the military?**
    - *the President*

33. **Who signs bills to become laws?**
    - *the President*

34. **Who vetoes bills?**
    - *the President*

* If you are 65 years old or older and have been a legal permanent resident of the United States for 20 or more years, you may study just the questions that have been marked with an asterisk.

USCIS List of 100 Questions and Answers (continued)

35. **What does the President's Cabinet do?**
    - *advises the President*

36. **What are <u>two</u> Cabinet-level positions?**
    - *Secretary of Agriculture*
    - *Secretary of Commerce*
    - *Secretary of Defense*
    - *Secretary of Education*
    - *Secretary of Energy*
    - *Secretary of Health and Human Services*
    - *Secretary of Homeland Security*
    - *Secretary of Housing and Urban Development*
    - *Secretary of the Interior*
    - *Secretary of Labor*
    - *Secretary of State*
    - *Secretary of Transportation*
    - *Secretary of the Treasury*
    - *Secretary of Veterans Affairs*
    - *Attorney General*
    - *Vice President*

37. **What does the judicial branch do?**
    - *reviews laws*
    - *explains laws*
    - *resolves disputes (disagreements)*
    - *decides if a law goes against the Constitution*

38. **What is the highest court in the United States?**
    - *the Supreme Court*

39. **How many justices are on the Supreme Court?**
    - *nine (9)*

40. **Who is the Chief Justice of the United States now?**
    - *John Roberts (John G. Roberts, Jr.)*

41. **Under our Constitution, some powers belong to the federal government. What is <u>one</u> power of the federal government?**
    - *to print money*
    - *to declare war*
    - *to create an army*
    - *to make treaties*

42. **Under our Constitution, some powers belong to the states. What is <u>one</u> power of the states?**
    - *provide schooling and education*
    - *provide protection (police)*
    - *provide safety (fire departments)*
    - *give a driver's license*
    - *approve zoning and land use*

* If you are 65 years old or older and have been a legal permanent resident of the United States for 20 or more years, you may study just the questions that have been marked with an asterisk.

www.uscis.gov

USCIS List of 100 Questions and Answers (continued)

43. **Who is the Governor of your state now?**
    - *Answers will vary. [District of Columbia residents should answer that D.C. does not have a Governor.]*

44. **What is the capital of your state?***
    - *Answers will vary. [District of Columbia residents should answer that D.C. is not a state and does not have a capital. Residents of U.S. territories should name the capital of the territory.]*

45. **What are the <u>two</u> major political parties in the United States?***
    - *Democratic and Republican*

46. **What is the political party of the President now?**
    - *Democratic (Party)*

47. **What is the name of the Speaker of the House of Representatives now?**
    - *Paul D. Ryan*
    - *(Paul) Ryan*

C: Rights and Responsibilities

48. **There are four amendments to the Constitution about who can vote. Describe <u>one</u> of them.**
    - *Citizens eighteen (18) and older (can vote).*
    - *You don't have to pay (a poll tax) to vote.*
    - *Any citizen can vote. (Women and men can vote.)*
    - *A male citizen of any race (can vote).*

49. **What is <u>one</u> responsibility that is only for United States citizens?***
    - *serve on a jury*
    - *vote in a federal election*

50. **Name <u>one</u> right only for United States citizens.**
    - *vote in a federal election*
    - *run for federal office*

51. **What are <u>two</u> rights of everyone living in the United States?**
    - *freedom of expression*
    - *freedom of speech*
    - *freedom of assembly*
    - *freedom to petition the government*
    - *freedom of religion*
    - *the right to bear arms*

52. **What do we show loyalty to when we say the Pledge of Allegiance?**
    - *the United States*
    - *the flag*

---

* If you are 65 years old or older and have been a legal permanent resident of the United States for 20 or more years, you may study just the questions that have been marked with an asterisk.

USCIS List of 100 Questions and Answers (continued)

53. **What is <u>one</u> promise you make when you become a United States citizen?**
    - *give up loyalty to other countries*
    - *defend the Constitution and laws of the United States*
    - *obey the laws of the United States*
    - *serve in the U.S. military (if needed)*
    - *serve (do important work for) the nation (if needed)*
    - *be loyal to the United States*

54. **How old do citizens have to be to vote for President?***
    - *eighteen (18) and older*

55. **What are <u>two</u> ways that Americans can participate in their democracy?**
    - *vote*
    - *join a political party*
    - *help with a campaign*
    - *join a civic group*
    - *join a community group*
    - *give an elected official your opinion on an issue*
    - *call Senators and Representatives*
    - *publicly support or oppose an issue or policy*
    - *run for office*
    - *write to a newspaper*

56. **When is the last day you can send in federal income tax forms?***
    - *April 15*

57. **When must all men register for the Selective Service?**
    - *at age eighteen (18)*
    - *between eighteen (18) and twenty-six (26)*

AMERICAN HISTORY

A: Colonial Period and Independence

58. **What is <u>one</u> reason colonists came to America?**
    - *freedom*
    - *political liberty*
    - *religious freedom*
    - *economic opportunity*
    - *practice their religion*
    - *escape persecution*

59. **Who lived in America before the Europeans arrived?**
    - *American Indians*
    - *Native Americans*

* If you are 65 years old or older and have been a legal permanent resident of the United States for 20 or more years, you may study just the questions that have been marked with an asterisk.

USCIS List of 100 Questions and Answers (continued)

60. **What group of people was taken to America and sold as slaves?**
    - *Africans*
    - *people from Africa*

61. **Why did the colonists fight the British?**
    - *because of high taxes (taxation without representation)*
    - *because the British army stayed in their houses (boarding, quartering)*
    - *because they didn't have self-government*

62. **Who wrote the Declaration of Independence?**
    - *(Thomas) Jefferson*

63. **When was the Declaration of Independence adopted?**
    - *July 4, 1776*

64. **There were 13 original states. Name <u>three</u>.**
    - *New Hampshire*
    - *Massachusetts*
    - *Rhode Island*
    - *Connecticut*
    - *New York*
    - *New Jersey*
    - *Pennsylvania*
    - *Delaware*
    - *Maryland*
    - *Virginia*
    - *North Carolina*
    - *South Carolina*
    - *Georgia*

65. **What happened at the Constitutional Convention?**
    - *The Constitution was written.*
    - *The Founding Fathers wrote the Constitution.*

66. **When was the Constitution written?**
    - *1787*

67. **The Federalist Papers supported the passage of the U.S. Constitution. Name <u>one</u> of the writers.**
    - *(James) Madison*
    - *(Alexander) Hamilton*
    - *(John) Jay*
    - *Publius*

68. **What is <u>one</u> thing Benjamin Franklin is famous for?**
    - *U.S. diplomat*
    - *oldest member of the Constitutional Convention*
    - *first Postmaster General of the United States*
    - *writer of "Poor Richard's Almanac"*
    - *started the first free libraries*

* If you are 65 years old or older and have been a legal permanent resident of the United States for 20 or more years, you may study just the questions that have been marked with an asterisk.

www.uscis.gov

USCIS List of 100 Questions and Answers (continued)

69. **Who is the "Father of Our Country"?**
   - *(George) Washington*

70. **Who was the first President?***
   - *(George) Washington*

B: 1800s

71. **What territory did the United States buy from France in 1803?**
   - *the Louisiana Territory*
   - *Louisiana*

72. **Name <u>one</u> war fought by the United States in the 1800s.**
   - *War of 1812*
   - *Mexican-American War*
   - *Civil War*
   - *Spanish-American War*

73. **Name the U.S. war between the North and the South.**
   - *the Civil War*
   - *the War between the States*

74. **Name <u>one</u> problem that led to the Civil War.**
   - *slavery*
   - *economic reasons*
   - *states' rights*

75. **What was <u>one</u> important thing that Abraham Lincoln did?***
   - *freed the slaves (Emancipation Proclamation)*
   - *saved (or preserved) the Union*
   - *led the United States during the Civil War*

76. **What did the Emancipation Proclamation do?**
   - *freed the slaves*
   - *freed slaves in the Confederacy*
   - *freed slaves in the Confederate states*
   - *freed slaves in most Southern states*

77. **What did Susan B. Anthony do?**
   - *fought for women's rights*
   - *fought for civil rights*

C: Recent American History and Other Important Historical Information

78. **Name <u>one</u> war fought by the United States in the 1900s.***
   - *World War I*
   - *World War II*
   - *Korean War*
   - *Vietnam War*
   - *(Persian) Gulf War*

* If you are 65 years old or older and have been a legal permanent resident of the United States for 20 or more years, you may study just the questions that have been marked with an asterisk.

USCIS List of 100 Questions and Answers (continued)

79. **Who was President during World War I?**
    - *(Woodrow) Wilson*

80. **Who was President during the Great Depression and World War II?**
    - *(Franklin) Roosevelt*

81. **Who did the United States fight in World War II?**
    - *Japan, Germany, and Italy*

82. **Before he was President, Eisenhower was a general. What war was he in?**
    - *World War II*

83. **During the Cold War, what was the main concern of the United States?**
    - *Communism*

84. **What movement tried to end racial discrimination?**
    - *civil rights (movement)*

85. **What did Martin Luther King, Jr. do?***
    - *fought for civil rights*
    - *worked for equality for all Americans*

86. **What major event happened on September 11, 2001, in the United States?**
    - *Terrorists attacked the United States.*

87. **Name <u>one</u> American Indian tribe in the United States.**
    [USCIS Officers will be supplied with a list of federally recognized American Indian tribes.]
    - *Cherokee*
    - *Navajo*
    - *Sioux*
    - *Chippewa*
    - *Choctaw*
    - *Pueblo*
    - *Apache*
    - *Iroquois*
    - *Creek*
    - *Blackfeet*
    - *Seminole*
    - *Cheyenne*
    - *Arawak*
    - *Shawnee*
    - *Mohegan*
    - *Huron*
    - *Oneida*
    - *Lakota*
    - *Crow*
    - *Teton*
    - *Hopi*
    - *Inuit*

* If you are 65 years old or older and have been a legal permanent resident of the United States for 20 or more years, you may study just the questions that have been marked with an asterisk.

www.uscis.gov

USCIS List of 100 Questions and Answers (continued)

INTEGRATED CIVICS

A: Geography

88. **Name <u>one</u> of the two longest rivers in the United States.**
    - *Missouri (River)*
    - *Mississippi (River)*

89. **What ocean is on the West Coast of the United States?**
    - *Pacific (Ocean)*

90. **What ocean is on the East Coast of the United States?**
    - *Atlantic (Ocean)*

91. **Name <u>one</u> U.S. territory.**
    - *Puerto Rico*
    - *U.S. Virgin Islands*
    - *American Samoa*
    - *Northern Mariana Islands*
    - *Guam*

92. **Name <u>one</u> state that borders Canada.**
    - *Maine*
    - *New Hampshire*
    - *Vermont*
    - *New York*
    - *Pennsylvania*
    - *Ohio*
    - *Michigan*
    - *Minnesota*
    - *North Dakota*
    - *Montana*
    - *Idaho*
    - *Washington*
    - *Alaska*

93. **Name <u>one</u> state that borders Mexico.**
    - *California*
    - *Arizona*
    - *New Mexico*
    - *Texas*

94. **What is the capital of the United States?***
    - *Washington, D.C.*

95. **Where is the Statue of Liberty?***
    - *New York (Harbor)*
    - *Liberty Island*
    - *[Also acceptable are New Jersey, near New York City, and on the Hudson (River).]*

* If you are 65 years old or older and have been a legal permanent resident of the United States for 20 or more years, you may study just the questions that have been marked with an asterisk.

USCIS List of 100 Questions and Answers (continued)

B: Symbols

96. **Why does the flag have 13 stripes?**
    - *because there were 13 original colonies*
    - *because the stripes represent the original colonies*

97. **Why does the flag have 50 stars?***
    - *because there is one star for each state*
    - *because each star represents a state*
    - *because there are 50 states*

98. **What is the name of the national anthem?**
    - *The Star-Spangled Banner*

C: Holidays

99. **When do we celebrate Independence Day?***
    - *July 4*

100. **Name <u>two</u> national U.S. holidays.**
    - *New Year's Day*
    - *Martin Luther King, Jr. Day*
    - *Presidents' Day*
    - *Memorial Day*
    - *Independence Day*
    - *Labor Day*
    - *Columbus Day*
    - *Veterans Day*
    - *Thanksgiving*
    - *Christmas*

* If you are 65 years old or older and have been a legal permanent resident of the United States for 20 or more years, you may study just the questions that have been marked with an asterisk.

Overcoming Disability When Applying for Citizenship

I f you have a physical or mental disability that makes applying for U.S. citizenship very difficult, don't give up. USCIS must make allowances and arrangements for people with permanent disabilities—a responsibility that the agency has been paying increasing attention to in recent years. USCIS offers the following types of assistance:

- If at any point in the process you need help from a guardian or family member, USCIS may allow this person to act as your "designated representative" (see Section A, below).

- If you can meet the basic requirements, but need a little help at the interview or swearing-in (oath) ceremony, USCIS can provide accommodations (see Section B, below).

- If your physical or mental condition makes it impossible to learn English or U.S. history and government, USCIS can waive these exam requirements (see Section C, below).

- For a person whose condition is so severe that he or she can neither understand nor repeat the Oath of Allegiance, which is the final step toward making someone a citizen, USCIS can waive the oath requirement (see Section D, below).

You may have a disability that requires both accommodations and an exam waiver. That's fine; you can ask for both. But before we go any further, understand that nothing is automatic. Even if you have been declared disabled by a doctor, the Social Security Administration, or some other authority, USCIS will want to make its own decision. USCIS is not concerned whether you can work or do the other things usually evaluated in a disability exam; the agency's main concern is whether your disability interferes with your ability to complete the citizenship application requirements.

SEE AN EXPERT

If you are uncomfortable dealing with the procedures described in this chapter on your own, hire an immigration attorney. You may not need to pay full price—a number of nonprofits serving immigrants and refugees have attorneys or highly qualified paralegals who help people with disabilities apply for U.S. citizenship. For more on how to find helpful nonprofits, see Chapter 10.

A. How to Become the Applicant's Designated Representative

This section is for people trying to help a disabled person who may not be able to make it through the naturalization process on his or her own. Your help is not only allowed, but welcomed, so long as you have been appointed the applicant's designated representative. Depending on the level of the applicant's disability, you, as the designated representative, may be allowed to help with various tasks, including filling in the Form N-400, accompanying the applicant to the naturalization interview, interpreting, sometimes even answering questions on the applicant's behalf, and more.

Allowing you to assist in these ways not only helps the applicant, but it helps USCIS, whose officers don't want to waste time or mistreat an applicant simply because they didn't understand his or her special needs.

Only one person can act as the applicant's designated representative at a time, so your first task is to make sure that you're the right person for the job. USCIS requires that the designated representative be one of the following types of caretakers, in this order of priority:

- legal guardian or surrogate
- U.S. citizen spouse
- U.S. citizen parent
- U.S. citizen adult son or daughter who acts as the applicant's primary caretaker, or
- U.S. citizen adult brother or sister who acts as the applicant's primary caretaker.

TIP

More than one person may be able to help, without being a designated representative. For example, if the applicant has a legal guardian who needs to speak for him at the interview, but the applicant's brother is the best one at administering regularly needed injections, the applicant could have the legal guardian appointed designated representative, but ask that the brother also be allowed to attend the interview, as a reasonable accommodation. (See Section B, below, for more on requesting accommodations.)

In order to have yourself appointed as designated representative, you'll need to ask USCIS for this, preferably in a letter accompanying the applicant's N-400, or in a paragraph in the cover letter. (There's no need to ask before submitting the N-400—USCIS won't mind if you fill out the form and the applicant signs it, but you should enter your name in the preparer's box.)

If you come into the picture after the N-400 has been filed, don't hesitate to send your letter separately (remembering to mention the applicant's A-number in your letter) or even arrive at the applicant's interview and hand the letter to the person at the appointment desk.

In addition to making your request and stating your relationship to the applicant, your letter should state that, to the best of your knowledge and belief, no other person has been granted legal guardianship or authority over the affairs of the applicant. Along with your letter, you'll need to provide proof that your relationship to the applicant qualifies you to be a designated representative, as follows:

- If you're the applicant's **legal guardian or surrogate**, include a copy of the court order or evidence from another state authority granting you guardianship or custody. Make sure the order is from the same state in which the applicant is applying for citizenship.

- If you're the applicant's U.S. citizen **spouse**, include a copy of proof of your citizenship status (such as a birth certificate, passport, naturalization certificate, or other official document), a copy of your marriage certificate, and a sworn statement that you're still married.

- If you're the applicant's U.S. citizen **parent**, include a copy of proof of your citizenship status (such as a birth certificate, passport, naturalization certificate, or other official document) and a copy of your child's birth certificate.

- If you're the applicant's U.S. citizen **adult son or daughter**, include a copy of proof of your citizenship status (such as a birth certificate, passport, naturalization certificate, or other official document), a copy of your birth or adoption certificate, and evidence that you have primary custodial responsibility for the applicant, such as an executed power of attorney, or tax returns reflecting that the applicant has been declared a dependent in your household.

- If you're the applicant's U.S. citizen **brother or sister**, include a copy of proof of your citizenship status (such as a birth certificate, passport, naturalization certificate, or other official document), proof that you have the same parents (such as copies of both your birth certificates), and evidence that you have primary custodial responsibility for the applicant, such as an executed power of attorney, or tax returns reflecting that the applicant has been declared a dependent in your household.

If you submit your letter by mail and hear nothing back from USCIS, it's safe to assume that the agency has either accepted your request to act as designated representative, or that it will make the final decision at the applicant's interview. Go ahead and accompany the applicant to the interview, if that was part of your request.

> **TIP**
> **Bring complete copies of your request, as well as original documents, to the interview.** USCIS may want to review your request at that time, and your mailed documents may have gotten separated from the applicant's file. Also, USCIS likes to view original versions of documents such as court orders and marriage certificates to be sure that they're the real thing.

B. Accommodating Your Disability

In a normal USCIS interview, you must get to the USCIS office, wait an hour or more for your interview (without food or water), make your way into the USCIS officer's cubicle or space, sit by the officer's desk, raise your hand to take an oath, answer questions, and generally cope with a stressful situation. Any of these tasks, which might seem simple to another person, can seem like giant challenges to someone with physical or mental disabilities.

Fortunately, you can ask for accommodations in advance. If these accommodations are reasonable, and you can prove your need for them (particularly with reports from your doctor), USCIS will make an effort to grant them.

Not all accommodations need to relate to the interview (though many do). An accommodation can be any change to normal USCIS policy and procedures that helps you participate in the naturalization process and reduces the disadvantages you'd otherwise face. For example, if you need USCIS to come up with a method other than fingerprinting to check your background for criminal activity, perhaps because your fingers have been badly burned or amputated, you can ask for that.

1. What You Can Ask For

Although you know best what you might need in the way of help, we include some examples below of the type of accommodations others might reasonably request. In general, the accommodations that USCIS will arrange usually have to do with the physical setting of the interview—where it's held, how quickly you're called in, whether your wheelchair will fit, whether you can bring a caregiver or guardian, whether someone will show you the way if you're blind (or you can bring your guide dog), whether someone will interpret for you if you're deaf, speak loudly if you're hard of hearing, give you a large-print version of the English reading test if you're visually impaired, give you more time to answer and mostly yes/no questions if you're cognitively impaired, and more.

> **EXAMPLE 1:** Dante's entire right side is paralyzed. He gets around using a motorized wheelchair and advises USCIS that he will be arriving in it. (Although federal buildings are required by law to be wheelchair accessible, it's worth advising them you'll be needing access, just in case.) Since Dante fatigues easily, he requests that USCIS interview him as soon as possible after he arrives. He explains that he will not be able to raise his right hand when swearing to tell the truth at the beginning of the interview. Under these circumstances, USCIS will allow him to take the oath using his left hand. Because he has difficulty making himself understood, Dante asks permission for a close friend to accompany him—someone who is accustomed to his mode of speech and can repeat his words to the USCIS officer.

EXAMPLE 2: Athena is severely developmentally disabled and hard of hearing. She was sexually abused as a child and now refuses to talk when any man speaks to her. She (or a guardian acting for her) requests that USCIS provide a female officer who is comfortable speaking loudly and clearly. In addition, Athena requests that USCIS allow her mother to accompany her into the interview to help Athena and the officer understand each other's words and to maintain Athena's comfort. (Athena separately requests waivers of the exam requirements, as covered in Section C, below.)

EXAMPLE 3: Kim has an advanced kidney ailment, and is confined to a hospital bed. His long-term prognosis is not good. Kim asks USCIS to send an officer to interview him in his hospital room. (USCIS can also send someone to swear Kim in if he passes.) In addition, since Kim is afraid he won't survive until the regularly scheduled interview date and wants very badly to become a U.S. citizen, he requests an expedited (speeded up) interview date—and assuming he passes, requests that the USCIS officer swear him in as a citizen at the same time. (Note: USCIS usually grants these expedited interviews only in life-or-death situations.)

Many applicants might find it helpful to ask for extra time—for example, for a mentally impaired applicant, or one with arthritic hands —to complete the written portion of the exam.

For various reasons, USCIS has been seeing more requests for accommodations recently, so don't worry that your situation will seem unusual. If you truly need assistance, don't be shy about making your request.

2. Requesting Accommodations

In order to alert USCIS that you need accommodations, check the "yes" box on Part 2, Question 10, of the citizenship application form (Form N-400). Below that, you are given a few options, or you can specifically explain what accommodations you'll need in the blank lines by the fourth box. If this isn't enough space, attach a more complete explanation on a separate piece of paper and in your cover letter.

Be as specific as you can in your request. For example, instead of saying "I need a friend with me because I am sick," say "I need a friend to accompany me into the interview in case I have a seizure and need an injection administered quickly."

PAPERWORK REMINDER

Make sure USCIS notices your request. Regardless of the information provided on the application form, it's a good idea to repeat your accommodations request in your cover letter and to include a doctor's letter in your application packet. Also write in big letters across the top of your Form N-400, "Accommodations Needed." And then call to talk over what you need with the Customer Service Center, at 800-375-5283 (TDD 800-767-1833).

Ask your doctor to write a letter—there's no special form to use in this situation—explaining your condition in medical terms and confirming the assistance you will need at the interview and swearing-in ceremony. (Although doctor's letters are not required, they're very helpful in convincing USCIS that you need certain accommodations. You could also simply use copies of test results.) Note: If your doctor is already filling out an exam waiver request for you on Form N-648 (discussed in the next section), he or she won't need to separately discuss your medical condition in this letter.

CAUTION

If you're asking to be interviewed soon after arrival at the USCIS office, alert a USCIS officer in person. Most people, upon arriving for their interview, are told to put their interview notice in a basket. This would result in your being interviewed in the same order as everyone else, usually after a long wait. Tell the USCIS officer in charge of the intake desk you're asking for a "special accommodation interview." Give the officer your interview notice, along with copies of your request letter and the explanatory letter from your doctor or your Form N-648 (if you filed one—this is the form requesting waivers of the exam requirements, discussed in Section C2, below). Don't leave this desk until you're sure the officer understands your request.

House Calls: When to Ask

It is unusual for USCIS to visit someone at their home or hospital. The agency—already backed up with applications—is afraid that if one person receives a home visit, everyone who is in less than great shape will want one too.

Nevertheless, if you really can't leave your home or your hospital bed, USCIS can arrange to come to you for every element of the citizenship application process. It has the power to send a fingerprinting specialist to take your fingerprints, and to send a USCIS officer to conduct your interview and to swear you in for citizenship. (The interview and the swearing-in can sometimes be done by the same officer on the same day.)

Unfortunately, in some districts, USCIS is not very responsive—for example, consider the case of the 87-year-old bedridden resident of a nursing home who waited two years for an interview and eventually had to file a lawsuit to get action on her request.

To request home services, follow the procedures described in this chapter. After you make your request, USCIS may take the unusual step of calling you or your family on the phone and asking for more details about your illness and your needs.

If USCIS seems inattentive to your requests—for example, if you receive a normal fingerprint appointment notice—write a letter reminding the agency of the situation and repeating your request. Some USCIS regions have a special staff person dedicated to helping people with disabilities. You may need to ask a friend or relative to go to the local USCIS office and ask who that person is. When making the inquiry, have your friend or relative bring a complete copy of your citizenship application and your receipt notice. Local nonprofits serving immigrants and refugees may also provide you with this information.

If USCIS refuses to make the accommodations that you requested, talk to a lawyer, a nonprofit organization serving immigrants and refugees, or a disability advocate. Hopefully, a third party will be able to help resolve any USCIS misunderstandings.

C. Obtaining a Disability-Based Waiver of the Exam Requirements

Many medical conditions make it difficult to learn English or the necessary U.S. history and government information. Besides permanent conditions—for example, developmental disability, severe learning disability, deafness, and blindness—a severe illness can bring on long-term pain and decreased functioning that interfere with your ability to learn. In addition, prescription medications may impair your concentration and memory. Some conditions may confine you to home, making it impossible to attend classes and prepare for the exams.

Psychological conditions can have as serious an impact as physical ones. In particular, it's not uncommon for refugees to have post-traumatic stress disorder (PTSD) and to experience problems with concentration and memory as a result.

If you have such a disability, and a "reasonable accommodation" won't help you pass your citizenship exams, you can request a waiver of the English requirement, the U.S. history and government requirement, or both. You cannot request the exam waiver(s) by yourself; your doctor must prepare a detailed form that explains your situation to USCIS.

Not every medical problem qualifies you for a waiver, however. Old age or illiteracy, for example, won't be enough by themselves to get you a disability waiver. And USCIS reportedly rejects about half of the waiver requests it receives. That's why it's important for you to review this chapter carefully and work closely with your doctor to prepare your waiver request convincingly.

CAUTION
The disability waiver excuses you from the citizenship exams, but not from other U.S. citizenship requirements discussed in Chapter 2. For example, you will still need to fulfill continuous residence, physical presence, green card, and moral character requirements.

You will not find out whether USCIS will grant your disability waiver until your interview. (It's rare for the agency to even look at your file until that date). However, the N-648 is supposed to be the first thing the USCIS officer looks at during the interview. If the officer finds that the N-648 is insufficient to grant you a disability waiver, the officer is supposed to tell you this, and give you a choice of either proceeding with the interview or rescheduling to a later date. The officer may also prepare a written statement clarifying the issue and perhaps requesting that your doctor provide additional information.

Note that the USCIS officer is not supposed to act like a doctor and rethink your medical diagnosis, but merely review what the doctor said and decide whether it makes a convincing case for granting you a waiver. In other words, the USCIS officer is not supposed to say, "You look fine to me," or "PTSD doesn't sound like a big deal, you should have just studied harder," and then proceed with the normal interview.

Some applicants have experienced a situation where the officer doesn't directly say yes or no to the N-648, but simply launches into asking the applicant U.S. history and government questions despite your waiver request.

They're probably not doing this to make your life difficult—they're just hoping that they can grant you citizenship without having to make a decision on the waiver, having noticed some problems with your N-648. Perhaps the officer also has observed that you speak a reasonable amount of English. If the officer can get you to answer six questions correctly (and they'll always choose the easiest questions), everyone will win. You'll be approved for citizenship, and the officer won't have to deal with the waiver application. If this process causes you too much stress, however, you can protest and ask the officer to follow normal procedures.

1. Qualifying Disabilities

To qualify for a disability waiver, your condition must, at a minimum, be "medically determinable." That means that your doctor must have diagnosed it using medically accepted clinical and laboratory techniques. The tests must show anatomical, physiological, or psychological abnormalities. If it's a mental disability, then USCIS will want your doctor to provide what's known as a "DSM" diagnostic code (which comes from a professional manual of mental disorders). Also, your condition must not be temporary—in fact, it must be expected to last for at least 12 months. And, it must not be the result of illegal drug use.

> **CAUTION**
> **If your doctor believes your condition comes from illegal drug use, don't ask for an exam waiver.** Alerting USCIS to your drug use can result in your being denied citizenship and being placed in removal (deportation) proceedings.

Medical conditions such as deafness, blindness, developmental disabilities, severe illness or injury (physical or psychological), memory, and concentration problems, might all qualify a person for a waiver of the English or U.S. history and government exams. A combination of such medical conditions might also qualify you for the waiver, even if each one taken alone wouldn't be severe enough to require a waiver.

Other conditions might also qualify—for example, learning disability, depression and hypertension, though these can be tougher. You'll have to prove that the condition truly impairs your functioning to the point where you can't learn the material on the tests.

USCIS does not grant the disability waiver automatically for any particular illnesses and the agency does not maintain a list of medical conditions recognized as worthy of waivers. USCIS knows that every person's medical history and life circumstances are unique. Factors such as age, the severity of the medical condition, its combination with other conditions or illnesses, and the type of medication prescribed can make a huge difference in a person's ability to study or learn.

Fraud-Based USCIS Denials of Disability Waivers

USCIS keeps watch for any patterns of fraud or misrepresentation in the submission of Form N-648. Some issues that it has spotted and denied cases on the basis of include:

- In cases of applicants with depression or post-traumatic stress disorder (PTSD), USCIS wanted more explanation of the nexus between the illness and the applicant's inability to learn or to demonstrate the necessary knowledge to qualify for citizenship.
- In the past, when the applicant applied for a green card, he submitted an I-693 medical exam that didn't mention the claimed disability.
- The applicant was able to pass a drivers' license test during the same time period that the N-648 said that she was disabled.
- The applicant has been able to manage his financial matters.

If any of the above situations might describe you, talk it over with your doctor. Your doctor is the most important voice in explaining why you're truly disabled. You may also want an attorney's help—the attorney can separately discuss these issues with the doctor.

USCIS is also well aware that modern training techniques can help some people overcome certain disabilities—for example, a blind or deaf person might be taught English and eventually be able to study for the U.S. history and government exam.

For these reasons, USCIS relies heavily on your doctor to tell it what you can and can't do. And that's why you will need to work closely with your doctor to make sure your doctor understands your situation and presents it completely and accurately.

CAUTION

USCIS can reject your doctor's recommendation. If your doctor doesn't give a good explanation of why your condition impedes you from learning the necessary material, or didn't personally examine you, or is under investigation for filling these forms out fraudulently, your waiver request will be rejected. We advise you on how to get what you need from your doctor in Section C2, below.

2. Requesting Disability-Based Waivers

To request a disability-based waiver, first check the "yes" box in Part 2, Question 12, of Form N-400. Then schedule an appointment with your medical doctor, osteopath, or clinical psychologist—whichever one is best qualified to diagnose and discuss your disability. (Other medical professionals, such as chiropractors, are not authorized to fill out an N-648.) Explain to the appointment desk that you'll need sufficient time—your appointment will resemble a full physical. Your doctor will be examining you in preparation for filling out Form N-648, Medical Certification for Disability Exceptions.

> **CAUTION**
> **Don't ask your doctor to prepare Form N-648 more than six months before you submit it to USCIS.** Otherwise, you might have to get your doctor to redo the form. Once it's submitted, however, it doesn't expire.

a. Working With Your Doctor

Before you go to your doctor's office, copy or print out Form N-648 and the USCIS instructions to it. On Part I of the form, fill out your name and other identifying information. On the last page, you need to give permission for the doctor to release information, by filling out the "APPLICANT (PATIENT) ATTESTATION/RELEASE OF INFORMATION" box.

If your disability prevents you from writing or signing your own name (for example, because your hands don't work, or because of cognitive difficulties), you can have someone else fill in most of the information for you—except for your signature. For the signature, you have two choices. You can either make a mark such as an "X" in place of your signature, or your legal guardian can sign for you. (After the signature, guardians should put in parentheses "signed by [guardian's name], designated representative.")

Take the form to your medical appointment. Your request on Form N-400 and the doctor's report on Form N-648 are all you'll need to request this waiver.

RESOURCE

Form N-648 is available from USCIS by phone at 800-870-3676. You can also download it from the USCIS website (www.uscis.gov/n-648). There is no separate fee to file this form.

PAPERWORK REMINDER

Include Form N-648 with the application packet that you submit to USCIS. If unable to do that, you can also take it to your interview, but USCIS will probably need to reschedule the interview in that case, and it will take a harder look at your request. Keep a copy of the Form N-648 for your records.

Another thing to bring to your doctor appointment is a copy of the medical exam (on Form I-693) that you submitted with your green card application. If your current disability was not mentioned on that exam (perhaps because it arose later), your doctor will need to explain this on the N-648. Failure to explain this may result in USCIS denying or delaying your application out of suspicion that your disability isn't real, or is less severe than you're claiming.

You should ideally use your own doctor for this exam—USCIS doesn't provide a list of doctors for disability exams. However, your doctor must be a U.S.-licensed physician, osteopath, psychiatrist, or clinical psychologist. Any doctor you normally see—either your primary care (or family) doctor or a specialist (such as an ophthalmologist, audiologist, or neurologist)—can fill out Form N-648, so long as he or she has access to the appropriate medical records and test results.

CAUTION

Don't go to a special doctor just because you hear that she is "easy" about giving out disability waivers. USCIS quickly picks up on patterns of abuse, and if the agency sees many waivers from the same doctor, it will look on your case more suspiciously. For example, USCIS may ask you to see a specialist—at your own expense.

If your doctor hasn't done disability waiver evaluations before, he or she will need your help. So, don't just hand the doctor Form N-648 and say, "Please fill it out."

Most doctors are accustomed to having their instructions followed, so they often believe that they can just write "patient has X condition, is disabled, and merits a waiver of the citizenship exam requirements" and be done with the matter. They're wrong. USCIS will not be convinced by this type of statement and will not grant a disability waiver unless the doctor has stated a *connection* or *nexus* between your illness and your inability to take the exam. Another way of expressing this is that the doctor must state the illness's "cause, connection, and consequences."

The best way to explain all of this is to copy the two-page letter below and hand it to your doctor at your appointment. (Read the letter yourself, too, so as to better understand the process.)

One more thing: Some doctors decide that they'd rather write a letter than fill out Form N-648. Unfortunately, that won't work. They must fill out the form, though they can attach sheets of paper if they need more space.

TIP

What if your doctor says you don't qualify for a disability exception? Don't give up on applying for citizenship. You can still ask that the USCIS officer who interviews you give "due consideration" to factors in your case such as age, efforts to learn the material, and anything else that's relevant. Then, if appropriate, the officer can give you an easier-than-usual civics/history test. If you feel you need such consideration, explain this in your cover letter when you submit your Form N-400.

b. When to Submit Form N-648

Ideally, you should submit Form N-648 with your citizenship application. However, if you picked up this book after submitting your citizenship application to USCIS, but now realize you need a disability waiver, it's not too late. You can ask your doctor to prepare a Form N-648 and submit it at your interview (though USCIS may then postpone your interview to another day and give it a harder look than it otherwise would have).

Letter to Doctor Performing Exam for Disability Waiver

Dear Physician:

Your patient plans to submit an application for U.S. citizenship to U.S. Citizenship and Immigration Services (USCIS). Part of the application process normally involves taking exams covering the English language (in writing and orally) and U.S. history and government (orally). However, your patient feels that his or her physical or psychological condition makes it unduly difficult to prepare for or pass these exams. Your patient will be asking for a waiver of one or both of these exams. In support of this waiver request, the patient asks that you assess his or her disability and fill out government Form N-648.

This letter is to give you an introduction, or perhaps a reminder, of what USCIS needs to see on Form N-648 in order to consider or grant the waiver. In particular, three key things must emerge from your statements on the form—or the waiver will be denied, even if, in your professional opinion, it should have been granted. These three critical things include:

1. a full explanation of your patient's condition(s), physical or mental, including its origin, nature, and severity or DSM code, with a list of the medically acceptable clinical or laboratory diagnostic tests used to reach your diagnosis (no need to include copies of test results now, but USCIS may later request them)

2. an explanation of how this condition(s) affects the patient's ability to study, learn, or remember the exam material (the more detail, the better), and

3. your opinion on whether a waiver of the exam requirements is appropriate.

Please give special attention to the second item on this list, since it's the one that most often causes USCIS to reject a doctor's disability waiver recommendation. USCIS feels that many doctors don't answer the question, "Why should having this condition excuse this person from taking these exams?" The instructions to Form N-648 provide some good examples of doctors' statements that USCIS found either insufficient or sufficient.

The more you can do to tie the patient's condition to an inability to study, learn, or memorize words or concepts, the better. Many doctors have found that it's helpful to report what they've observed during office visits, or have learned about the patient's daily living, such as "Patient is unable to recognize me, and perpetually forgot appointments or got lost on the way until his daughter began driving him." Also, you'll be reducing the chances that USCIS will request follow-up information from you!

Letter to Doctor Performing Exam for Disability Waiver (continued)

A few other points to consider:

- You're dealing with government bureaucrats, not doctors. Please write in plain English, avoiding or explaining technical jargon whenever possible.

- Also avoid using boilerplate-type language from other patients—USCIS may take this as a sign of fraud.

- For mental impairments, you must provide the DSM-IV code.

- Because there are two separate exams, one covering English and one covering U.S. civics, please specify whether the patient is unable to learn one or both of these subjects.

- If you believe the patient's impairment is due to illegal drug use, please stop now and tell the patient you can't fill out this form. Submitting a form with this information could cause your patient to be deported from the United States.

- If you believe the patient's medical condition will not last at least twelve months, please stop now and tell the patient you can't fill out this form. Temporary disabilities will not qualify applicants for the waiver.

- Avoid referring to the patient as illiterate, lacking in formal education, or being of advanced age if you can point to a separate or more fundamental medical reason that he or she can't learn—otherwise USCIS may deny the waiver, believing that illiteracy, age, etc., is the only problem.

- Although old age alone is not sufficient to qualify a person for a disability waiver, diseases caused by old age, such as Alzheimer's, Parkinson's, or senile dementia, are often sufficient.

- You don't need to attach medical records, though USCIS reserves the right to request them later.

- USCIS has been complaining that it can't read doctors' handwriting, and it has been rejecting waiver requests as a result. Please print or type legibly! Return the form directly to the patient, unsealed.

- A final, logistical matter: You may not have enough space on Form N-648. It's fine to include an attachment, but you must still put something in the blanks, such as "Please see attached letter." Your attachment should be on your office's letterhead paper, and signed by you.

Thank you very much for your attention to this letter and for assisting your patient to become a U.S. citizen.

The "six months" rule still applies, however—the doctor's signature on the form can't be more than six months old when you submit it. Since you can't be sure when your interview will be scheduled, timing your doctor's signature can be a bit tricky. You wouldn't want to have your doctor fill out the form now, only to wait eight months for your interview.

Explain the situation to the person making appointments at your doctor's office, and make sure that the doctor can schedule you for an appointment as soon as you receive your interview notice (you'll have about a two-week window). Alternately, find out when USCIS "normally" calls people for interviews in your area and schedule a medical appointment close to that time—recognizing, of course, that the interview could occur earlier or later than the "normal" date.

> **TIP**
>
> **If you've already submitted your N-648, but your condition has since gotten significantly worse, bring an updated N-648 to your interview.** This will, of course, require attending another doctor's appointment, but it will make your waiver case stronger. But don't do this unless there's been a big change. USCIS has expressed irritation at getting multiple N-648's from waiver applicants.

D. Requesting a Waiver of the Oath of Allegiance Requirement

The last step in becoming a U.S. citizen is to attend a ceremony in which you take an oath, swearing allegiance to the United States. Despite their disabilities, many applicants successfully attend the ceremony and take the oath. However, for some, particularly those with severe developmental or cognitive difficulties, understanding or repeating the Oath of Allegiance will be impossible.

Although the former INS refused citizenship to many applicants who couldn't take the oath, a law passed in 2000 fixed the problem by providing a waiver of the oath requirement. The waiver applies to people who are "unable to understand, or to communicate an understanding of [the oath's] meaning because of a physical or developmental disability or mental impairment." (See I.N.A. § 337(a), 8 U.S.C. 1448(a).)

If you are the naturalization applicant, and you are reading and understanding this paragraph, you don't need this waiver. It's also not meant for people who would find it physically very difficult to attend the ceremony—USCIS prefers to find a way to accommodate such people, including visiting them at home if absolutely necessary.

The oath waiver is most appropriate for people who are virtually beyond communication, or who must depend on others to do their thinking for them. Normally, such people have a friend or family member act as their designated representative during the naturalization interview. For example, I once met an applicant who was both severely mentally retarded and deaf, and who had been unable to learn any sort of sign language other than pressing her mother's hand. She is a classic example of someone who would qualify for a waiver under the new law.

Unfortunately, the oath waiver isn't automatic. The applicant (or whoever is preparing the application for him or her) must separately request the waiver. Moreover, USCIS has not created any form with which to make this request. You (presumably, the applicant's representative) should check "No" to Part 12, Question 46, of Form N-400, then write a separate statement explaining the situation. If USCIS needs more information before the interview, it will send you a written request. If the designated representative is the one to fill out Form N-400, he or she must fill out and sign Part 15, as a "Preparer."

1. Drafting a Request Letter

As designated representative, you must draft a written request for the Oath Waiver, and ideally submit it with the N-400 (though you can submit it later if necessary). Your job here is an important one, because you must explain that you are willing to complete the naturalization process for the applicant and state that you know the facts pertinent to the applicant's eligibility for naturalization and can attest that he or she is, in fact, eligible.

2. Obtaining a Written Evaluation From a Medical Professional

In addition, you'll need to obtain a separate written evaluation from the applicant's doctor (medical doctor, osteopath, or clinical psychologist) supporting the Oath Waiver request. The evaluation must be written by the doctor who has had the longest relationship with the applicant, or who is most familiar with his or her medical history. Here's what the doctor should put into the evaluation:

- an explanation of the applicant's condition and disability, in lay terms, which can be easily understood by the applicant's representative and the USCIS officer
- a thorough statement of why and how the applicant's disability makes the applicant unable to understand or communicate an understanding of what the oath means
- an indication of how likely it is that in the near future, the applicant will be able to communicate or show an understanding of the oath's meaning, and
- the doctor's signature and state license number.

At the applicant's naturalization interview, a USCIS officer will decide whether to grant the Oath Waiver. The interviewing officer will not only review the written materials you have submitted, but will also attempt to communicate with the applicant directly. In particular, the officer will want to discover whether the applicant understands that he or she is:

- becoming a U.S. citizen
- giving up allegiance to his or her home country, and
- personally and voluntarily agreeing to this change.

The officer is allowed to try all sorts of things in attempting to communicate with the applicant. For example, the officer may use the applicant's family members as interpreters, asking them to convey the above three concepts in a way the applicant can understand. The officer may also ask the applicant to give "yes" or "no" responses to simplified questions about these concepts. If the only way the applicant can communicate is through physical motions or signals, that's okay; these will be relied on.

If it turns out that the applicant can understand, at some basic level, the idea of becoming a U.S. citizen, the Oath Waiver may be denied—but don't worry, this is good news in its own way. It means that the applicant can go forward to the oath ceremony, and, probably with the help of the applicant's designated representative and other accommodations (such as having the oath language put into simple words, or allowing the applicant to respond nonverbally, such as through nodding or tapping), take the oath to become a U.S. citizen.

If the Oath Waiver is granted, that's also good—the applicant's citizenship can be granted right away. Although applicants who are granted the waiver need not attend the oath ceremony, USCIS will allow them or their designated representatives to participate if they so desire. ●

The Interview

Your appointment notice—when you finally receive it—will tell you where and when to present yourself for your citizenship interview. An example is provided below. After you receive this notice, you have only one major hurdle left to citizenship—a successful interview.

In this chapter, we'll help you prepare for your interview by discussing:

- what to bring, what to wear, and what to do before your interview (see Section A)

- what to expect and how to handle yourself at the interview (see Section B), and

- how to deal with difficult interviews and unpleasant officers (see Section C).

If your interview appointment arrives and you aren't ready—that is, you haven't learned as much English as you thought you would, or you are having trouble remembering the exam questions and answers—we recommend that you attend anyway. For one thing, the interview might be easier than you think. Remember, the USCIS officer is supposed to take into account any factors related to your education or age that would make the interview difficult for you. As we'll discuss in Section C, below, you'll get a second chance if you fail the exam portion of the first interview, so, in that case, consider this first interview as a practice round.

If, however, you are afraid to attend the interview because you now realize you are ineligible for citizenship or are putting your green card at risk by continuing with your application, reschedule your interview. (In your request letter, you'll have to simply say that circumstances beyond your control require you to miss the scheduled interview.) Then consult with a lawyer immediately. If the situation is serious enough, the lawyer may recommend that you withdraw your application to remove it from USCIS's attention.

Sample Interview Notice

Department of Homeland Security U.S. Citizenship and Immigration Services	I-797C, Notice of Action

	NOTICE DATE
Request for Applicant to Appear for Naturalization Initial Interview	August 25, 2016

CASE TYPE			INS A#
N400 Application For Naturalization			A 075 123 456

APPLICATION NUMBER	RECEIVED DATE	PRIORITY DATE	PAGE
WSC*001634567	March 09, 2016		1 of 1

APPLICANT NAME AND MAILING ADDRESS	Please come to:
PATRICK LEUNG CHAN c/o ILONA BRAY 950 PARKER ST BERKELEY CA 94710	USINS SAN FRANCISCO DISTRICT OFFICE 630 SANSOME ST 2ND FLOOR RECEPTION WAITING ROOM A SAN FRANCISCO CA 94111

On (Date): Wednesday, October 12, 2016
At (Time): 10:45 AM

You are hereby notified to appear for an interview on your Application for Naturalization at the date, time, and place indicated above. Waiting room capacity is limited. **Please do not arrive any earlier than 30 minutes before your scheduled appointment time.** The proceeding will take about two hours. If for any reason you cannot keep this appointment, return this letter immediately to the USCIS office address listed below with your explanation and a request for a new appointment; otherwise, no further action will be taken on your application.

If you are applying for citizenship for yourself, you will be tested on your knowledge of the government and history of the United States. You will also be tested on reading, writing, and speaking English, unless on the day you filed your application, you have been living in the United States for a total of at least 20 years as a lawful permanent resident and are over 50 years old, or you have been living in the United States for a total of 15 years as a lawful permanent resident and are over 55 years old, or unless you have a medically determinable disability (you must have filed form N648 Medical Certification for Disability Exception, with your N400 Application for Naturalization).

You MUST BRING the following with you to the interview:
- This letter.
- Your Alien Registration Card (green card).
- Any evidence of Selective Service Registration.
- Your passport and/or any other documents you used in connection with any entries into the United States.
- Those items noted below which are applicable to you:

If applying for NATURALIZATION AS THE SPOUSE of a United States Citizen;
- Your marriage certificate.
- Proof of death or divorce for each prior marriage of yourself or spouse.
- Your spouse's birth or naturalization certificate or certificate of citizenship.

If applying for NATURALIZATION as a member of the United States Armed Forces;
- Your discharge certificate, or form DD 214.

If copies of a document were submitted as evidence with your N400 application, the originals of those documents should be brought to the interview.

PLEASE keep this appointment, even if you do not have all the items indicated above.

If you have any questions or comments regarding this notice or the status of your case, please contact our office at the below address or customer service number. You will be notified separately about any other cases you may have filed.

USCIS Office Address:	**USCIS Customer Service Number:**
US CITIZENSHIP AND IMMIGRATION SERVICES 630 SANSOME ST SAN FRANCISCO CA 94111-	(800) 375-5283 REPRESENTATIVE COPY

Form I-797C (Rev. 01/31/05) N

How to Reschedule an Interview

If it's truly impossible to make the scheduled appointment, ask for a new date. But we recommend that you try your hardest to make the initial appointment. If you reschedule, you could wait a long time for a new date—possibly many months. If you must reschedule, either go to the office where the interview was scheduled and explain the situation, or write the office a letter. You can use the form letter, below, as a guide. (Don't send the letter to the same address that you first sent your application—that's a USCIS Service Center, and once it has transferred your file to the local USCIS office, it has no power over your case.)

In order to qualify for a new appointment, you'll need to show that you are prevented from attending for reasons beyond your control. "I'm not ready" is not an acceptable excuse. (If you're not ready, we recommend that you attend anyway; see the discussion later in this chapter.)

If you fail to appear at your initial interview and take no other action, USCIS will not reschedule your interview—it will simply close your file.

[*Your address and the date*]

U.S. Citizenship and Immigration Services
Citizenship Unit
[*Address from which the interview notice came*]

RE: [*Your full name and A-number*]; Request for Reschedule

Dear Sir/Madam:

I am unable to attend the citizenship interview that you set for [*date*]. The reason is that [*explain your reason*].

Please reschedule me for a later date. I can be reached at the address above, or by telephone at [*your number*].

Thank you for your attention to this matter.

Very truly yours,
[*sign your name*]
[*type your name*]

A. Final Preparation

The key to a successful interview is preparation. Hopefully, you've been studying English and U.S. history during the months leading up to the interview. Now, you'll need to:

- review your application
- assemble the documents you'll bring with you
- decide what else to bring and what to wear, and
- make sure you know where you're going.

1. Review Your Application and Note Any Changes

A surprising amount of your naturalization interview will be spent going over your written application, particularly Form N-400. The USCIS officer uses the simple inquiries on your form such as "Your current legal name" and "What is your current marital status?" to test your English and to confirm that the information you have given is correct.

Before the interview, go over your copy of Form N-400 carefully. Then, simulate the interview at home. Have a friend ask you each one of the questions.

Be on the lookout for any mistakes you accidentally made or changes to your life after you entered the information on the form. The officer at your interview may ask near the beginning, "Are there any changes to your application?" Be prepared to provide corrections—most are not a problem.

If, for example, you have had another child, be prepared with the child's exact name and a copy of the birth certificate. If you've taken a trip outside the United States, memorize or write down the exact dates and other information that the N-400 asks for regarding trips (and, of course, make sure that none of those trips broke the continuity of your U.S. stay; see Chapter 2, Section B2). If you've changed jobs, it would be helpful to have a business card, pay stub, or other document handy to show your new employer's name and address.

> CAUTION
>
> **If you bring written material to your interview, be prepared to share it with the USCIS officer.** An officer may ask to see any personal notes you've brought to avoid suspicion that you've got the answers to the U.S. history and government exam.

Two particular changes to your Form N-400 could have a serious impact on your citizenship chances:

- If you've recently been divorced from the person who sponsored you for a green card, see "If You Divorce" in Chapter 1, Section A.
- If you've recently been arrested or done anything else that would cause you to change your answer on the questions in Part 12 of the Form N-400 to "yes," see an immigration attorney immediately.

If either of the above are true, it may not only affect your eligibility for citizenship, but your right to remain in the United States.

2. What to Bring

Assemble the items on the "N-659, Naturalization Interview Document Check List" that USCIS sent you. (See the sample below.) The USCIS officer may not ask for all of them, but it's better to be over-prepared. Most of this list is "boilerplate"—in other words, USCIS includes it on everyone's letter, even if items on it don't apply to you. Occasionally, however, USCIS will identify something particular to your case that you must bring. (See sample below.)

> CAUTION
>
> **Whatever you do, don't forget to bring the interview notice from USCIS.** Without it, you won't even get past the security desk!

Sample Interview Document Check List

<table>
<tr>
<td>Department of Homeland Security
U.S. Citizenship and Immigration Services</td>
<td align="right">N-659, Naturalization
Interview Document Check List</td>
</tr>
</table>

Notice to Naturalization Applicants

Bring the **original and a photocopy** of the applicable items listed below to your naturalization interview. Any document in a foreign language must be accompanied by an English language translation. The translator must certify that he or she is competent to translate and that the translation is accurate.

You must be on time for your interview. Late arrival may result in the need to reschedule your interview. Rescheduling can cause significant delays in the processing of your application. Bring all the required documents to avoid delays in processing your case. This is a general check list and since each case is unique, you may be required to submit additional documentation.

Document Check List

1. **You must be properly attired and bring:**

   A. Your Permanent Resident Card (previously known as "Alien Registration Card" or "Green Card"); **and a**

   B. A government issued photo identification; **and**

   C. All passports and travel documents (including expired and current) issued to you by any government.

   D. Although not required, it is recommended that you bring two additional passport-style photos (2"x2"). The photos must be in color with full face, frontal view on a white to off-white background. Head height must measure 1" to 1 3/8" from top of hair to bottom of chin, and eye height is between 1 1/8" to 1 3/8" from bottom of photo. For additional specifications, refer to **<http://travel.state.gov/passport/pptphotos/ondex.html>**.

2. **If your current name is different than the name on your Permanent Resident Card, bring:**

   The document that legally changed your name (e.g., marriage license, divorce decree, court document).

3. **If you are applying for naturalization on the basis of marriage to a U.S. citizen, bring:**

   A. Proof that your spouse has been a U.S. citizen for at least the past three years (birth certificate, naturalization certificate, certificate of citizenship, your spouse's valid U.S. passport, or Form FS-240, Report of Birth Abroad of a Citizen of the United States of America); **and**

   B. Your current marriage certificate registered by a civil authority; **and**

   C. Proof of the termination of all previous marriages for **both** you and your spouse (divorce decree, death certificate, etc., registered by a civil authority); **and**

   D. An original Internal Revenue Service (IRS) Form 1722 listing tax information for the past three years (call IRS toll-free at **1-800-829-1040**), or copies of the income tax forms you filed for the past three years; **and**

   E. Proof of marital union as well as proof of residence; **and**

   D. Certified copies of birth certificates of all your children born in the United States.

4. **If you have ever been in the U.S. military, or are applying based on military service (see sections 328 and 329 of the INA), and have not previously submitted the two forms listed below with your Form N-400, bring:**

   A. An **original** Form N-426, Request for Certification of Military or Naval Service; **and**

   B. An **original** Form G-325B, Biographic Information.

5. **If you have taken a trip outside the United States that lasted for six months or more since becoming a Permanent Resident, bring:**

   A. Evidence showing that you did not abandon your residence or terminate your employment in the United States nor abandon your U.S. abode; **and**

(Continued on Next Page)   Form N-659 (Rev. 01/22/07)N

Sample Interview Document Check List (cont'd)

Document Check List *(Continued)*

    B. An **original** IRS 1722 letter (call IRS toll-free at **1-800-829-1040**), listing tax information for the past five years (or for the past three years) if you are applying on the basis of marriage to a U.S. citizen.

6. **If you have taken a dependent spouse or children and have been ordered to provide financial support, bring:**

    A. Copies of the court or government order to provide financial support; **and**

    B. Evidence that you have complied with the court or government order (cancelled checks, money order receipts, a court or agency printout of child support payments, or evidence of wage garnishments).

7. **If you have ever been arrested or detained by any law enforcement officer for any reason and *no charges were filed*, bring:**

    An official, certified statement from the arresting agency or applicable court indicating that no charges were filed.

8. **If you have ever been arrested or detained by any law enforcement officer for any reason and *charges were filed*, bring:**

    An **original** or certified copy of the arrest record(s) and the complete court disposition for each incident (dismissal order, conviction record, or acquittal order).

9. **If you have been convicted or placed in an alternative sentencing program or rehabilitative program, bring:**

    A. The sentencing record for each incident; **and**

    B. Evidence that you completed your sentence, such as probation record, parole record, or evidence that you completed an alternative program or rehabilitative program. **Copies must be certified copies from the issuing agency.**

10. **If you have ever had any arrest or conviction vacated, set aside, sealed, expunged, or otherwise removed from your records, bring:**

    An **original** or certified copy of the court order vacating, setting aside, sealing, expunging, or otherwise removing the arrest or conviction.

    NOTE: Unless a traffic incident was alcohol or drug related or serious personal injury to another person occurred, you do not need to submit documentation for traffic fines and incidents that did not involve an actual arrest if the only penalty was a fine of less than $500 and/or points on your driver's license.

11. **If you have any Federal, State, or local taxes that are overdue, bring:**

    A. A signed agreement from the IRS, State, or local tax office showing that you have filed a tax return and have arranged to pay the taxes you owe; **and**

    B. Documentation from the IRS, State, or local tax office showing the current status of your repayment program.

12. **If you are applying for a disability exception to the testing requirement and have not submitted Form N-648, bring:**

    An **original** Form N-648, Medical Certification for Disability Exceptions, completed by a licensed medical doctor, licensed clinical psychologist, or licensed doctor of osteopathy.

13. **If registered with the Selective Service, bring proof of such. If you did not register with the Selective Service and you are (1) male, (2) over 26 years old, (3) were born on or after January 1, 1960, and (4) were a Permanent Resident between the ages of 18 and 26 when you failed to register, explain your failure to register and bring:**

    A "Status Information Letter" from the Selective Service. (Call the Selective Service at **1-847-688-6888** for more information.)

14. **If you are requesting expeditious naturalization under section 319(b) of the INA through military service, bring:**

    The U.S. citizen's travel orders that include the name of the alien spouse and establish that the overseas assignment will end no less than 12 months beyond the date of the naturalization interview.

Sample Supplement to Interview Check List

U.S. Department of Homeland Security
P.O. Box 648006
Lees Summit, MO 64064

**U.S. Citizenship
and Immigration
Services**

Date: 3/17/2015

BRAY, ILONA
ILONA BRAY, ATTORNEY AT LAW
950 PARKER ST.
BERKELEY, CA 94710

File:

NBC*001454321

In RE: OSMAN, ARMAGAN

Case File Review Notice / Interview Document Check List

After a complete review of your file and Application for Naturalization (Form N-400), this office has found additional documentation may be needed. **Unless previously submitted,** please bring the below requested documents to your naturalization interview. Please **do not** mail in these requested items.

Along with this **original** notice, please bring the applicable items listed below to your naturalization interview. All documents must be clear and legible. If you have a document in any language other than English, it must be provided with a full English translation. The translator must certify that the translation is complete and accurate, and that he or she is competent to translate. You must provide both the foreign language document and the English translation.

You should be properly attired and be on time for your interview. Late arrival may result in the need to reschedule your interview. Please note that rescheduling can cause significant delays in the processing of your application. Bring all required documents to avoid delays in processing your case. **Please do not mail in your required documents**. This is a general checklist and since each case is unique, you may be required to produce additional documentation at the time of your interview. If your situation requires further details, you will be notified.

[X]   If you are a male who lived in the United States at any time between your 18th and 26th birthdays in any status except as a lawful nonimmigrant and are still under 26 years of age, you must register before you apply for naturalization and provide your Selective Service Number and date registered. If already registered with the Selective Service, bring proof of such showing Selective Service Number and date registered.

If you did not register with the Selective Service and you are (1) male, (2) over 26 years old, (3) were born on or after January 1, 1960, and (4) were a Permanent Resident between the ages of 18 and 26 when you failed to register, explain your failure to register and bring a "Status Information Letter" from the Selective Service. For more information, call the Selective Service toll-free at 1-847-688-6888. The Selective Service internet site can be reached at www.sss.gov.

Questions may be directed to the USCIS National Customer Service Center at 1-800-375-5283. Thank You.

REMINDER: bring this **original** notice with your documents.

NBC November 15, 2006 Revision 8   **Page 1 of 1**

If you qualify for and have requested a waiver of the English language requirements, you'll need an interpreter. Ask the USCIS office whether you can bring your own interpreter (allowed in some, but not all, districts) or whether USCIS will hire an interpreter. (See 8 C.F.R. § 312.4.) USCIS often uses telephone interpreters for citizenship interviews. The interpreters will be on speakerphone and may be difficult to hear, so if you have a choice, you might want to bring an interpreter.

You don't necessarily have to hire a professional—a friend or relative who is older than 18 and sufficiently fluent in both English and your native language to translate word for word will do. Also, make sure the person has a flexible enough schedule to stay for many hours, if need be. (Long waits are common.) Your interpreter must also be in the U.S. lawfully and have a photo identity card to prove it.

CAUTION

Don't hold side conversations with your interpreter. The USCIS officer may conclude that your interpreter is supplying answers or coaching you, and thus stop the interview or deny your case.

But, if USCIS decides that your interpreter isn't good enough for the job or isn't a "disinterested party," it can refuse to use that person and reschedule your interview. (For example, you wouldn't want to bring a close family member who is a obviously protective of you and argues with the officer over whether to grant you citizenship.)

CAUTION

Unless you are disabled or need an interpreter and have arranged for this in advance, USCIS will not allow friends or family members at your interview. Any friends or family who accompany you will be required to sit in the waiting room—and USCIS discourages this as well. See Chapter 7 regarding accommodations for the disabled.

3. What to Wear—And What to Leave at Home

It's improper for the USCIS officer's decision about citizenship to be affected by your appearance, but it's also hard to believe that it's not a factor—at least at some level. Although we don't want to limit your ability to express your personal style, we recommend that you dress neatly, professionally, and conservatively—in short, look the way you might if going for an important job interview.

In any case, avoid wearing T-shirts or jewelry that might make the officer wonder about your lifestyle or morals. We've known people who attended their USCIS interview wearing a T-shirt that said "S*** happens!" or a necklace with a gold marijuana leaf hanging from it. Those style decisions are likely to distract the interviewer and lead to unwanted personal questions.

> CAUTION
> **Remember the metal detector.** When you go into a federal building, you'll be subject to a security search. Don't carry anything that resembles a weapon, or you'll have to check it with the security guard. (Of course, if it *is* a weapon, you'll be arrested.) Don't suffer the same result as the author of this book, who lost her favorite Swiss Army knife when the door guards checked it in and then accidentally gave it to another visitor.

4. Know Where You're Going

Why is it that buses run late and parking spots are hardest to find on days when you're desperate to get somewhere? Whatever the reason, make sure you know how to get to the USCIS office listed on the letter, and leave plenty of extra time to get there. It's better to spend some extra time in the waiting room than to arrive at the last minute in a panic, or worse, to miss your interview.

Also, keep in mind that the address on your appointment letter may not be the central USCIS office that you're accustomed to visiting. In some regions, USCIS has arranged for extra offices to handle citizenship interviews—for example, in the San Francisco Bay Area, some people are sent to the USCIS's San Francisco District office, while many others are sent to an office in Oakland that handles only citizenship interviews.

B. The Interview

When you get to the USCIS office, the usual procedure is for you (after getting through security) to place your interview notice in a box and wait for your name to be called. You may have to wait a very long time, since USCIS often schedules many people for the same block of time.

When it's your turn, a USCIS officer will call you in to the inner office. In this section, we discuss what the officer will say and do (Section B1) and the best ways for you to respond (Section B2).

> **TIP**
>
> **If you're disabled and have asked for an immediate interview, don't put your notice in the box.** Find a USCIS officer and hand him your appointment notice personally, and explain that you have a disability and are requesting an immediate interview.

1. A Sample Interview

A single USCIS officer will most likely bring you to his or her desk to interview you. (The exception, however, would be if your local USCIS office is among those that split the interview up, by having one officer test you on civics as well as English, and then another one do the actual interview. In such cases, if your English is too poor to make it through the first half, they'll probably send you home without doing an interview on that day, but reschedule you to come back on another day.)

Don't sit down when you get to the desk—the officer will probably want you to remain standing until he or she tells you it's time to sit down. (As we explained in Chapter 5, your ability to follow instructions is important in proving that you speak English.)

If the officer does not tell you his or her name, ask for it, and write it down or do your best to remember it (USCIS officers don't give out business cards). If anything goes wrong and you later need to consult with a lawyer, it will help if you can then tell your lawyer the name of the officer. Experienced immigration lawyers often know the personalities of the various USCIS officers, and that information may assist in preparing your case.

First, the interviewing officer will ask you to stand up, raise your right hand, and swear to tell the truth. After that, you'll sit down and the officer will proceed with three tasks:

- verifying the information on your Form N-400
- determining whether you speak, read, and write English, and
- testing you on U.S. history and government.

The tasks may flow together—that is, the officer won't necessarily tell you "this is step one," etc. The interview usually takes about 20 minutes in total.

To see how this works, let's look at the script of a typical interview—one in which the applicant did a good job of handling herself. Because the applicant speaks English well and has a college education, the USCIS officer gave her more difficult questions than would be given to someone with less ability.

USCIS: Right this way, please. Remain standing; I'll need to put you under oath. Now raise your right hand. Do you swear or affirm that during today's interview you'll tell me the truth, the whole truth, and nothing but the truth?
Applicant: Yes. [Or, "I do."]

USCIS: You may sit down. May I see your green card, passports, and photo identification?
Applicant: Yes, here they are.

USCIS: Okay, what is your full name?
Applicant: My name is Xena Nassopoulous.

USCIS: Have you used any other names??
Applicant: No.

USCIS: What is your address?
Applicant: I live at 459 Gooseberry Drive, in Jay, Vermont.

USCIS: When and where were you born?
Applicant: I was born in Greece on July 12, 1972.

USCIS: You say on your application that you've taken only two trips outside the United States since you became a permanent resident in 1994. Is that true?
Applicant: Yes, I just took two trips home to Greece.

USCIS: Are you sure? What about short trips to Mexico or Canada?
Applicant: We live near the Canadian border, so we sometimes go visit there for a day. But we've never spent a night there.

USCIS: What is your husband's name?
Applicant: His name is Ernest Birnbaum.

USCIS: Are there any changes to the rest of the personal information on your application?
Applicant: Yes, my husband and I had a daughter last year, named Artemis. Here is a copy of her birth certificate.
USCIS: Thank you. [*Officer writes the information from the birth certificate onto the application.*]

USCIS: Have you ever failed to file your federal income taxes?
Applicant: I'm sorry, could you say that in another way? I didn't quite understand it.

USCIS: Have you ever failed to send the IRS an annual tax form and any payments owing?
Applicant: No, that is, I've paid taxes every year since I've been here.

USCIS: Did you bring copies of your tax returns today?
Applicant: Yes, here they are.

USCIS: Your application form says that you are a member of Amnesty International. Are you involved in any other groups or organizations?
Applicant: Not formally. I attend religious services with my husband sometimes, and I contribute to some charities, but I'm not really a member of anything else.

USCIS: Have you ever been a member of the Communist Party?
Applicant: No.
USCIS: [*Reviews the rest of the questions on Part 12 of the N-400; Xena answers "no" to all of them. The USCIS officer opens the results of her fingerprint check with the FBI and confirms that Xena has no record of criminal or USCIS violations.*]

USCIS: Now I'll ask you a few questions about U.S. history and government. Why does the flag have 13 stripes?
Applicant: Because there were thirteen original colonies. [*Correct.*]

USCIS: Name three of the thirteen original states.
Applicant: Connecticut, New Hampshire, and … and … oh dear, I'm blanking on the rest. [*Incorrect.*]

USCIS: Who was President during World War I?
Applicant: Woodrow Wilson. [*Correct.*]

USCIS: What are the two parts of the Congress?
Applicant: The Senate and House of Representatives. [*Correct.*]

USCIS: What is the supreme law of the land?
Applicant: The Constitution. [*Correct.*]

USCIS: Name one problem that led to the Civil War.
Applicant: Slavery. [*Correct.*]

USCIS: Who is the Governor of our state, Vermont?
Applicant: Peter Shumlin. [*Correct.*]

USCIS: Okay, you've answered six correctly, that's enough. Now take this pencil and write the sentence, "People vote for President in November."

[*Xena writes the sentence correctly.*]

USCIS: Please read this passage of text.
[*Xena reads the passage correctly.*]

USCIS: Do you believe in the U.S. Constitution?
Applicant: Uh, huh.

USCIS: Please state "Yes" or "No" clearly.
Applicant: I meant, yes.

USCIS: Are you willing to take the Oath of Allegiance?
Applicant: Yes.

USCIS: If the law requires it, will you fight and defend the United States, or assist those who do?
Applicant: Yes.

USCIS: That's all for today, I'm going to approve your application. Please sign here, and sign your photographs here, and take this sheet explaining when you'll be called for the swearing-in ceremony.
Applicant: Thank you!

USCIS: Congratulations, and good-bye.

RESOURCE
Want to watch a sample citizenship interview? USCIS has created one, which you can view at its website, at www.uscis.gov/us-citizenship. Click "Naturalization Test" and then look for "The USCIS Naturalization Interview and Test Video."

2. Interview Tips

For you, the interview may be one of the most important events of your life. But keep in mind that, to the USCIS officer who is at work, you're just one person in a long day full of people. That doesn't mean the officer doesn't care about you—but in order to maintain efficiency, the officer will appreciate it if you're prepared, organized, and professional. Wait for the officer's questions and answer them as briefly as you can while still using full sentences.

> **💡 TIP**
>
> **If you don't understand a question, ask the officer to rephrase it.** Rather than guessing at what the officer is saying—which could get you into trouble—simply say, "I'm sorry, could you repeat that using different words?" In fact, USCIS has instructed officers "to repeat and rephrase questions until the officer is satisfied that the applicant either fully understands the question or does not understand English."

a. Avoid Putting on an Act

Some immigrants cynically conclude that they can win the officer's favor through tactics like personal compliments or pro-American statements. Telling the officer, "My, that's a lovely outfit you're wearing today" is unnecessary, and could seem like an effort at distraction.

One applicant showed up for his USCIS interview wearing a tie covered with U.S. flags, and peppered the interview with comments about America's greatness. (The interviewing officer obviously felt that the applicant was pushing this too far.)

USCIS certainly wants you to act courteously and be supportive of the United States, but self-serving speeches are a waste of the officer's time and an insult to the officer's intelligence.

b. Honesty Is the Best Policy

One of the worst things you can do at your interview is to lie. If you're caught—and USCIS has a surprising number of ways at catching people in lies—the effect on your application may be devastating—far worse than if you had told the truth. Even if you're caught years later, your citizenship can be taken away at that time.

On the other hand, don't view the USCIS office as a confession booth. Only answer what you are asked, and avoid volunteering information unless it is needed to better understand the information provided on the application.

c. Present Yourself Confidently

In some cultures, it is impolite to look someone in the eyes when you speak. That's not the case in the United States, where looking away or at the floor is often perceived as a sign of deception.

At your interview, look straight at the officer's eyes when the two of you speak. (If you find this difficult, try looking at the officer's forehead or nose.) Speak confidently and, if possible, try to relax. Think positive! The USCIS officers are usually pleased to meet someone like yourself who has prepared the paperwork carefully and studied hard.

C. If the Interview Goes Badly

Although a good number of USCIS officers are helpful and interested in seeing you become a citizen, you may run into one whose manner is rude or hostile. First, remember that it's probably not personal. Some USCIS officers become jaded and cynical after years of investigating fraudulent citizenship claims.

Second, try not to get angry. Remain respectful and answer honestly if you don't know or remember something. You might encounter an officer who makes irrelevant or unfounded accusations, acts in a discriminatory manner based on your race or gender, becomes uncontrollably angry, or persists with a line of questions or statements that is completely inappropriate.

Another problem is when the USCIS officer does something that deviates from normal procedures. For example, if you realize that one of the U.S. government questions the officer asked you is not from the list of 100 sample questions—for example, the officer asked you the name of a U.S. President's wife—that's a violation of procedure.

If any of these things happens, politely ask to see a supervisor before continuing with the interview. Explain the situation to the supervisor and ask him or her to intervene or reschedule you with a different officer.

If you deal with an irate officer who demands information or documents that you don't have on hand, ask to either reschedule the interview or to be allowed to submit supplemental documents by mail.

The latter approach may avoid having an angry officer make a final decision on the spot. (Hopefully, by the time the officer receives your follow-up materials, he or she will have cooled down.)

If you believe that a USCIS officer behaved improperly, write down as many details as you can remember of the interview, while it's fresh in your mind. Then consider consulting an attorney about your experience, to learn what you can do to improve USCIS's reaction to your application.

Even if you don't speak to or hire a lawyer, you can write a letter to the USCIS office. USCIS supervisors assume that officers act appropriately unless you tell them otherwise, so alert the supervisor to any inappropriate behavior and ask that the supervisor consider the officer's conduct when making a final review of your case.

> **EXAMPLE:** At Johan's interview, the USCIS officer barrages him with personal questions, such as why he got divorced, what he did wrong to drive his wife away, why people of his religion always have so many children, and finally, why he isn't paying child support. Although Johan explains that the court did not require him to pay child support and his wife makes a better income than he does, the officer denies his application on moral character grounds. Johan writes a letter asking the supervisor to consider the officer's hostile and discriminatory attitude and overturn the denial.

D. Approval or Denial: What's Next?

If all goes well at your interview, the officer will tell you that you've been approved and may hand you a piece of paper with information about your upcoming oath or swearing-in ceremony.

In some areas, you have a choice between going to a court-run or a USCIS-run ceremony, and the officer will show you the schedule and ask you to choose a date. (Remember to choose a court ceremony if you're requesting that your name be changed.)

Most USCIS offices notify you about the swearing-in ceremony by mail. In a few USCIS offices, oath ceremonies are held on the same day as the interview. In any case, you're probably no more than one or two months away from citizenship.

> TIP
>
> **Know you'll be traveling or have other unbreakable conflicts in the coming weeks?** If so, mention that fact to the officer (if you weren't already given a choice of dates.) That will help make sure that the officer schedules you for an oath ceremony date when you'll be available, and avoids the hassles of trying to reschedule.

If the interview goes badly, the officer may deny your citizenship application on the spot. Again, you should receive a piece of paper explaining the reasons—see the sample below. If the basis for denial was that you failed the English or U.S. history and government exam, you'll automatically get a second-chance interview.

If there is some other problem regarding your case, the officer may give you a chance to provide follow-up documents rather than deny your citizenship. In some cases, the officer may need to think about your case before making a decision.

If the officer doesn't make a decision on your case at your interview, you are supposed to receive a decision within 120 days of your interview. (See I.N.A. § 366(b), 8 U.S.C. § 1447(b).) However, as with all USCIS responses, you may have to wait longer than expected. If the officer requested more documents, the time period for the decision may get dragged further into the future.

Security checks may also add to the wait time. USCIS may run your name and fingerprints through a security check several times once you file your application, again before your interview, and often a third time before your swearing-in ceremony.

If you've waited well past 120 days and have an urgent need for citizenship, you may want to consult with an attorney, who can file an action in federal court. The court can either decide your case on its own or send it back to USCIS for an immediate decision.

If you aren't scheduled for a follow-up interview, you will get your approval or denial by mail. If you are approved, see Chapter 11 for details on the swearing-in ceremony and your new rights as a citizen. If you are denied citizenship, see Chapter 9 for information on how to appeal the decision.

Sample Interview Decision

U.S. Department of Homeland Security
San Francisco, CA 94111

**U.S. Citizenship
and Immigration
Services**

A12345678

On **December 11, 2015** you were interviewed by CIS Officer Nelson

☑ You passed the tests of English and U.S. history and government.

☐ You passed the test of U.S. history and government and the English language requirement was waived.

☐ The Service has accepted your request for a Disability Exception. You are exempted from the requirement to demonstrate English language ability and/or knowledge of U.S. history and government.

☐ You will be given another opportunity to be tested on your ability to _____ speak / _____ read / _____ / write English.

☐ You will be given another opportunity to be tested on your knowledge of U.S. history and government.

☑ Please follow the instructions on the Form N-14.

☑ CIS will send you a written decision about your application.

☐ You did not pass the second and final test of your _____ English ability / _____ knowledge of U.S. history and government. You will not be rescheduled for another interview for this N-400. CIS will send you a written decision about your application.

☐ Your application is pending completion of background checks. You will be notified when the checks are completed.

A) _____ **Congratulations! Your application has been recommended for approval.**
At this time, it appears that you have established your eligibility for naturalization. If final approval is granted, you will be notified when and where to report for the Oath Ceremony.

B) ___✗___ **A decision cannot yet be made about your application.**

It is very important that you:

✓ Notify CIS if you change your address.

✓ Come to any scheduled interview.

✓ Submit all requested documents.

✓ Send any questions about this application in writing to the named above. Include your full name, A-number, and a copy of this paper.

✓ Go to any oath ceremony that you are scheduled to attend.

✓ Notify CIS as soon as possible in writing if you cannot come to any scheduled interview or oath ceremony. Include a copy of this paper and a copy of the scheduling notice.

www.dhs.gov

Denials, Appeals, and Repeat Interviews

f USCIS does not grant your U.S. citizenship at your first interview, don't despair. It happens to many people—and many of them are later approved. (You may improve your ability to analyze and deal with the problem by hiring an attorney, however.)

If USCIS is giving you some sort of a last chance, you can still turn things around. For example:

- If the officer delayed making a decision until you provide additional documents, complying with the officer's request will give you a good shot at gaining approval. In Section B, we'll give you advice on preparing and submitting these documents.

- If you failed the English or U.S. history and government exam, you'll get one chance at a repeat interview. (See Section A.)

If you are issued a final denial, USCIS will tell you its reason, either during your citizenship interview or in a subsequent letter. In Section C, we'll help you determine the appropriate next step, based on USCIS's reasoning and other factors. That step may be to appeal, as described in Sections D and E; or it may be to submit a new application for citizenship, as described in Section F.

A. Retaking the Exams

If you failed your first interview because you lacked sufficient English language skills, couldn't answer enough U.S. history and government questions, or both, it's time for intensive study. USCIS automatically gives you a second chance at the exam(s)—but you won't have much time to prepare. You could be scheduled for your second interview anytime between 60 to 90 days after your first one. (See 8 C.F.R. § 312.5(a).)

So, if you didn't attend a preparatory course, you should quickly enroll in one—see Chapter 5, Section C, for advice on finding a good one.

At your second interview, you will probably meet with a different officer, who will concentrate on the exam and not repeat the rest of the interview. Your meeting shouldn't last more than a few minutes.

If you don't pass on the second try, that's it—your citizenship application will be denied. But don't sit around moping. File an appeal or get a new citizenship application into the mail while the process is still fresh in your mind. (See Sections C and F, below, to help you choose between these procedural options.)

B. Providing More Documents

The USCIS interviewer may need additional documentation before making a decision about your application. In that case, the officer will give you a written request describing the documents needed—for example, the officer might ask for a copy of your recent tax transcript or returns, more proof or explanation of disability from your doctor, or proof of your dates of travel outside the United States. See the sample form below, requesting the applicant to return for a new interview and bring new documents, from the San Francisco USCIS office.

Normally, you'll send these documents by mail. However, if the USCIS officer wants an opportunity to discuss the documents with you, you will be asked to bring them to another interview. In general, however, USCIS prefers not to interview applicants a second time.

Being asked for more documents can be seen as a good sign—it means that the officer believes there are good reasons to pursue your case further. Now you must do your best to swing things in your favor.

1. To Provide or Not to Provide?

Don't automatically provide requested documents until you have closely reviewed the request and decided that the situation doesn't call for an attorney's help. If you are convinced that the document will help your quest for citizenship, go ahead and send it in. For example, if the document is one that you knew you should have brought to your interview, but forgot—such as a letter from your church exempting you from the Oath of Allegiance—that's easy, and you can take care of it on your own.

Sample Re-Interview Notice

Request for Applicant to Appear for Naturalization Re-Interview			NOTICE DATE February 27, 2014
CASE TYPE N400 Application For Naturalization			USCIS A# A 022 456 789
APPLICATION NUMBER WSC*003331233	RECEIVED DATE November 12, 2014	PRIORITY DATE November 12, 2014	PAGE 1 of 1

APPLICANT NAME AND MAILING ADDRESS

ROBERTO ORTIZ
c/o ILONA BRAY
950 PARKER ST.
BERKELEY, CA 94710

Please come to:
USCIS SAN FRANCISCO FIELD OFFICE
630 SANSOME ST
2ND FLOOR RECEPTION
CITIZENSHIP
SAN FRANCISCO CA 94111

Ildadlllaadladllallaldaldd

On (Date):   Tuesday, April 28, 2017
At (Time):   09:40 AM

You are hereby notified to appear for an interview at the date, time and place indicated above, for the following reason(s):

Re-Examination for Reading, Writing or Speaking English
Re-Examination on Government/History of the United States
Naturalization Re-Interview

Waiting room capacity is limited. Please do not arrive any earlier than 30 minutes before your scheduled appointment time. If for any reason you cannot keep this appointment, return this letter immediately to the USCIS office address listed below with your explanation and a request for a new appointment; otherwise, no further action will be taken on your application.

You MUST BRING the following with you to the interview:
- This letter.
- Your Alien Registration Card (green card).
- Your driver's license or State I.D.
- Your passport and/or any other documents you used in connection with any entries into the United States.

PLEASE keep this appointment, even if you do not have all the items indicated above.

If you have any questions or comments regarding this notice or the status of your case, please contact our office at the below address or customer service number. You will be notified separately about any other cases you may have filed.

USCIS Office Address:
U.S. CITIZENSHIP AND IMMIGRATION SERVICES
630 SANSOME ST
SAN FRANCISCO CA 94111-

USCIS Customer Service Number:
(800) 375-5283

REPRESENTATIVE COPY

Sample Request for More Documents

U.S. Department of Homeland Security
630 Sansome Street, CB
San Francisco, CA 94111

**U.S. Citizenship
and Immigration
Services**

ROBERTO ORTIZ
HAND DELIVERED

File No: A 08567891013

Officer: Quezon

Date: February 27, 2017

cc:

Examination of your application (N400) shows that additional information, documents or forms are needed before your application can be acted upon. Please ***BRING WITH YOU, THE COMPLETED FROM N-648 BY YOUR PHYSICIAN, AT YOUR RE-EXAMINATION.***

Failure to do so may result in the denial of your application.

The standard for the disability exception requires that the doctor establish that the applicant has <u>a physical or mental abnormality that has impaired an individual's functioning *so severely* that the individual is unable to learn the English language and the civics.</u>

Enclosures checked:

- A new N-648 Medical certicification, to be completed by your doctor: Explain in detail and describe how the applicant's disabilities affect her ability to learn. Need connection or a NEXUS between the impairments and her ability to learn and severity. Including diagnoses.
- Any attachment submitted with Form N-648 need to be on a letter head and signed by the doctor.

www.dhs.gov

Similarly, if the document is one that the officer has clearly described, such as your certificate of divorce from your first husband or a police certificate showing that you haven't been arrested, obtaining it should be within your power (unless, of course, no such document exists).

However, you should think twice about your next step if:

- you don't understand the reason for the request
- the request implies that the officer has serious doubts about your eligibility for naturalization or even for a green card, or
- the only documents you can come up with are likely to get you in deeper trouble.

If you can't understand why the officer requested a specific document, you should not furnish the document until your attorney has reviewed the request. You may make a serious error furnishing a document affecting your right to stay in the United States—for example, providing a certificate from your home country saying that you were convicted of child abuse will get you a quick denial and a plane ticket home.

The same is true for requests that cast doubts on your right to citizenship. For example, if you were divorced from the spouse through whom you got your green card, brought documents to prove that the marriage was bona fide, but are now being asked for more such documents, you may have a problem. The USCIS officer may believe that you've committed marriage fraud. Instead of just putting some more documents in the mail and hoping for the best, consult an attorney to get to the root of what's bothering USCIS.

Of course, if you just ignore the officer's request for documents, your citizenship application will be denied automatically. In the worst-case situation, USCIS may refer your case for investigation into your right to continue having a green card.

2. Preparing Documents

The USCIS officer may give you an exact description of the documents he or she wants to see—such as a letter from the IRS saying you owe no taxes—or the officer may leave the exact choice of documents to your imagination. If, for example, the officer requests "documents to prove your good moral character for the last five years," you'll have to decide what documents will serve this purpose. (In Chapter 2, Section D, we describe suitable documents concerning good moral character.)

After you've gathered the necessary documents, put them together in an orderly manner. Each document must be readable and contain your name or other identifying information. If there are any items that belong in a series, such as your paychecks over the last six months, put them in chronological (date) order.

If you don't believe the officer can tell from looking at a document what it is or why it's important, add a Post-It note or a cover letter. For example, if the officer asked for evidence that you returned to the United States before August 2016 and you include photos of yourself at a July 4th barbecue in Cincinnati, make sure the photos are dated and that you are clearly recognizable in them.

The first item in your document packet should be a copy of USCIS's written request for documents. A separate cover letter is not usually necessary, though adding one would be helpful if the documents are not self-explanatory. (A cover letter, if you include it, should go second in the packet.) Then add copies of the documents themselves—remember, send originals only if you don't need them back … ever. Make a copy of everything for your records.

3. Documents by Mail

You'll find the mailing address to which you'll need to send the documents on the USCIS officer's written request. (It will be the same office as where you had your interview, not the office to which you originally submitted your Form N-400 citizenship application.)

Always add the officer's name to the letter—or, if you don't know the name, include your A-number in the letter—so that your letter will be put on the correct officer's desk.

Use a trackable sending method, such as FedEx, or U.S. Priority Mail or certified mail with a return receipt requested. This is especially important at this stage, since delays are common and you may need evidence of the date when you submitted your documents in order to follow up with USCIS. (But beware if the USCIS address is at a post office box, FedEx and similar courier services cannot deliver there.)

4. The Decision

Sometimes the USCIS officer will make a decision within a few weeks of your sending in your documents—other times it could be months. If three or more months pass and you haven't heard from USCIS, see an attorney or write an inquiry letter and send it to the same officer and address to which you sent your documents.

After the USCIS officer decides your case, you will be notified by mail. If the decision is favorable, congratulations—you can move on to Chapter 11, which describes your swearing-in ceremony and your new rights as a citizen. If the decision is negative, see Sections C and F, below, to help you decide whether to appeal or start over and file a new application.

C. Choosing to Appeal or Reapply

If your citizenship application is denied, you will receive a written explanation from USCIS as to why, along with information on how to file an administrative appeal.

You should seek legal assistance if:

- The reason for denial is confusing.
- The reason for denial is difficult for you to overcome on your own.
- USCIS has indicated that it will refer you to immigration court for removal proceedings.

In these instances, the stakes are too high for self-help efforts. Consult an attorney.

If, however, you believe that with a minimum of time and effort you can win your case—for example, you suddenly discover a document that could prove your foreign trip lasted less than a year—then continue reading.

Before filing an appeal, you'll need to consider two things:

- whether you have any basis on which to appeal (see Section C1, below), and
- whether filing an appeal is any better than starting over and reapplying (see Section C2, below).

1. Determining Whether You Have a Basis for Appeal

Before filing an appeal, you need to determine whether you have solid grounds upon which to appeal the decision—that is, you must be able to demonstrate that a mistake was made and that you are eligible for citizenship. Keep in mind that appeals are appropriate *only* when you believe that the USCIS officer who interviewed you made a mistake or acted inappropriately. For example, if the officer confused your belief in "communes" with a belief in "communism," an appeal is a fine way to ask that the error be corrected. However, if your denial resulted from your own actions, reapplying is more appropriate (after correcting the problem).

EXAMPLE 1: During her citizenship interview, Olga told the USCIS officer that, during a period of unemployment, she had regularly eaten dinner at a church soup kitchen. The officer took this as a sign of bad moral character and denied Olga's application. However, since Olga was not at fault in being unemployed, and eating at a soup kitchen is perfectly legal, the officer's decision was wrong. Olga has solid grounds upon which to appeal the denial.

EXAMPLE 2: When preparing his application, Fyodor included the proper dates of travel on his form, but he miscalculated when adding up the time spent abroad. At the interview, the officer determined that Fyodor had actually spent more than six months outside the U.S. and had, therefore, broken the continuity of his U.S. stay. Fyodor was ineligible for citizenship and had no basis on which to appeal. (Chapter 2 explains how to deal with such problems in order to reapply.) If the USCIS officer believed that Fyodor had lied on his application or was deliberately concealing information, Fyodor would definitely need an attorney's help before reapplying.

As noted, you can appeal only if you can demonstrate that the officer was wrong or made a mistake when denying your citizenship application. Therefore, if you didn't study for the U.S. history and government exams before your first two interviews, you shouldn't look at an appeal as your third chance. Similarly, if you aren't eligible for citizenship and didn't realize this at the time you submitted your application, an appeal is not the way to cure the problem.

If you don't have strong grounds for an appeal and you're not sure whether you would prevail, the wisest course is to file a new application for citizenship, as described in Section F, below.

2. Appeal or New Application?

As mentioned above, an appeal is not your only option. You can, if you wish, skip the appeal and reapply by submitting a new N-400 application (see Section F, below).

For many people, the most important factor to consider when making this decision is the length of time each option will take. There's no blanket rule regarding which will take less time—an appeal or a new application—because the answer will differ depending on the USCIS district in which you live. In some USCIS districts, applicants rarely file appeals because USCIS consistently takes longer to act on them than it does to call applicants in for a new interview.

You can find out about USCIS's comparative timing on your own by doing a little legwork. Talk to the staff at local nonprofits serving immigrants and refugees, or visit your local USCIS office and ask in person. If you determine that you'll wait longer for your appeal interview than for a new interview (after reapplying), it's probably better to reapply. This may not be the case, however, if you're one of those people who want a long time to go by before the interview—for example, to get the maximum time to learn English or to make sure that ten years have passed since their involvement in the Communist Party.

Another factor to consider is cost. You'll pay a little less for filing an appeal (currently $650; but free for veterans or U.S. Armed Forces members) than for filing a new citizenship application ($595, plus $85 for fingerprints, totaling $680).

A final factor in deciding whether to appeal or reapply is your relationship with USCIS. If you file a new N-400 application, the dynamics between you and USCIS will change. You're no longer trying to prove that USCIS was wrong, and USCIS is no longer trying to prove you shouldn't be a citizen. By reapplying, you'll start over with a different interviewer and an application specially tailored to deal with the problems that previously sank your application. (You won't, however, be able to hide the previous citizenship application from the new interviewing officer.) For information on reapplying, see Section F, below.

D. How to Appeal

If you choose to go the administrative appeal route, you must act quickly. Your appeal notice is due at USCIS within 30 days of the date your citizenship was denied. (The date you were denied is shown on your written denial notice.)

Some applicants receive this notice in person, on the day they are interviewed, while others receive it by mail from USCIS. If you receive your notice by mail, your appeal notice must be sent within 33 days of the date on the USCIS letter, because USCIS presumes that you received its letter within three days after mailing.

In order to persuade a second (or third) USCIS officer to view your case positively, we recommend that you include a standard appeal form and an accompanying sworn statement and supporting documents.

The necessary and recommended paperwork for filing an administrative appeal includes:

- Form N-336, Request for a Hearing on a Decision in Naturalization Proceedings Under Section 336 of the Act (see line-by-line instructions in Section D1, and the sample, below)
- fee (currently $650, but check for changes on the USCIS website, at www.uscis.gov/n-336). Send a check or money order made out to U.S. Department of Homeland Security—do not send cash.

- documents to overcome the basis for the denial (see Section D2, below), and

- your sworn statement to overcome the basis for the denial (see Section D3, below).

You'll also need to choose whether or not to appear in person, as described in Section D5, below.

> TIP
>
> **If someone else pays by check for you, make sure that your name and A-number appear on the line at the lower left corner of the check.** That way, if the check gets separated from your application, USCIS will be able to trace it, and you won't have to pay twice.

1. Completing Form N-336

Form N-336—a three-page form—is the only form you'll need to fill out for your appeal. As with all USCIS forms, it's best to type the information. If that's not possible, write clearly, using black ink.

> RESOURCE
>
> **Form N-336, pictured below, is available from USCIS by calling 800-870-3676, or by visiting the USCIS website.** Go to www.uscis.gov/n-336; you have a choice of printing the form out or downloading it and filling it out on your computer.

When completing Form N-336, follow the line-by-line instructions below. Although the form is easy to complete, we recommend that you make a copy before entering information. That way you can use one as a draft and one as a final version.

Sample Request for Hearing on Decision (Page 1)

OMB No. 1615-0050: Expires 01/31/2016

Form N-336, Request for a Hearing on a Decision in Naturalization Proceedings
(Under Section 336 of the INA)

Department of Homeland Security
U.S. Citizenship and Immigration Services

Print or type all your answers fully and accurately in black ink. Write "N/A" if an item is not applicable. Write "None" if the answer is none. Failure to answer all of the questions may delay your Form N-336.

Part 1. Information About You, the Naturalization Applicant	Your A-Number:
	A 876 - 543 - 212

1. Current Legal Name (do *not* provide a nickname)

For USCIS Use Only

Family Name (last name)

BENSUSAN

Given Name (first name)

Ercan

Middle Name (if applicable)

Bar Code	Date Stamp

2. Date of Birth (mm/dd/yyyy)

05/17/1991

Remarks

☐ Re-Affirm N-400 Denial

3. Home Address

Street Number and Name (do *not* provide a P.O. Box in this space unless it is your **ONLY** address.)

876 48th St.

☐ Re-Determine N-400 Denial

Apartment Number	City
A	Detroit

County	State
Wayne	MI

ZIP Code	Province (foreign address only)
48207	

Country (foreign address only)	Postal Code (foreign address only)

4. Mailing Address

C/O (in care of name)

(same as above)

Street Number and Name	Apartment Number

City	State	ZIP Code

Province (foreign address only)	Country (foreign address only)	Postal Code (foreign address only)

5. Daytime Phone Number

(313)555-1212

Work Phone Number (if any)

(313)545-1212

Evening Phone Number

(313)555-1213

Mobile Phone Number (if any)

(313)515-1212

6. E-Mail Address (if any)

ercan27@email.com

Form N-336 (Rev. 01/07/13) N

Sample Request for Hearing on Decision (Page 2)

Part 2. Information About Form N-400 (Application for Naturalization) Denial On Which You Are Requesting a Hearing

A 876 - 543 - 212

1. **Form N-400 Receipt Number**

   NBC 0141234567

2. **Date of Form N-400 Denial Notice** *(mm/dd/yyyy)*

   01/23/2017

3. **USCIS Office That Issued Form N-400 Denial Notice**

   Detroit, MI

Part 3. Reason You Are Requesting a Hearing

Provide the reason(s) you are requesting a hearing on your denied Form N-400. If extra space is needed to provide an explanation, attach an additional sheet(s) of paper. You must write your A-Number, the date, the question number, and sign the top of each additional sheet(s).

NOTE: Refer to Form N-336 Instructions, Page 1, Document Submission, for documents to submit with your Form N-336.

Please see attached statement.

Sample Request for Hearing on Decision (Page 3)

Part 4. Accommodations for Individuals With Disabilities and/or Impairments

A _876_ - _543_ - _212_

Are you requesting an accommodation for the Form N-336 hearing because of a disability and/or impairment? (*see Part 4, Specific Form Instructions, in the Form N-336 instructions for some examples of accommodations*)

☐ Yes   ☒ No

If you checked "Yes," check the box(es) below that apply:

☐ I am deaf or hearing impaired and need a sign language interpreter who uses the following language (e.g., American Sign Language (ASL)):

☐ I use a wheelchair.

☐ I am blind or sight-impaired.

☐ I will need another type of accommodation. Explain:

Part 5. Your Signature *(USCIS will reject your Form N-336 if it is not signed.)*

I certify, under penalty of perjury under the laws of the United States, that this request, and the evidence submitted with it, is all true and correct. I authorize the release of any information that U.S. Citizenship and Immigration Services needs to determine eligibility for naturalization.

Your Signature

Ercan Bensusan

Date *(mm/dd/yyyy)*

02/01/2017

Part 6. Signature of Person Who Prepared This Form N-336 For You *(if applicable)*

I declare that I prepared Form N-336 at the request of the above person. The answers provided are based on information of which I have personal knowledge or were provided to me by the above-named person in response to the questions contained on this Form N-336.

Preparer's Printed Name

Preparer's Signature

Date *(mm/dd/yyyy)*

Preparer's Firm or Organization Name *(if applicable)*

Preparer's Daytime Phone Number

(   )

Preparer's Address

Street Number and Name

City

State

ZIP Code

Province *(foreign address only)*

Country *(foreign address only)*

Postal Code *(foreign address only)*

Preparer's E-Mail Address *(if any)*

Preparer's Fax Number

(   )

Form N-336 (Rev. 01/07/13) N Page 3

Part 1: Enter your full name, exactly as you entered it on your Form N-400. (The exception would be if your name has changed since then, for example through marriage or divorce. In such a case, you should attach a document that explains this, such as a marriage or divorce certificate.) Don't forget to write your A-number on the right of the same line.

Enter your birth date and home address in the spaces immediately below. Following that is space for your mailing address. If you don't use a separate mailing address, you may write "same" here. Fill in your contact information.

Part 2: This asks you for details regarding your application and the office that dealt with it, to help USCIS match your appeal request to your file.

Part 3: Here, USCIS asks you to state your reasons for requesting an appeal and another meeting (hearing) with USCIS. You will want to describe the mistake that you believe USCIS made and the evidence you plan to submit in order to overcome the denial. If you can fit your explanation within this limited space, do so. If not, do NOT leave it blank, but instead write "Please see attached statement," and follow the instructions in Section D2, below.

Part 4: Don't forget to fill in your A-number again, at the top right. Then check the "yes" or "no" box, answering the question of whether you need any special accommodations to help you at the appeal interview.

Part 5: Enter your signature and the date.

2. Preparing Supporting Documents

As you may have noticed, USCIS officers love documents. A convincing document in your file gives the USCIS officer an outside authority on which to base decisions and a defense against doubting supervisors. Unless the basis of your appeal involves something that can't be proven on paper—such as your English ability—assemble documents that will prove your point.

To organize your ideas for documents, get a piece of scratch paper and write down every document you've thought of that might help your case. For example, let's take an applicant named Sara, who is trying to convince the USCIS officer that her marriage to the spouse who got her a green card was not a sham. Sara might write up the following list of potential supporting documents:

Sara's List of Possible Documents

☐ my sworn statement

☐ photos of me and my husband on summer vacation in Mexico

☐ letters from friends addressed to both of us

☐ sworn statement by neighbors saying that they saw us sharing the house, taking out the garbage, barbecuing together, etc.

☐ copies of records from meetings with marriage counselor

☐ copies of bills and receipts sent to our address in both our names

☐ medical records from fertility specialist showing that we were both tested to find out why I hadn't gotten pregnant yet

---

CAUTION

The above list doesn't include video. The USCIS officers rarely have a time or place to view video, so there's no point in sending them.

After you've made your own list, put check marks next to the five or six strongest, most convincing items. The idea is to give enough information to be convincing, but to avoid burying USCIS in a mountain of paperwork.

Looking at Sara's list above, which entries strike you as the most convincing? We believe the strongest document is the last one—medical records from the fertility specialist. This document is almost enough by itself, because it is from an independent, outside source; it was created for a separate purpose, not just for sending to USCIS; and it shows that Sara and her husband were attempting to have children together—a classic sign of a real marriage. The records from the counselor are also excellent evidence, for similar reasons.

All of the other entries on Sara's list are good ideas, however. Given the strength of the other documents this applicant will obtain, she might choose to drop the idea of bothering the neighbors for sworn statements.

You aren't limited in the type or number of documents you can present during your appeal. If there were gaps in your previous documents or other evidence, you now have an opportunity to fill them.

Think creatively about what documents will most convincingly show that USCIS got its facts wrong. Letters or records from official, trustworthy sources such as doctors, government officials, or schools are the best. See, for example, the list of documents included in the Sample Statement in Support of Appeal in Section D4, below. This person was able to show that, although USCIS may not have believed that his trips to Canada lasted fewer than 24 hours, he had independent confirmation from his credit card company, a hotel, and a kennel—none of whom would be expected to lie for him. He also included a sworn statement from a friend. The friend's statement is weaker evidence, but when added to the rest, it persuasively rounds out the picture.

If you use letters or sworn statements from friends and relatives, make sure they include as much detail as possible and are signed. For example, having your husband say in a letter that, "I swear that my wife has never abused drugs," is not strong evidence by itself. However, he will provide a more convincing statement if he writes, "I swear that my wife has never abused drugs—in fact, she's so opposed to unnatural chemical substances that I have to beg her to take an aspirin when she has the flu."

In Chapter 2, we provide a sample letter by a friend or relative. This sample was written for someone attempting to prove her good moral character for her original application—and such an issue might also come up on appeal. The sample shows an appropriate letter format and level of detail. To make the letter more legally convincing, the writer can turn it into a sworn statement by adding the following language at the bottom:

> I swear, under penalty of perjury, that the contents of the foregoing statement are true and correct to the best of my knowledge.

(See below, for a full sample of a sworn statement, which can be tailored for use by a friend or relative.)

It's always a good idea to start with your own sworn statement, explaining the situation and giving an overview of the documents you're presenting.

3. Preparing a Sworn Statement

Form N-336 provides a large box in which to explain the basis for your appeal. It's possible your case can be explained within this area. If not, however, say "Please see attached statement," and then use a separate page or two in which to fully explain why USCIS was wrong and you truly deserve U.S. citizenship. Write your statement in plain English with specific and convincing details and avoid legal-sounding language.

In addition, you can use this statement as a way to summarize and explain the documents that you've enclosed in support of your appeal. Look at the sample statement below for ideas on formatting and the appropriate level of detail, then write your own.

You might be wondering why, if USCIS already doubts your right to citizenship, would it take your word on appeal and grant you citizenship? Obviously, if you've lied to USCIS or another government official in the past, USCIS will look skeptically at your sworn statement. But it is not always possible for an applicant to come up with a document that covers every relevant life issue, and USCIS knows it. The USCIS officer will carefully consider your sworn statement—check it for detail, completeness, and internal logic—and could, potentially, give it great weight in deciding your case.

4. Submitting Your Appeal

Submit your appeal by mail to the USCIS; P.O. Box 20100; Phoenix, AZ 85036. Or, if you're submitting via Express Mail or courier, send it to: USCIS; Attn: Form N-336; 1820 E. Skyharbor Circle S, Suite 100; Phoenix, AZ 85034. The address will be shown your denial notice. (You can also find the address, including the separate one for members of the military, at www.uscis.gov/n-336.)

Sample Statement in Support of Appeal

876 48th Street, Apartment 9A
Detroit, MI 48207

March 7, 20xx

U.S. Citizenship and Immigration Services
Detroit District Office
333 Mt. Eliot
Detroit, MI 48207

RE: Citizenship Appeal
    A#87654321

Dear Sir/Madam:

I am requesting an appeal of my citizenship application because the USCIS officer who heard my case made a mistake. I explained during the interview that I had not entered my trips to Canada on the N-400 application form because none of my trips were for longer than 24 hours. The officer assumed that I was lying and denied the application.

I do not understand why the officer believed that I was lying. My USCIS file shows I have always been truthful in my dealings with USCIS and other government officials and I am telling the truth in this instance. Though it may seem unlikely that I would never stay in Canada for more than 24 hours, the fact of the matter is that I drive up there only for the purpose of meeting an old friend for dinner at our favorite restaurant. I stay the night at a hotel afterwards and return the next morning. Also, I hate to stay away too long, since my dog, Richie, suffers greatly during my absences and the kennel is expensive.

In fact, I can prove that my trips to Canada were short ones. Enclosed please find the following:

• credit card bills showing purchases of gas and other items north and south of the Canadian border before, during, and after each of my brief trips

• a letter from the friend with whom I have dinner, confirming our regular meetings

• a letter from the hotel where I always stay, showing the dates of all my stays over the past five years and confirming that I've never stayed for more than one night, and

• a sworn statement from the kennel that boards my dog, Richie, while I'm away, confirming that, on all the dates of my Canadian trips, I picked up Richie within 26 hours (the two extra hours represent the time it takes to get from the Canadian border to the kennel).

Thank you for this opportunity to clarify matters and to show my eligibility for U.S. citizenship.

Ercan Bensusan
Ercan Bensusan

As always, protect your packet from loss by keeping a copy for your records and by sending it via courier, Priority Mail, or certified mail with a return receipt requested.

5. Attending Your Interview

The agency has 180 days to call you in for an appeal interview. (Don't panic if more time passes, however—USCIS often fails to meet its scheduling obligations.) Be sure to bring copies of all your appeal materials as well as all the documents you brought to your original USCIS interview.

There's not much difference between your original interview and an appeal. When you appeal, you return to the USCIS office and meet with a different USCIS officer—one who may be higher ranking or of equal rank to the one who originally denied your application.

Look again at Chapter 8 for tips on getting through a USCIS interview. The appeal proceedings are usually as informal as your initial interview. The officer may conduct the whole interview over, as if the first one never happened. Or the officer may simply focus on the problem area. Be prepared to make a brief statement about why you should not have been denied citizenship.

6. Your Decision

USCIS may tell you its decision on your appeal at the end of the interview or it may send you a decision by mail. (See the sample decision below.) If you're waiting for a decision by mail, we can't predict how long you'll wait—it varies by local offices.

If you win your appeal and USCIS approves you for U.S. citizenship, see Chapter 11 for information on the swearing-in ceremony and your new rights as a citizen. If USCIS still refuses to grant you U.S. citizenship, see Section E, below.

E. What to Do If You Lose the Appeal

If your citizenship appeal is denied for a reason that clearly doesn't affect your eligibility to remain in the United States with a green card —for example, failing the English exam—the easiest thing to do is fix the problem and submit a new citizenship application (see Section F), or simply decide to do nothing for now. Presuming you don't do anything to endanger your green card status (such as getting arrested or abandoning your U.S. residence), you are allowed to live in the United States permanently, without ever becoming a U.S. citizen.

If, however, your case is denied for a reason that does affect your right to remain in the United States—for example, because you committed a crime, abandoned your U.S. residence, or smuggled aliens—seek skilled legal help immediately. Depending on the basis for the denial, you could be put into removal proceedings and lose your green card altogether. The attorney may also be able to help you file an appeal in federal court. For information on finding a good attorney, see Chapter 10.

F. Reapplying for Citizenship

If you've decided to skip the appeal and reapply for citizenship, or if your appeal was denied but you still feel sure you qualify for citizenship, go back to Chapter 3 and start fresh—but use the lessons you learned during this application process. Examine USCIS's written reasons for your denial and make sure that your next application corrects the problem.

While you're at it, review your USCIS interview in your mind. Was there anything about your application that bothered the USCIS officer? If, for example, an officer had trouble reading your handwriting, it would probably be worth typing the application this time around.

Some applicants wonder whether they should wait a while to reapply, to give their case a "rest." Given the many months or years you'll wait for your interview and the strong likelihood that your case will be handled by a different USCIS officer, there is no advantage to waiting. The only reasons to wait are if:

Sample Review Hearing Decision

U.S. Department of Justice
Immigration and Naturalization Service

San Francisco District Office
630 Sansome Street,, Citizenship Branch
San Francisco, Ca. 94111

EUGENIA KAIRYS
111 OAK ROAD, APT. 2
BERKELEY, CA 94710

Refer to File Number
A 12 395 678/CB

OCT -9 2004

N-336 HEARING DECISION

On July 21, 2004, your application for naturalization was denied. You have filed timely a "Request for Hearing on a Decision [in] Naturalization Proceedings," Form N-336, under Section 336 of the Immigration & Nationality Act.

Your application was denied because *you failed to demonstrate ability to speak and understand the English language sufficiently to answer the questions in your interview and on your application, and you failed to establish that you were exempt from this requirement.*

On October 02, 2004, you appeared for a Review Hearing. You submitted a Form N-648, Medical Certification For Disability Exceptions and your English and civics requirements were waived. It is determined that you have sufficiently overcome the reasons for the denial of your application for naturalization, and your application is now GRANTED. You will become a citizen upon taking the Oath of Allegiance to the United States, and you will receive an appointment notice by mail scheduling you for the oath-taking ceremony.

ORDER: It is hereby ordered that your application for naturalization be granted and that you be scheduled for an oath-taking ceremony.

David N. Still
District Director

cc: Attorney Ilona Bray

- you need extra time to prepare for the exams, or
- you were denied for a time-sensitive reason, such as failure to complete probation or failure to show a sufficient number of years with good moral character.

In these cases, you should not reapply until the appropriate length of time has passed.

In terms of procedures, your new application won't be treated any differently than your previous application. You will wait the same length of time and will be randomly assigned a USCIS officer for your interview.

> **CAUTION**
>
> **Your old file will not be forgotten.** The USCIS officer will have a chance to review your old citizenship application before making a decision concerning the new one. So don't view your new application as an opportunity to hide past problems with your application.

There is no limit on how many times you can reapply for citizenship— but we sincerely hope that you won't have to put this rule to the test! ●

Legal Help Beyond This Book

Many people apply for and receive U.S. citizenship without opening a law book or consulting a lawyer. Unfortunately, not everyone's citizenship case is an easy one. Thorny issues can arise regarding your eligibility for citizenship, the impact of criminal convictions, time spent outside the United States, membership in certain political organizations, and more. In such instances, you may need good legal help, and fast. In this chapter, we'll explain:

- when applicants need to consult an attorney (see Section A)
- how to find suitable counsel (see Sections B and C)
- how to hire, pay, and (if necessary) fire your lawyer (see Sections D, E, and F), and
- how to do some legal research on your own (see Section G).

> **CAUTION**
>
> **If you are or have ever been in removal or deportation proceedings, you must see a lawyer.** If the proceedings aren't over or are on appeal, your entire immigration situation is probably in the power of the courts—and you are not allowed to apply for citizenship through naturalization. Even if the proceedings are over, you should ask a lawyer whether the outcome affects your current application.

A. When Do You Need a Lawyer?

The most common reasons that applicants consult or hire an attorney are:

- basic eligibility issues—for example, there is an issue as to whether you have lived in the U.S. for the required time period or have valid lawful permanent resident status
- issues about moral character—for example, you were arrested for a drug offense or other crime
- exceptions to citizenship application rules—for example, you are unsure whether you qualify for an exception to the residency requirements as the former spouse of a deceased member of the U.S. military

- delays—for example, you filed form N-400 on your own, but USCIS has failed to act on your application for over six months
- requests for additional evidence by USCIS
- because you want to be accompanied by a lawyer at the citizenship interview, or
- simply because your case has gotten messy and you need more personalized advice than this book can give.

Lawyers can assist and advise you on all of these issues. We absolutely recommend you seek a lawyer's assistance for the first three.

But be warned, an attorney won't have as much power as you might like when it comes to the fourth issue—assisting you with USCIS delays. In some cases, lawyers may have access to inside email inquiry lines, where they (and only they) can send in questions about delayed or problematic cases—but even lawyers have trouble getting answers to such inquiries.

Experienced lawyers may also have contacts inside USCIS who can give them information or locate a lost file. But the bottom line is that a lawyer has no magic words that will force USCIS into taking action or approving your application. So you'll have to decide whether it's worth it to pay a lawyer to address USCIS's failure to act on your application. The answer may simply be that you have to wait longer.

Do you need an attorney to represent you at your citizenship interview? If you know that there is a problem in your case, then having a lawyer there is a good idea. However, the lawyer's main role will be to help clear up misunderstandings, point out the law to USCIS if it's got it wrong, protect you from harassment, and help you later understand what happened. This is all helpful, and it can make you feel more comfortable —but it leaves out one important thing. The lawyer cannot stop USCIS from asking you whatever questions it finds relevant to your case. If there is something you are hoping USCIS won't delve into, bringing a lawyer is not going to help.

Also keep in mind that despite the popular perception, your lawyer will not lie for you. Lawyers have an ethical obligation to tell the truth and can lose their licenses if they violate it.

> (!) CAUTION
>
> **Beware of legal advice provided by USCIS.** It's possible that a USCIS information officer, an examining officer, or a USCIS higher-up may give you advice about your case. Keep in mind that USCIS employees cannot best represent your interests—that's what your attorney does—and their information may be partially or wholly inaccurate—for example, an information officer answering the phones may misunderstand your inquiry or misstate the law. Even if the advice is accurate, language barriers may cause you to misinterpret the information. And the agency takes no responsibility for bad advice—it won't treat you with greater sympathy later. Whenever in doubt as to a legal course of action, seek your attorney's opinion, not the advice of a USCIS officer.

B. Gather Names of Prospective Attorneys

Immigration law is a specialized area with many subspecialties. So, you will need to find a qualified immigration lawyer—someone whose practice is concentrated in the area of immigration and who has experience dealing with USCIS.

You're most likely to find a reliable attorney by asking a trusted person for a referral. You probably know someone in the United States who is sophisticated in practical affairs and has been through an immigration process. Perhaps this person can recommend a lawyer or can ask that lawyer to recommend another.

Local nonprofit organizations serving immigrants can also be excellent sources for referrals. A nonprofit organization is a charity that seeks funding from foundations and individuals to help people in need. Since they exist to serve others rather than to make a profit, they charge less and are usually staffed by people whose hearts and minds are in the right places.

Most nonprofits keep lists of lawyers who they know do honest immigration work for a fair price—or the nonprofit itself may be able to take your case, if you have a low income. In the immigrant services field, examples of nonprofits include Northwest Immigrant Rights Project (Seattle), El Rescate Legal Services (Los Angeles), the International Institutes (nationwide), and Catholic Charities (nationwide).

For a list of USCIS-approved nonprofits, ask your local USCIS office or Immigration Court (EOIR), or go to www.justice.gov/eoir and under "Action Center," click "Find Legal Representation," then "List of Pro Bono Legal Service Providers."

If you hope to use the services of a nonprofit, you don't need to use one from the EOIR list, but it may be wiser to do so. Some nonprofits may be unscrupulous or may be for-profit businesses in disguise—and charge you the same rates as an attorney would, for possibly substandard services. The EOIR can't guarantee that the organizations on its list are reputable, but usually if a group is on the list, it's because it's fairly established—in other words, it won't pick up and disappear tomorrow.

Another good resource is the American Immigration Lawyers Association (AILA). Go to at www.aila.org and click "Public" then "Find an Immigration Lawyer." AILA's member lawyers have passed a screening process, which keeps out less-scrupulous practitioners. On the other hand, don't reject an attorney just because he or she is not an AILA member. Membership is pricey, and not all good immigration lawyers have joined.

Also check out:

- **Nolo's Lawyer Directory (www.nolo.com/lawyers).** Nolo has an easy-to-use online directory of lawyers, organized by location and area of expertise, and offering comprehensive individual profiles.

- **Lawyers.com.** Here, you'll find a user-friendly search tool that allows you to tailor results by area of law and geography. You can also search for attorneys by name. Attorney profiles prominently display contact information, list topics of expertise, and show ratings—by both clients and other legal professionals.

- **Martindale.com.** This site has an advanced search option allowing you to sort not only by practice area and location, but also by criteria, like law school. Whether you look for lawyers by name or expertise, you'll find listings with detailed background information, peer and client ratings, and profile visibility.

Once you have a list of a few good lawyers, meet or talk to each one before you choose. We'll talk more about lawyers' fees below.

C. Avoid Sleazy Lawyers

Some immigration attorneys are candidates for sainthood—they put in long hours dealing with a difficult bureaucracy on behalf of a clientele that typically can't pay high fees.

Unfortunately, some immigration attorneys are a nightmare—and there are more than a few of them. Their practice is based on high volume, not quality, and they churn out the same forms for every client regardless of the situation. These lawyers can get you into deep trouble, by overlooking critical issues in your case or failing to submit applications or other materials on time. One thing they never seem to forget is to send you a huge bill for their supposed help. Some signs to watch for are:

- **The lawyer approaches you in a USCIS office or other public location and tries to solicit your business.** Direct, in-person, for-profit solicitation by a lawyer—when the lawyer has no family or prior professional relationship with you—is illegal and unethical. More importantly, in-person solicitation is a sure sign that you're dealing with a loser. A competent lawyer doesn't need to find clients this way.

- **The lawyer makes big promises, such as, "I guarantee I'll win your case" or "I've got a special contact who will put your application at the front of the line."** USCIS is in ultimate control of your application, and lawyers who imply they have special powers are misleading you and could be involved in something dishonest.

- **The lawyer has a super-fancy office and wears expensive jewelry.** A high-rent office and a $2,000 suit aren't necessarily signs of a lawyer's competence. These trappings may just be a sign that the lawyer charges high fees and believes that clients are impressed by appearance, not performance.

- **The lawyer encourages you to lie on your application.** A lawyer who advises you to lie—for example, by suggesting that you deny or conceal trips outside the United States—isn't ethical and may permanently endanger your chances for citizenship. Keep in mind that USCIS may already know this lawyer's reputation and will apply closer scrutiny to your application because of it.

You might think that the unethical lawyers would be put out of business. Sad to say, neither the attorney bar associations, nor the courts or police take much interest in going after people who prey on immigrants. Absent this threat of official scrutiny, there is little deterrent for such unethical behavior.

> **TIP**
> **If you are the victim of an unscrupulous lawyer, complain!** Law enforcement won't go after lawyers who prey on immigrants until there is sufficient community pressure. If a lawyer acts unethically, report it to the state and local bar association and the local district attorney's office. Ask your local nonprofits if anyone else in your area is collecting such information.

D. Choosing Among Lawyers

Once you've got your "short list" of lawyers, try to contact each attorney's office, either by phone or email. Ask the lawyer, receptionist, or paralegal who handles new clients the following questions:

- Does your practice include citizenship cases?
- Are you accepting new cases now?
- What is your initial consultation fee, if any?

Many lawyers charge initial consultation fees, to cover the time that they spend meeting with people and evaluating their cases. The initial consultation fee is usually $50 to $250.

Some lawyers provide free consultations, but many have found that they can't afford to offer this free service, since immigrants often have no visa or remedy available to them—that is, the lawyer gets no work after the consultation. Pay a reasonable fee for your initial consultation, but do not sign any contracts for further services until you're confident you've found the right lawyer. This usually means meeting and consulting with several lawyers.

> CAUTION
> **Don't expect a lawyer to quote you a fee estimate until your first meeting.** Most lawyers can't determine the fee until they've met with you, discussed your individual situation, and determined the number of hours your case is likely to take.

Most lawyers will conduct the initial consultation in person. That's good for you, because you'll get a better sense of whether the lawyer is right for you. Below are some important factors to consider as you consult with prospective lawyers.

1. Immigration Law Experience

To learn how much experience a lawyer has in issues concerning U.S. citizenship, ask practical questions, such as:

- How long do you expect my application to take?
- What is the reputation of the citizenship unit at the USCIS office that will be handling my case?
- How many citizenship cases did you handle this year?

The more experience the lawyer has, and the more detailed the answers, the better. A lawyer's expertise in immigration law is not something that can be gained from reading law books alone. An experienced lawyer is more likely to anticipate and know how to deal with problems than a novice, and will know the procedural quirks of the local USCIS offices. This doesn't mean you should avoid a lawyer who is new to the profession—just make sure he or she comes recommended by other immigration lawyers and charges fees that are reasonable compared to more experienced attorneys.

> TIP
> **Choosing a novice immigration attorney?** You're better protected if the new lawyer shares an office with more experienced immigration lawyers who can provide backup advice or is an AILA member.

2. Client Rapport

Don't assume that you should find the meanest, toughest shark to fight for your case. This approach—though common in some types of litigation—isn't necessarily the best choice in immigration matters. You may need to share some highly confidential information with your lawyer, and you'll want someone who is discreet and thoughtful. Also, realize that a lawyer's politeness goes a long way with immigration officials, while sharks often produce a bureaucratic backlash. Lawyers with a sense of decorum and civility are more likely to enjoy a good working relationship with USCIS.

No matter what type of legal problem you have, don't expect your lawyer to make all your decisions for you. There are many situations in which the law doesn't provide clear guidance, and you, not your attorney, will have to make the final decision about your course of action. For example, if you've been outside the United States for a year and are worried that applying for citizenship will cause you to lose your green card, the lawyer can't decide whether you should take the risk of applying. A good lawyer will accurately describe the legal paths that are available to you, but will ask you to make the final decision.

3. Access to Your Lawyer

A lawyer's accessibility—that is, whether it's easy or hard to reach the lawyer—may be tough to judge before you make your hiring decision, but some factors may give you an indication. For example, listen to the lawyer's receptionist as you wait in the office. If the receptionist is rude, pushing clients off, or giving flimsy excuses about why the lawyer hasn't returned their calls, don't hire that lawyer.

In your first meeting, ask the lawyer how quickly he or she will normally get back to you. If the lawyer regularly breaks his or her promise, you'll have grounds on which to complain. Of course, you also have a responsibility not to pester your lawyer with frequent calls.

4. Explaining Services and Costs

Toward the end of your consultation, the lawyer should explain the charges for handling your case from start to finish. Make sure you understand exactly what is and is not included—for example, the fee probably won't include filing an appeal. (This should be made clear. Ask whether the lawyer is willing to handle appeals if necessary.) Hiring an attorney is a business arrangement, so ask questions and negotiate. We talk about typical fee structures in Subsection a, below.

In addition to fees, you will probably be responsible for paying the lawyer's expenses for handling your case—for example, photocopying, postage, transportation, and parking during your USCIS interview. In some cases, these expenses may mount quickly—for example, charging per page for copying your paperwork or faxing to a USCIS office.

Make sure you are clear about what will be charged for each expense. Some lawyers have been known to turn a tidy profit by charging, for example, 20 cents a page for a photocopy job that cost them only three cents a page. If the charges seem unreasonable compared to other attorneys, don't choose that lawyer.

Cost is important, but it's only one factor in choosing your lawyer. If you've got a complicated case, and you've found an experienced lawyer whom you'd like to handle it, paying that lawyer a little more will be worth the investment. However, don't assume that a higher rate means a better lawyer. Some attorneys who charge less may be keeping their overhead low or may be philosophically opposed to charging high fees.

A fee that's *far* less than others have quoted you, however, may be a sign of a nonlawyer attempting to pass as an attorney (see "When Nonlawyers Offer Immigration Assistance," below). Get as much independent information as you can about the quality of the lawyer you hope to hire—and then decide whether the fee is affordable and reasonable.

a. Flat Rates and Hourly Rates

Many immigration lawyers charge flat rates—that is, fixed fees that do not change regardless of the number of hours spent. Flat fees are particularly common where the case is not complicated. The flat fee for a standard citizenship application (including representation at the interview) usually ranges between $800 and $2,000. Even with flat fees, a lawyer will preserve the right to charge you for expenses and for additional time spent on unexpected tasks.

Flat fees do, however, give you an opportunity to compare prices between lawyers—even with the add-on fees and expenses, you'll get a general sense of the lawyer's fee structure. If the lawyer quotes an hourly rate instead, expect to pay between $100 and $300 per hour.

> **TIP**
> **Don't pay the whole flat fee up front.** Human nature being what it is, if you give your money up front, there will be less incentive for the lawyer to please you. And if you don't like the lawyer later on, you'll have a hard—if not impossible—time getting your money back. Ask if you can pay in installments—for example, monthly payments, or half at the outset and half at the time of your interview. Alternatively, ask if you can initially pay for a few hours' service (perhaps to be deducted against the flat fee). That way, if you don't like the lawyer's work, you can end the relationship with less hassle and more money.

b. If You Can't Afford Legal Fees

If the fees you are being quoted are beyond your reach, but you definitely need legal help, you have a couple of options:

- arrange a work-splitting arrangement with an attorney, or
- obtain low-cost help from a nonprofit organization.

In a work-splitting arrangement, the lawyer consults with you solely about the issue causing you difficulty, reviews a document, or performs some other key task, at the hourly rate, while you do the follow-up work, such as filling out the application forms and translating or writing documents, statements, letters, or more. Be forewarned, though: Most lawyers won't want to get into a mixed arrangement unless they are sure they won't end up correcting any problems you may cause by doing something wrong. For example, some lawyers won't agree to represent you in a USCIS interview if they weren't hired to review your forms and documents before you submitted them to USCIS.

A second option is to look for a nonprofit organization offering free immigration services or reduced rates. In addition, some law schools run immigration law clinics where law students take on immigrant cases under the supervision of a professor. But don't get your hopes too high. The U.S. government does not fund organizations that provide services to undocumented immigrants (except for very limited types of services), which means that most nonprofits depend on private sources of income and are chronically underfunded. Meanwhile, the demand for such services is very high. The result is that many nonprofits as well as law school clinics have long backlogs of cases and may not be able to take your case at all.

If you presently can't afford a lawyer, but your case is tricky enough that you need one, don't risk applying for citizenship on your own. As we've discussed, you can live in the United States permanently with your green card, by obeying certain rules. The safest route is to wait and save your money until you can pay a lawyer. Otherwise, you may find yourself in Immigration Court, where you'll have no choice but to hire a lawyer—and you risk losing your green card altogether.

E. Signing Up Your Lawyer

Many lawyers will ask you to sign an agreement—known as a fee agreement—covering their services and the fees you will pay them. A fee agreement can help prevent misunderstandings, but in order for it to be effective, it should be understandable—not written in confusing legal jargon—and the lawyer should explain the contract to you, not just push it under your nose, saying, "Sign here." A fee agreement usually provides for:

- **Scope of work.** The agreement will describe what the lawyer will do for you. To protect yourself from abuse, make very sure that the contract specifies in detail all the work that will be included. For example, a contract for a lawyer to help you with your citizenship application might specify that the lawyer will be responsible for "preparation and submission of N-400 application, reasonable follow-up with USCIS, and representation at one interview." If the lawyer agrees to include work on any special documents, make

When Nonlawyers Offer Immigration Assistance

Be careful whom you consult with or hand your case over to. Unless you see certification that the person you're dealing with is a lawyer, an "accredited representative," or a paralegal working under the direct supervision of a lawyer, that person may simply be a typist—and may know just enough about immigration law to get you into deep trouble.

To check on whether someone is really a lawyer, ask for his or her bar number and call the state bar association.

An accredited representative is a nonlawyer who has received training from a lawyer and has been recognized by USCIS as qualified to prepare USCIS applications and represent clients in court. Many accredited representatives know as much as any lawyer—but do your research and make sure that person can show you a certificate of accreditation or evidence of which lawyer is supervising him or her.

A paralegal is a nonlawyer who has acquired some legal knowledge and performs basic legal tasks—for example, filling out forms. Although there are many educational programs for learning paralegal skills, there is no accreditation process for paralegals—that is, anyone can claim to be one. In the immigration context, it's risky to hire a paralegal who isn't affiliated with a law firm.

Don't be misled by people using the title "notary public" or "notario." Although in some countries a notary public may have legal skills, in the U.S., the title is reserved for a fairly menial service—verifying the identity of those who sign legal documents. Titles like "Paralegal," "Notary Public," and "Immigration Consultant" are usually meaningless when it comes to providing you with legal advice about immigration—these people do not have a law degree or the necessary training or supervision. Some of them are outright crooks.

Hiring a nonlawyer or nonaccredited representative is appropriate only if you want help with the form preparation, and no more. But as you know from reading this book, even the most innocent questions on USCIS forms can have important legal consequences.

sure these are mentioned in the contract—for example, a sworn statement from a friend or family member.

- **Fees.** The agreement will establish the amount you'll pay, either as a flat fee (a lump sum you pay for a stated task, such as $1,000 for a citizenship application) or at an hourly rate, with a payment schedule. If you hire an attorney at an hourly rate, the contract can specify that you be told when the hours reach a certain limit.

- **Expenses.** You will probably be required to pay incidental expenses associated with work on your case. These expenses may include phone calls, postage, photocopying, and more. When possible, the amounts for each expense—for example, ten cents per page photocopying—should be set out in the agreement.

- **Effect of nonpayment.** Many lawyers charge interest if you fail to pay on time. This is normal and probably not worth making a big fuss about. If it turns out you do have trouble paying on time, the attorney may be willing to forgo the interest if it's clear you're taking your obligation seriously and making arrangements for payment.

- **Exclusion of guarantee.** The lawyer will probably warn you in the agreement that there's no guarantee he or she will win your case. This may appear as if the lawyer is preparing an excuse in case you lose, but it is actually a common and responsible way for the lawyer to let you know that no one can ever guarantee success. After all, USCIS is the ultimate decision maker on your case.

- **Effect of changes in your case.** Most fee agreements will include a provision stating that if there is something you didn't tell the attorney, or if something new arises relevant to your case—for example, you concealed that you are the head of your local anarchist group, and/or you get arrested after you've already submitted your citizenship application—the attorney can charge you additional fees (likely at an hourly rate) to deal with the work resulting from these revelations or concealments. This is normal; but to protect yourself against abuse, make sure that the initial scope of work is described accurately as we discussed, above.

F. Firing Your Lawyer

You have the right to fire your lawyer at any time. But before you do, make sure that the lawyer is truly at fault. Don't blame your lawyer for delays actually caused by USCIS.

You can always consult with another lawyer if you believe your case has been mishandled. Before you seek a second opinion, ask your lawyer for a complete copy of your file first (you have a right to have it any time). If it appears that your case was mishandled, or if relations with your lawyer have deteriorated, firing the lawyer may be the healthiest thing for you and your immigration case.

You will have to pay the fired lawyer for any work that has already been done on your case. If you originally paid a flat fee, the lawyer is permitted to keep enough of the fee to cover the work already done, at the lawyer's standard hourly rate, limited by the total flat fee amount. Ask for a complete list of hours worked and how those hours were spent. Don't count on getting any money back, however—flat fees are often artificially low, and it's very easy for lawyers to show that they used up your fee on the work that was done.

Firing your lawyer will not affect the progress of your application with USCIS. However, send a letter to the last USCIS office you have heard from, directing it to send all future correspondence to you (or to your new lawyer). (Once you hire a new lawyer, he or she can correspond directly with USCIS asking for this.)

G. Do-It-Yourself Legal Research

At some point, you may wish to look at the immigration laws yourself. We applaud your interest in the law, but beware! A government spokesperson once called the immigration laws a "mystery, and a mastery of obfuscation." (Spokeswoman Karen Kraushaar, quoted in *The Washington Post,* April 24, 2001.)

Researching the immigration laws is something even the experts find difficult, so you may be wading into murky waters if you try it on your own. Figuring out local USCIS office procedures and policies can be even more difficult. This doesn't mean that you shouldn't ever look further than this book.

Some research inquiries are quite safe—for instance, if we've cited a section of the law and you want to read the exact language or see whether that section has changed, there's no magic in looking up the law and reading it. But in general, be cautious when researching. If possible, look at several sources to confirm your findings.

Immigration laws are federal, meaning they are written by the U.S. Congress and do not vary from one state to another (though procedures and priorities for carrying out the laws may vary among USCIS offices in different cities or states). Below we give you a rundown on the most accessible research tools—and not coincidentally, the ones that immigration lawyers most often use.

> **TIP**
> **Law libraries aren't just for lawyers.** Many law libraries, particularly those connected with public law schools, are state funded. These libraries must make federal statutes and regulations available to the public. Don't be shy about using such libraries as a resource. (This is not the case with all law school libraries— private law school libraries are not always open to the public.)

1. The Federal Code

Federal immigration law is located in the Immigration and Nationality Act (I.N.A.) which is set forth within Title 8 of the United States Code. The U.S. Code consists of federal laws passed by Congress and applicable throughout the United States.

The easiest way to access the I.N.A. is at www.uscis.gov (click "Laws"). You will, however, need the section number.

Alternatively, any law library (such as the one at your local courthouse or law school) should have a complete set of the U.S. Code (traditionally abbreviated as U.S.C. or U.S.C.A.). The library may also have a separate volume containing exactly the same material, but called the Immigration and Nationality Act, or I.N.A.

Unfortunately, the two sets of laws are numbered a bit differently, and not all volumes of the I.N.A. cross-reference to the U.S. Code and vice versa. For this reason, when code citations are mentioned in this book, we include both the U.S.C. and I.N.A. numbers.

2. USCIS Regulations and Guidance

Another important source of immigration law is the Code of Federal Regulations, or C.F.R. Federal regulations are written by the agencies responsible for carrying out federal law. The regulations are meant to explain in greater detail just how the federal agency is going to carry out the law. You'll find the USCIS regulations at Title 8 of the C.F.R.

The USCIS regulations are helpful, but certainly don't have all the answers. Again, the easiest way to access these rules is via www.uscis. gov. If you already know the title (which is 8) and section, you can enter them and pull up the text immediately. If you don't have access to the Internet, your local law library will also have print copies of the C.F.R.s.

3. Information on the Internet

On the USCIS website (www.uscis.gov), you can obtain information on various immigration benefits and applications (including citizenship through naturalization), download most immigration forms, view the laws and regulations, and check current fees.

You'll also find sites provided by immigration lawyers as well as immigrants. The quality of these sites varies widely, so we don't attempt to review all of them here. Many of the lawyers' sites are blatant attempts to bring in business by providing a little information. That said, a couple of lawyer sites that contain useful information include:

- shusterman.com (by Los Angeles-based attorney Carl Shusterman, with daily news of immigration law changes as well as evergreen articles concerning immigration law matters)
- www.cyrusmehta.com (by the New York–based firm of Cyrus D. Mehta and Partners, PLLC, and including a blog, overviews on immigration law matters, and recent news articles)

- www.visalaw.com (by the firm of Siskind Susser PC, and including ABCs of Immigration, blogs, and regular updates on immigration law matters), and
- www.ilw.com (a privately run website that includes news, blogs, and discussion boards).

Sites created by immigrants offering immigration information and experiences, although well meaning, are not always reliable when it comes to legal or procedural facts.

4. Court Decisions

Immigrants who have been denied citizenship may appeal these decisions to the federal courts. The courts' decisions in these cases are supposed to govern the future behavior of USCIS.

Hopefully, you will never have to argue with a USCIS official that your case should (or should not) fit within a particular court decision. For one thing, the officials are not likely to listen until they get a specific directive from their superiors or until the court decision is incorporated into the USCIS regulations (the C.F.R.). For another thing, such discussions probably mean that your case has become complicated enough to need a lawyer. For these reasons, we do not attempt to teach you how to research federal court decisions here. For more information on performing that type of research, read *Legal Research: How to Find & Understand the Law,* by Attorney Stephen Elias and the Editors of Nolo (Nolo).

Internet Resources

This list summarizes the useful Internet sites that have been mentioned in this book:
- U.S. Citizenship and Immigration Services (USCIS) (www.uscis.gov)
- Attorney Carl Shusterman (shusterman.com)
- Attorney Cyrus Mehta (www.cyrusmehta.com)
- Siskind Susser (www.visalaw.com)
- www.ilw.com, and
- Lists of overseas embassies in the U.S (www.embassy.org).

After You Are Approved

If you have been approved for U.S. citizenship, congratulations! This chapter will guide you through the final phases of the citizenship process and help you claim some of the rights that are now owed to you. (For a review of those rights, see Chapter 1.) We'll discuss:

- the swearing-in ceremony—where to go, what to bring, and what will happen (Section A)
- how to prove your citizenship (Section B)
- how to register to vote (Section C)
- how your children can become citizens automatically (Section D), and
- how you can help certain family members to immigrate (Section E).

A. The Swearing-In Ceremony

You are not a citizen until you attend a swearing-in (or "oath") ceremony. Either at your USCIS interview or soon after, you will receive a written notice (Form N-445) telling you the date and time at which the ceremony will be held. (Some offices conduct "same-day" ceremonies, as well.) See the sample notice from the San Francisco USCIS office, below. USCIS usually holds such ceremonies twice a month. Or, it may hold the formal ceremonies less often, but supplement those with less formal swearings-in held at USCIS district offices.

CAUTION

You do not become a citizen until the ceremony. So you must continue to maintain your eligibility for citizenship until that time. In fact, you will be asked before the ceremony to sign a paper assuring USCIS that you are still eligible for citizenship. Now is not the time to jeopardize your chances for citizenship by getting arrested or by suddenly divorcing the person through whom you obtained your green card.

If you won't be able to make the appointment for the swearing-in ceremony, return the notice to USCIS along with a letter explaining why you're unable to attend and asking the agency to reschedule you. Make a copy of both items for yourself before mailing them. Send the request by FedEx, certified mail, or some other method with delivery tracking to the USCIS office where you had your interview—you'll find the address on the swearing-in notice. The USCIS office will reschedule you and send you a new Form N-445 appointment notice to tell you when your swearing-in ceremony will be.

We recommend trying to attend the appointment, however, because rescheduling always seems to produce delays. Also note that if you simply don't show up for more than one swearing-in ceremony (and didn't request rescheduling), USCIS may simply deny your citizenship at this point.

1. When and Where the Oath Ceremony Will Be Held

Depending on where you live and the oath ceremony schedule in your district, you could be scheduled as soon as the same day you pass your interview; or you might have to wait several months before taking the oath of allegiance. Also, you might be told the date of your swearing-in at the time of approval, or might have to wait for notification by mail.

The ceremony may be held at any of a variety of locations. The possibilities range from a small room or courtroom in a government building to a large stadium or convention center. Sometimes special ceremonies are scheduled in locations of historical significance, such as Independence Hall or the U.S.S. *Constitution*.

The ceremony may be presided over by a judge or a USCIS officer. (In either case, your citizenship will be equally valid!)

You may be given a choice of swearing-in location, a choice that may be more important than you'd think. In some parts of the U.S., for example, USCIS has been working to have more naturalization oath ceremonies at its own offices. The plus side of that is a shorter wait before you become a citizen.

The downsides include that you wouldn't be able to do a legal name change (which can be done only at court ceremonies) and that federal buildings often have a no-camera policy. So if your proud friends and family members want to join the occasion and take pictures to remember it by, they'll be sorely disappointed, and perhaps a little anxious when required to check their valuable camera equipment at the front door. How many guests you can bring is also an important consideration for different locations.

So if the USCIS officer approving your case offers you more than one option for the ceremony location, be sure to think about what's most important to you on that day, and ask about ramifications such as those described above.

2. What to Bring

As you can see from the sample appointment notice, USCIS asks you to bring a variety of things to your swearing-in ceremony, including:

- **The swearing-in notice, with the back side of the notice filled in.** You're expected to fill this in just before you go to your swearing-in ceremony. Take a look at the questions you'll be asked on the sample—questions about whether you've recently married, divorced, traveled outside the United States, and more. These questions are designed to make sure that nothing has changed since your citizenship interview—most importantly, that you still have the same name and are still eligible for U.S. citizenship. If your answer to any of the questions impacts your citizenship eligibility (see Chapter 2) or if you aren't sure, consult a lawyer. If it's a minor matter (for example, you got married or took a brief trip outside the U.S.), bring documents proving and explaining your answer (such as your marriage certificate or passport). An officer will review your documents, and if everything is in order, you'll be allowed to continue with the swearing-in ceremony that day.

- **Your green card (Alien Registration Card or I-551).** To avoid any fraudulent uses of your green card, you must return it to USCIS at the swearing-in ceremony. You won't need it once you're a citizen. If you've lost it, expect some heavy questioning. If it was stolen, USCIS may want to see a copy of the police report, indicating that you took action on the matter.

Sample Swearing-In Notice

Department of Homeland Security
U.S. Citizenship and Immigration Services

OMB No. 1615-0054; Expires 10/31/05

Form N-445, Notice of Naturalization Oath Ceremony

A#	A075123456	WSC*001234567

Date ____October 18, 2015____

REPRESENTATIVE COPY

PATRICK LEUNG CHAN
c/o ILONA BRAY
950 PARKER ST
BERKELEY CA 94710

You are hereby notified to appear for a Naturalization Oath Ceremony on:

Tuesday, November 8, 2015

at:

US CITIZENSHIP AND IMMIGRATION SERVICES
1111 CALIFORNIA (MASONIC CENTER)
SAN FRANCISCO, CA 94108
MASONIC AUDITORIUM, FIRST FLOOR, GATE: NONE

Please report promptly at ____9:00 AM____ .

You must bring the following with you:

[X] This letter, WITH ALL THE QUESTIONS ON PAGE 2 ANSWERED.   TYPE OR PRINT ANSWERS IN BLACK INK.
[X] Permanent Resident Card.
[X] Reentry Permit or Refugee Travel Document.
[X] Any Immigration documents you may have.
[X] If the naturalization application is on behalf of your child (children), bring your child (children).
[ ] Other.

Proper attire should be worn.

If you cannot come to this ceremony, return this notice immediately and state why you cannot appear. In such case, you will be sent another notice of ceremony at a later date. You must appear at an oath ceremony to complete the naturalization process.

Form N-445 (Rev. 09/12/03)N

Sample Swearing-In Notice (continued)

In connection with your application for naturalization, please answer each of the questions by checking "Yes" or "No". You should answer these questions the day you are to appear for the citizenship oath ceremony. These questions refer to actions since the date you were first interviewed on you <u>Application for Naturalization</u>. They do not refer to anything that happened before that interview.

After you have answered every question, sign your name and fill in the date and place of signing, and provide your current address.

You must bring this completed questionnaire with you to the oath ceremony, as well as the documents indicated on the front, and give them to the Immigration employee at the oath ceremony. You may be questioned further on your answers at that time.

AFTER the date you were first interviewed on your Application for Naturalization, Form N-400:

ANSWERS

1. Have you married, or been widowed, separated, or divorced? (If "Yes" Please bring documented proof of marriage, death, separation or divorce.)

   1. ☐ Yes   ☐ No

2. Have you traveled outside the United States?

   2. ☐ Yes   ☐ No

3. Have you knowingly committed any crime or offense, for which you have not been arrested; or have you been arrested, cited, charged, indicted, convicted, fined, or imprisoned for breaking or violating any law or ordinance, including traffic violations?

   3. ☐ Yes   ☐ No

4. Have you joined any organization, including the Communist Party, or become associated or connected therewith in any way?

   4. ☐ Yes   ☐ No

5. Have you claimed exemption from military service?

   5. ☐ Yes   ☐ No

6. Has there been any change in your willingness to bear arms on behalf of the United States; to perform non-combatant service in the armed forces of the United States; to perform work of national importance under civilian direction, if the law requires it?

   6. ☐ Yes   ☐ No

7. Have you practiced polygamy; received income from illegal gambling; been a prostitute, procured anyone for prostitution or been involved in any other unlawful commercialized vice; encourage or helped any alien to enter the United States illegally; illicitly trafficked in drugs or marihuana; given any false testimony to obtain immigration benefits; or been a habitual drunkard.

   7. ☐ Yes   ☐ No

I certify that each of the answers shown above were made by me or at my direction, and that they are true and correct.

Signed at _____   ,On _____
                City and State   Date

_____   _____
      Full Signature   Full Address and ZIP Code

Authority for collection of the information requested on Form N-445 is contained in Sections 101(f), 316, 332, and 336 of the Immigration and Nationality Act (8 U.S.C. 1101(f), 1427, 1443, 1446, and 1447). Submission of the information is voluntary. The principal purposes for requesting the information are to enable examiners of the Immigration and Naturalization Service to determine an applicant's eligibility for naturalization. The information requested may, as a matter of routine use, be disclosed to naturalization courts and to other federal, state, local or foreign law enforcement and regulatory agencies, the Department of Defense, including any component thereof, the Selective Service System, the Department of State, the Department of the Treasury, the Department of Transportation, Central Intelligence Agency, Interpol and individuals and organizations in the processing of any application for naturalization, or during the course of investigation to elicit further information required by the Immigration and Naturalization Service to carry out its functions. Information solicited which indicates a violation or potential violation of law, whether civil, criminal, or regulatory in nature, may be referred, as a routine use, to the appropriate agency, whether federal, state, local or foreign, charged with the responsibility of investigating, enforcing or prosecuting such violations. Failure to provide all or any of the required information may result in a denial of the application for Naturalization.

Public Reporting burden for this collection of information is estimated to average 5 minutes per response, including the time for reviewing instructions, searching existing data sources, gathering and maintaining the data needed, and completing and reviewing the collection of information. Send comments regarding this burden estimate or aspect of this collection of information, including suggestions for reducing this burden to: US Department of Justice, Immigration and Naturalization Service, (Room 5304), Washington, DC 20536; and to the Office of Management and Budget, Paperwork Reduction Project: OMB No.1115-0052, Washington, DC 20503.

*U.S. GPO: 1992-312-328/51138

- **Your Reentry Permit or Refugee Travel Document.** If you have either of these documents, bring them so that USCIS can review your travel history and verify your continued eligibility for citizenship.

- **Any immigration documents you have.** Bring your passport with any U.S. visas you might once have obtained, as well as any other important INS or USCIS approvals or permits (such as old Employment Authorization Documents). Although USCIS isn't likely to examine these documents, you may be asked to show them or give them back. (Because you will now be eligible for a U.S. passport, you no longer need USCIS-issued travel or other documents.)

- **Other.** The items listed above are things that everyone will be asked to bring, if they have them. If USCIS wants you to bring anything additional, it will mention it in this Other category.

> **TIP**
>
> **The USCIS notice advises you to wear "proper attire."** This doesn't mean you have to go out and buy a suit—just avoid bare feet or flip-flops and disrespectful clothing, such as shorts or jeans.

The USCIS materials sent to you will explain whether you can bring family members to the ceremony. This will depend in part on the size of the hall where the ceremony is to be held. Unfortunately, not all halls are large enough for everyone in one's family to attend.

If USCIS permits your family members to watch the proceedings, they won't be allowed to sit with you—family members are the "audience" and are usually asked to sit in the balcony or in the seats to the rear of the hall. With over a thousand or more new citizens often sworn in at a single ceremony, space can be tight. You may need to arrive early to ensure your family members will get a seat.

3. What to Expect

The swearing-in is a group ceremony, which will probably last two to three hours.

When you first arrive, a USCIS officer or a volunteer will point you to an area where you'll turn in your appointment notice and meet briefly with an officer.

This may occur at a series of tables divided alphabetically; you'll need to go to the one that corresponds with your last name (surname). You'll need to know the English alphabet to figure out which table to go to—you may, for example, see signs saying "A–F," "G–L," "M–R," and "S–Z." Go to the table whose letters include the first letter of your last name. For example, if your last name is Yang, then you would go to the S–Z table.

The USCIS officer at the table will review your appointment notice, including the portion on the back that you filled in. He or she may ask to see other immigration documents. Assuming everything is acceptable, you will hand in your green card and receive any additional citizenship information. Then you'll proceed into the main hall for the ceremony.

The ceremony is meant to be a celebration—there may be speeches, television cameras, and more. You'll hear various people's ideas of what it means to be a U.S. citizen.

The crucial moment is when you raise your hand and repeat, together with the group, the Oath of Allegiance making you a U.S. citizen. (For information on how members of certain religious groups and conscientious objectors to military service can modify the oath to match their beliefs, see Chapter 2, Section G.) You've seen the oath elsewhere in this book, but here it is once more:

The Oath of Allegiance

I hereby declare, on oath,

that I absolutely and entirely renounce and abjure all allegiance and fidelity to any foreign prince, potentate, state or sovereignty, of whom or which I have heretofore been a subject or citizen;

that I will support and defend the Constitution and the laws of the United States against all enemies, foreign and domestic;

that I will bear true faith and allegiance to the same;

that I will bear arms on behalf of the United States when required by the law; and

that I take this obligation freely, without any mental reservation or purpose of evasion, so help me God.

TIP

Giving up your throne? As part of your oath, you'll have to add some language if you possess, and therefore must renounce, any foreign titles or orders of nobility. The exact language will be either "I further renounce the title of [*state your title or titles*] which I have heretofore held" or "I further renounce the order of nobility [*state your order of nobility*] to which I have heretofore belonged." (See 8 C.F.R. § 337.1(d).)

B. How to Prove Your Citizenship

At the end of your swearing-in ceremony, the judge or USCIS officer will call you up to receive your Naturalization Certificate or "N-550"—a document that looks like a college diploma and is more suitable for framing than for carrying around. You may be asked to sign it in front of a USCIS or court official (if you're changing your name, don't forget to use the new one).

Before you hang your certificate on the wall, however, make photocopies in case you want to help other family members immigrate. You'll need to send the copies to USCIS with the visa petitions you submit for them. Copying the certificate for any other purpose is illegal—but USCIS does not object to making copies for purposes of an immigration application. (It *is* illegal to forge additional copies of the certificate for other people to use.)

!

CAUTION

Check your Naturalization Certificate for errors. Even before you leave the ceremony hall, take a close look at your name and the other information on your certificate. If anything is wrong, look around for the Resolution Table or a USCIS officer who can help you. USCIS may be able to fix your certificate that same day. If you don't notice the error until you've gone home, go to your local USCIS office within five days, if possible—that's the time window within which USCIS is usually willing to fix any errors without your having to send in a form. After that you'll have to file Form N-565 and pay a fee—though you won't have to pay any fee if you can show that the error was USCIS's fault. (Get the form at www.uscis.gov/n-565.) Also plan for the fact that it can take USCIS several months to process an N-565. If you need your naturalization certificate sooner (perhaps because you need to apply for a U.S. passport for upcoming travel), include a letter explaining the issue and requesting expedited service.

Your U.S. passport is a more useful form of proof of citizenship status. If you are asked, at the swearing-in ceremony, whether you want to fill out a passport application, we recommend that you do so. You'll need a passport in order to travel and return to the United States, and it's convenient for showing to employers and the like. If you don't apply for a passport at the ceremony, you can obtain one later through the U.S. State Department (a different agency from the one that runs USCIS). For contact information, go to www.state.gov.

> **TIP**
>
> **At last, you can travel all you want!** Unlike green card holders, a naturalized U.S. citizen can't lose status solely on the basis of living outside of the U.S. for a long time. (You could, however, voluntarily renounce your U.S. citizenship and live in another country if you wanted to.)

You also need to get in touch with the Social Security Administration (SSA) to advise it that you have become a U.S. citizen, and, if you changed your name, of this fact as well. At your swearing-in ceremony, USCIS should give you SSA contact information.

C. Registering to Vote

After you have been sworn in as a citizen, you are eligible to vote in U.S. elections—national and local. We recommend taking advantage of this right, even if you distrust politicians, feel that you don't understand the issues, or are unsure of the English language.

There are ways of dealing with voting barriers. Community and ethnic organizations often hold seminars in other languages to help educate foreign-born voters. Organizations or newspapers that you trust will analyze the issues and explain the candidates' positions. And when you do go to vote, remember that you don't have to vote on every single item; you can choose to punch your ballot slip—or click the computer screen—only for those candidates or issues of importance to you.

To sign up to vote, contact your local registrar of voters (you have to be on the registrar's list in advance of the next election if you want to vote in it). National elections are commonly held on the Tuesday on or after the second day of November.

You can find the registrar's phone number by searching online or in the blue or white pages of your local phone book, usually under the city or county section. If this doesn't work, look for voter registration forms at local government offices—for example, departments of motor vehicles, post offices, fire stations, and city halls.

D. Citizenship for Your Children

If you give birth to a child in the United States (including in Guam, the Northern Mariana Islands, Puerto Rico, or the Virgin Islands), that child is a U.S. citizen. Of course, that was true even before you became a citizen. However, by becoming a citizen you have gained some important new rights, including the ability to pass citizenship automatically to:

- certain of your existing children born outside the United States (see Section D1), and

- your future children born outside the United States (see Section D2).

If, after reading the sections below, you don't see a way for your child to become a citizen automatically, don't give up—see an attorney. There are ways that children can become citizens that we don't describe here, because they are obscure and rarely used. Act quickly—certain opportunities available to your child may run out after he or she turns 18.

CAUTION

Do not use the information in this chapter to analyze the citizenship rights of anyone other than your own child or the child of someone just becoming a citizen. The laws have changed over the years, but the older laws remain in force for certain children, depending on when they were born, when their parents became citizens, and more. For more information, go to www.nolo.com and search for the article "U.S. Citizenship by Birth or Through Parents."

1. Citizenship for Existing Children

Certain children can become citizens automatically through their citizen parents under a legal concept called "derivation." The Child Citizenship Act of 2000 provides that your children will become U.S. citizens the moment that all of the following become true:

- The child has lawful permanent residence (a green card) and got that permanent residence before age 18.

- The child is living in the United States.
- The child is living in your legal and physical custody.
- You become a citizen before your child turns 18.

It doesn't matter when your child was born or whether the other parent is a U.S. citizen.

Adopted children are included among those who can derive citizenship under this provision. The child must have either been adopted as an orphan or been adopted before the age of 16 and have lived with you (an adopting parent), in your legal custody, for at least two years.

Although derivation of citizenship is "automatic," there is a downside to this: No one will actually check to see whether your children are citizens—and therefore no one will give you any proof of their new status as citizens. (Adopted children are an exception—USCIS will arrange citizenship certificates for them after they enter the U.S.) To resolve this, apply for Certificates of Citizenship for your children using Form N-600. You can obtain this form by calling USCIS at 800-870-3676, or downloading it at www.uscis.gov/n-600.

An alternative is for your child to apply for a U.S. passport, but because derivation is a complicated matter, the passport can be harder to get (and to renew). You should definitely apply for a passport for your child at some point, but see if you can get a Certificate of Citizenship as well. For information on obtaining U.S. passports, contact the State Department (www.state.gov).

2. Citizenship for Future Foreign-Born Children

If, in the future, one of your children is born outside the United States, that child may acquire U.S. citizenship, depending on whether your child's other parent is also a U.S. citizen (covered in Subsection a, below), and if not, whether you, the citizen parent, are the child's mother or the father (discussed in Subsection b, below). (In addition, it's possible that the child will gain citizenship in the country of birth—but that depends on the laws of that country; not all countries grant citizenship based on birth.)

a. If Both Parents Are U.S. Citizens

If both you and your child's other parent are U.S. citizens, your foreign-born child will acquire citizenship if:

- you and your child's other parent are married to one another, and
- either you or your spouse have lived in the United States before the birth date.

There is no time minimum on how long you or your spouse lived in the United States, but it needs to have been your primary home at some point—not just a temporary tourist destination. However, since you probably had to live in the United States for a time before you became a citizen, you have likely satisfied this requirement already.

If the two of you are not married when your child is born, and you are the father concerned with getting citizenship for your child, the same requirements as above apply—but you'll need to take an added step: Legitimate the child before his or her 18th birthday.

"Legitimation" is a legal term meaning that you accept the child as being yours under the laws of the country where you live. This may be as simple as putting your name on the child's birth certificate. If you're not sure what the local procedure is, an alternative is to acknowledge your paternity in writing under oath (again, before the child is 18). In addition, you'll need to sign a statement that you will provide financial support for the child until he or she reaches age 18. If you're overseas, the local U.S. consulate may be able to help you with this paperwork. If not, you may need the help of an experienced immigration attorney.

If the two of you are not married and you are the child's mother, and if the father refuses to admit that he's the father, then the residence requirements become a bit more strict: You must have lived in the United States for at least a full year before the child is born in order for the child to acquire citizenship. Again, however, since you probably already lived in the United States for that amount of time in order to become a citizen, this probably won't be a problem.

b. If Only One Parent Is a Citizen

If your child's other parent is not a U.S. citizen and you want the child to acquire your U.S. citizenship when born overseas, it is still possible. However, the requirements are slightly stiffer than if both parents had been U.S. citizens. If you're the mother and a U.S. citizen, you'll need to have been physically present in the United States or its outlying possessions for at least five years before the child's birth. At least two of those five years must have been after you reached age 14. It doesn't matter if you weren't a citizen during the entire five years.

If you are the child's father and a U.S. citizen, and you are married to the mother, then the same requirement described just above applies: You'll need to have been physically present in the United States or its outlying possessions for at least five years before the birth. At least two of those years must have been after you had reached age 14. Again, it doesn't matter if you weren't a citizen during the entire five years.

However, if you are the child's father and you aren't married to the mother, you'll also need to legitimate the child before his or her 18th birthday. (See Subsection a, above, for more about legitimation.) In addition, you'll need to sign a statement that you will provide financial support for the child until he or she reaches age 18. If you're overseas, the local U.S. consulate may be able to help you with this paperwork. If not, you may need the help of an experienced immigration attorney.

c. Obtaining Proof of Your Child's Citizenship

Although your child's citizenship acquisition is, in theory, automatic, you'll still want to be able to prove it. If you're overseas, ask your local U.S. consulate for a document called an FS-240, or Report of Birth Abroad of a Citizen of the United States of America. If you happen to have returned to the United States, you can apply to USCIS for a Certificate of Citizenship. This is done using Form N-600, which you can order from USCIS at 800-870-3676 or obtain online at www.uscis.gov/n-600.

Another alternative is to ask the U.S. State Department to give your child a U.S. passport. This may prove difficult, since State Department officials are less familiar with the details of the immigration laws than USCIS officials. In any case, you should definitely apply for a passport for your child at some point, and see if you can get a Certificate of Citizenship as well.

E. Helping Other Family Members Immigrate

Your ability to help your foreign-born family members immigrate to the United States improves dramatically after you become a U.S. citizen. While you had a green card, your rights were quite limited. You could sponsor (file a visa petition for) only your spouse and unmarried children—no one else. In fact, you may have filed visa petitions for these family members and still be waiting for them to immigrate.

Spouses and unmarried children of permanent residents, as well as various other family members, are called "preference relatives." That means that Congress has set annual limits on the number of visas available to them. Because the demand for these visas always exceeds the supply, preference relatives end up on waiting lists that last many years before they can immigrate to the United States.

But now that you're a citizen, the situation improves for:

- family members for whom you may have already started the immigration process, including your spouse and unmarried children, who will be able to immigrate faster (see Section E1), and
- other family members—including your parents, married children, brothers, and sisters—for whom you now can start the immigration process (see Section E2).

1. Helping Your Foreign-Born Spouse and Children

Once you're a citizen, your spouse and your unmarried children who are younger than age 21 turn from preference relatives into "immediate relatives"—so they can apply for lawful permanent residence right away, with no annual limits and no waiting lists to delay their progress. You can either start the immigration process for them now or, if you've already started it by filing an initial visa petition for them, have them continue the process at a faster pace.

Unfortunately, even immediate relatives must go through a lot of application paperwork before they can get their green cards—the application process often takes a year or more to complete. You can't avoid the paperwork. But at least you'll know that their cases are progressing.

If you have unmarried children who are already older than 21 (in visa preference category "2B"), your citizenship turns them into what are called "first preference relatives." This is not as beneficial as being an immediate relative—it means that they are subject to annual limits on the number of visas and will have to wait for an available visa before they can continue with their immigration process. However, they are fairly high on the priority list. The wait in this category averages about six to eight years (though longer if they're coming from India, China, Mexico, or the Philippines)—normally an improvement over when you were a permanent resident and the wait for a visa averaged seven to ten years. (In the rare cases where this conversion is not an improvement, however, your child can elect to remain in category 2B, assuming you filed a visa petition for him or her while you were still a permanent resident.)

If you've already filed a visa petition to start the immigration process for your spouse or children (Form I-130), but they're still on the waiting list for a visa or green card, you don't have to restart the process from the beginning, but can advance them forward. In other words, you don't have to file a new visa petition, and they don't have to lose their place in line. If they have become immediate relatives, they can jump straight to the head of the line and continue with the final stages of their applications for green cards. If your children are older than 21, they can (if it benefits them) go from the 2B waiting list to the first preference waiting list with full credit for the years they have already waited. (In technical terms, they can use the same "priority date" as they had before.) In either case, the usual procedure is to send a copy of your citizenship certificate and a letter explaining the situation to whichever office is currently handling your family members' files.

A further benefit to your citizenship is that as soon as your children become lawful permanent residents, they may also become instant citizens—so long as they're younger than age 18 when you become a citizen and they're living in the United States in your legal and physical custody. (For more information, see Section D, above, concerning derivation of citizenship.)

2. Helping Other Family Members

Becoming a citizen allows you to start the immigration process for certain family members other than your spouse and unmarried children. These include your parents, married children, and brothers and sisters. (Unfortunately, it doesn't include family members such as grandparents, aunts, uncles, cousins, nieces, and nephews.) Not all of your eligible family members will become immediate relatives, however; some of them will have to wait many years before having the opportunity to immigrate through you.

Your parents benefit the most. They become your immediate relatives and can apply to immigrate to the United States right away. (As described earlier, however, even immediate relatives must get through the paperwork of immigrating, which tends to take at least a year to complete.)

Your married children as well as your brothers and sisters benefit, because you can now file visa petitions starting the immigration process for them. However, they will be considered your preference relatives, meaning that your visa petition won't get them a visa or green card anytime soon. First, they'll be put on a waiting list and subject to an annual limit on the number of visas that are given out. Your married children will fall into the third preference category, your brothers and sisters into the fourth preference category. Both are fairly low on the priority list and are likely to wait many years before becoming eligible to immigrate to the United States.

See the chart below, "Bringing the Family Over," for a summary of whom you can help immigrate and how long they are likely to wait. Unfortunately, these estimates of waiting times are not exact—they merely show how long the wait was for people who are finally receiving visas now. Because the length of the wait depends on supply and demand, it is unpredictable and could be far different—probably longer—by the time your relatives apply.

Note also that the length of time your family members wait can be affected by which country they're coming from. For countries that have large numbers of visa applicants, the wait is longer, because the laws contain per-country limits. As a result, the State Department usually creates a separate (and longer) waiting list for Mexico, the Philippines, China, and India.

RESOURCE

A full discussion of the rules and procedures for assisting family members to immigrate is beyond the scope of this book. For more information on immigrating spouses, see *Fiancé & Marriage Visas: A Couple's Guide to U.S. Immigration*, by Ilona Bray (Nolo). For information on immigrating other family members, see *How to Get a Green Card*, by Ilona Bray (Nolo), or *U.S. Immigration Made Easy*, by Ilona Bray (Nolo). Family members who are either living in the United States illegally, have lived here illegally in the past, or have ever been in removal (deportation) proceedings will probably need the help of an experienced immigration lawyer.

Bringing the Family Over		
Relationship to U.S. Citizen	**Category Name**	**Approximate Length of Wait as of Early 2016**
Husband or wife	Immediate relative	No wait other than application processing time
Unmarried child younger than 21	Immediate relative	No wait other than application processing time
Parent	Immediate relative	No wait other than application processing time
Unmarried child older than 21	Family first preference	Eight years from most countries, 12 years if the child is from the Philippines, and 21 years if the child is from Mexico
Married child	Family third preference	Twelve years from most countries, 23 years if the child is from the Philippines, and 22 years if from Mexico
Brother or sister	Family fourth preference	Thirteen years from most countries, 24 years if they're from the Philippines, and 19 years if they're from Mexico

Words You Need to Know

A-number. An eight- or nine-digit number following the letter A (for Alien) that USCIS assigns to green card applicants, to people who apply for certain immigration benefits, and to people placed in removal (deportation) proceedings. Once an A-number is assigned, USCIS uses it to track an applicant's file. The A-number must be included on any correspondence with USCIS.

Aggravated felony. A crime so serious that it will permanently bar a person from U.S. citizenship. The immigration law counts a number of crimes as aggravated felonies, even if the criminal laws didn't call them felonies in the first place. (For more information, see Chapter 2, Section D1.)

Alien smuggling. Helping or encouraging someone to enter the United States illegally. People who have committed alien smuggling can be barred from U.S. citizenship. (For more information, see Chapter 2, Section D3.)

Appeal. An opportunity for a higher authority to review an immigration decision. In the citizenship context, the first appeal after a denial of one's application is called an "administrative appeal," meaning that it is heard by another officer of USCIS. If the administrative appeal is denied, the applicant can pursue further appeals in the federal courts, with the help of a lawyer.

Asylee. Someone who is permitted to live in the United States as a sanctuary from the persecution faced in the native country. Asylees can apply for green cards and later for U.S. citizenship. (For information on when asylees become eligible for citizenship, see Chapter 2, Section A3.)

Citizen (U.S.). A person who owes allegiance to the U.S. government, is entitled to its protection, and enjoys the highest level of rights due to members of U.S. society. People become U.S. citizens through their birth in the United States or its territories, through their parents, or through naturalization. Citizenship status cannot be taken away except for certain extraordinary reasons. (For more information, see the immigration articles on Nolo's website (www.nolo.com).)

Citizenship exam. A test that a lawful permanent resident must pass to become a naturalized U.S. citizen, covering the English language as well as U.S. civics, history, and government.

Conditional resident. A person whose status is almost identical to that of a lawful permanent resident, except that the status expires after a set period of time, usually two years. Before the expiration date, the conditional resident must submit an application asking USCIS to approve him or her for permanent residency.

Consulate. An office of the U.S. State Department located overseas and affiliated with a U.S. embassy in that country's capital city.

Continuous residence. One of the requirements for U.S. citizenship (referred to in this book as the "continuous U.S. stay" requirement). (For more information, see Chapter 2, Section B2.)

Continuous U.S. stay. See "Continuous residence," above.

Crime of moral turpitude. A crime that is morally wrong, such as murder, rape, or fraud. Such crimes will bar applicants from showing the good moral character necessary for citizenship. (For more information, see Chapter 2, Section D.)

Customs and Border Protection (CBP). Like USCIS, CBP is part of the Department of Homeland Security (DHS). Its primary functions include keeping the borders secure from illegal crossers, and meeting travelers at airports and border posts to check their visas and decide whether they should be allowed into the United States.

Department of Homeland Security (DHS). A government agency created in 2003 to handle immigration and other security-related issues. Its responsibilities include overseeing USCIS and other subagencies.

Department of Justice. An agency of the United States federal government that oversees the immigration courts.

Department of State. An agency of the United States federal government that oversees U.S. embassies and consulates.

Deportable. An immigrant or permanent resident who falls into one of the grounds listed in I.N.A. § 237, 8 U.S.C. § 1227, is said to be deportable, and can be removed from the United States after a hearing in Immigration Court.

Deport/deportation. See "Removal," below.

Deportation proceedings. Also known as removal proceedings. An Immigration Court hearing to determine whether a person should be deported or removed from the United States.

Dual citizenship. Maintaining citizenship in two countries at the same time. The United States currently allows dual citizenship with other countries, but the other country must also allow it.

Embassy. The chief U.S. consulate within a given country, and the residence of the U.S. ambassador, usually located in the capital city.

Executive Office for Immigration Review. See "Immigration Court," below.

G-325B (Biographic Information). An immigration form required of citizenship applicants who have served in the military. (For more information, see Chapter 3.)

Good moral character. A basic eligibility requirement for U.S. citizenship. (For more information see Chapter 2, Section D.)

Green card. Identification card carried by lawful permanent residents of the United States. The USCIS name for the green card is an I-551 or Alien Registration Receipt Card. A green card is different from the work permit card often carried by noncitizens (Employment Authorization Document). (In this book, we also use the term green card to refer to the card received by conditional residents.)

Green card holder. Commonly used term for an immigrant, or a lawful resident, whether permanent or conditional.

Immediate relative. The spouse, parent, or unmarried child under age 21 of a U.S. citizen. Immediate relatives can apply for green cards without worrying about quotas or waiting periods. Spouses include widows and widowers who apply for the green card within two years of the U.S. citizen spouse's death. Parents must wait until their U.S. citizen child is age 21 to apply. Children can include stepchildren and adopted children (subject to further requirements).

Immigrant. A term that the public generally uses to refer to any foreign-born newcomer to the United States. USCIS categorizes immigrants as those who have attained permanent residency or a green card.

USCIS categorizes nearly everyone else as a nonimmigrant, even though they're in the United States.

Immigration Court. Also known as the "Executive Office for Immigration Review" or "EOIR." The first court that will hear a case if an individual is placed in deportation (removal) proceedings. Cases are heard by immigration judges, and USCIS has its own crew of trial attorneys who represent the agency in court.

Immigration and Customs Enforcement (ICE). This agency of the Department of Homeland Security (DHS) handles enforcement of the immigration laws within the U.S. borders.

Immigration and Nationality Act (I.N.A.). A portion of the federal code containing all U.S. immigration laws. The I.N.A. can also be found in the United States Code (U.S.C.) at Title 8. (To find it online, visit www.uscis.gov and click "Laws.")

Immigration and Naturalization Service (INS). A defunct agency, formerly the main one responsible for controlling the United States borders, enforcing the immigration laws, and processing and judging the cases of immigrants living in the United States. Its responsibilities have been taken over by the DHS.

Inadmissible. A personal characteristic for which the U.S. government will deny a visa or admission to the United States because the individual falls into one of the categories listed at I.N.A. § 212, 8 U.S.C. § 1182. Broadly speaking, these categories of inadmissibility cover people who might be a burden on or risk to the U.S. government or public, for health, security, or financial reasons. (Replaces the formerly used term "excludable.")

Lawful permanent resident. See "Permanent resident," below.

Location requirements. The term used in this book to describe the three requirements relating to a citizen's physical location during the months and years leading up to citizenship, including: continuous residence (or continuous U.S. stay), physical presence, and state stay requirements. (For more information, see Chapter 2.)

Lockbox. A USCIS office responsible for accepting and making decisions on particular applications from people in specified geographical areas. Lockboxes are not open to the public; all communication must be by letter, and there is limited telephone access. Though inconvenient to work with, the applicant has no choice—an application that must be reviewed by a lockbox will not be accepted or decided by a local office. (The Lockbox addresses for citizenship applications are provided in Chapter 3. For more general information on lockbox locations and addresses for other applications, call the USCIS information line at 800-375-5283 or see the USCIS website, www.uscis.gov.)

N-336 (Request for Hearing on a Decision in Naturalization Proceedings Under Section 336 of the I.N.A). A form used to appeal a denial of one's application for citizenship. (For more information, see Chapter 9.)

N-400 (Application for Naturalization). A form used to apply for U.S. citizenship through the naturalization process. (For information on how to complete this form, see Chapter 3.)

N-426 (Request for Certification of Military or Naval Service). A form required of citizenship applicants who have served in the military.

N-470 (Application to Preserve Residence for Naturalization Purposes). A form used by certain categories of people to request permission to live outside the United States for a year or more without impacting their eligibility for citizenship. (For more information, see Chapter 2, Section B.)

N-648 (Medical Certification for Disability Exceptions). A form to be completed by a doctor in support of an applicant who requests a waiver of the citizenship exam requirements based on medical disability. (For more information see Chapter 7, Section B.)

Naturalization. An immigrant who succeeds in attaining United States citizenship by submitting an application and passing a citizenship exam is said to have "naturalized."

Oath of Allegiance. The statement of loyalty to the United States that immigrants approved for U.S. citizenship must recite at their swearing-in ceremony in order to become U.S. citizens.

Permanent residence. The status of being a permanent resident; see below.

Permanent resident. (Also known as a "green card holder.") A person approved to live in the United States for an unlimited amount of time. The status can be lost for certain reasons, such as having committed a crime or made one's home outside the United States. The green card must be renewed every ten years, although the actual green card status doesn't expire. After a certain number of years (usually five), a permanent resident can apply for U.S. citizenship. However, many people remain in the United States for decades without applying for citizenship. Although they cannot vote, permanent residents enjoy many other rights, such as the right to work and travel freely.

Physical presence. A condition for U.S. citizenship requiring that a resident be physically present in the U.S. for a fixed period of time. (For more information read Chapter 2, Section B.)

Preference relative. A relative of a U.S. citizen or permanent resident considered more distant than an "Immediate relative" (see "Immediate relative," above) and who does not have an immediate right to a U.S. visa or green card. Limits are placed on the numbers of visas and green cards issued to preference relatives each year, with the result that there is a waiting list often lasting many years, depending on the exact family relationship. Preference relatives include the adult children of U.S. citizens (first preference), the spouses and unmarried children under age 21 of lawful permanent residents (second preference), the married sons and daughters of U.S. citizens (third preference), and the brothers and sisters of U.S. citizens (fourth preference).

Public charge. An immigrant with insufficient financial support who receives welfare or some other form of need-based government assistance. This status can result in an immigrant being found inadmissible or, under certain circumstances, deportable.

Refugee. Someone permitted to enter and live in the United States in order to avoid persecution faced in the native country. (Refugees are similar to asylees except that refugees apply for their status from overseas, whereas asylees have already reached the United States on their own before submitting an application.) Refugees can apply for green cards and later for U.S. citizenship. (For information on when refugees become eligible for citizenship, see Chapter 2, Section A.)

Removal. The process of sending an alien back to his or her home country because he or she is (or has become) inadmissible or deportable. This term combines the former USCIS terms "exclusion," the term used for blocking someone's entry into the United States, and "deportation."

Resident. Someone residing legally in the United States, whether temporarily, permanently, or conditionally.

Selective Service System. A U.S. government agency that collects the names of young men in the United States who are between the ages of 18 and 26 in preparation for a U.S. military draft. Men must have registered for the Selective Service in order to qualify for U.S. citizenship, as discussed in Chapter 2, Section D13.

State stay requirement. Term used by Nolo to describe the requirement that an applicant must live in the same U.S. state or USCIS district for three months before applying to the USCIS there. (For more information, see Chapter 2, Section B.)

Swearing-in ceremony. Ceremony at which immigrants approved for U.S. citizenship recite the Oath of Allegiance, are formally granted U.S. citizenship by a judge or USCIS officer, and receive a Naturalization Certificate.

United States Code. See "Immigration and Nationality Act (I.N.A.)," above.

Waiver. When USCIS agrees to overlook one of the normal requirements of an immigrant's application. In the citizenship context, waivers of the English language and U.S. history and government exam requirements are available to applicants who are of advanced age or are medically disabled. (For more information, see Chapter 2, Sections E and F.)

Index

⚖ NOLO *Online Legal Forms*

Nolo offers a large library of legal solutions and forms, created by Nolo's in-house legal staff. These reliable documents can be prepared in minutes.

Create a Document

- **Incorporation.** Incorporate your business in any state.
- **LLC Formations.** Gain asset protection and pass-through tax status in any state.
- **Wills.** Nolo has helped people make over 2 million wills. Is it time to make or revise yours?
- **Living Trust (avoid probate).** Plan now to save your family the cost, delays, and hassle of probate.
- **Trademark.** Protect the name of your business or product.
- **Provisional Patent.** Preserve your rights under patent law and claim "patent pending" status.

Download a Legal Form

Nolo.com has hundreds of top quality legal forms available for download—bills of sale, promissory notes, nondisclosure agreements, LLC operating agreements, corporate minutes, commercial lease and sublease, motor vehicle bill of sale, consignment agreements and many, many more.

Review Your Documents

Many lawyers in Nolo's consumer-friendly lawyer directory will review Nolo documents for a very reasonable fee. Check their detailed profiles at **Nolo.com/lawyers**.

On Nolo.com you'll also find:

Books & Software

Nolo publishes hundreds of great books and software programs for consumers and business owners. Order a copy, or download an ebook version instantly, at Nolo.com.

Online Legal Documents

You can quickly and easily make a will or living trust, form an LLC or corporation, apply for a trademark or provisional patent, or make hundreds of other forms—online.

Free Legal Information

Thousands of articles answer common questions about everyday legal issues including wills, bankruptcy, small business formation, divorce, patents, employment, and much more.

Plain-English Legal Dictionary

Stumped by jargon? Look it up in America's most up-to-date source for definitions of legal terms, free at nolo.com.

Lawyer Directory

Nolo's consumer-friendly lawyer directory provides in-depth profiles of lawyers all over America. You'll find all the information you need to choose the right lawyer.

USCIT8